Shooter's Bible GUIDE TO Home Defense

Shooter's Bible GUIDE TO Home Defense

A Comprehensive Handbook on How to Protect Your Property from Intrusion and Invasion

Roger Eckstine

SKYHORSE PUBLISHING

Skyhorse Publishing books may be purchased in bulk at special discounts for sales promotion, corporate gifts, fund-raising, or educational purposes. Special editions can also be created to specifications. For details, contact the Special Sales Department, Skyhorse Publishing, 307 West 36th Street, 11th Floor, New York, NY 10018 or info@skyhorsepublishing.com.

Skyhorse® and Skyhorse Publishing® are registered trademarks of Skyhorse Publishing, Inc.®, a Delaware corporation.

Visit our website at www.skyhorsepublishing.com.

10 9 8 7 6 5 4 3

Library of Congress Cataloging-in-Publication Data is available on file.
ISBN: 978-1-62636-179-9

Printed in China

CONTENTS

PREFACE

*M*uch of the information in *The Shooter's Bible Guide to Home Defense* can be organized into one of three categories. These categories include preparation, taking action, and preparation for taking action. Preparation focuses on preparing your home with devices, such as key-operated dead bolts, double doors, alarm systems, and other precautions. Taking action deals with weaponry and how to use them, especially in the home environment. Preparation for action focuses on personal conditioning. If an expensive alarm system wakes you with blaring concussion, it won't do you any good if you are too rattled to remember where your gun is or where you planned to take cover.

So much of what it takes to survive—or better yet win—a confrontation has to do with mindset. When I was a Little League baseball player, my father coached me to start playing my position before the ball was hit. I was trained to think and decide, before the pitch was thrown, what I would do with the ball if I got it. But playing second base is a lot simpler than defending your home. While an infielder might face a line drive, pop-up, or bouncing ground ball, the person or persons you are likely to face in a home invasion are far less predictable.

Many people make the mistake of thinking, "If I were a criminal, I would…" If you are a law-abiding citizen of scruples and rational thought, you probably do not have the innate capacity to think or plan like a criminal. Relying upon a prediction instead of being fully engaged in the moment can cause you to zig when you should have zagged and take you out of the fight, rendering you unable to defend yourself or others. Even if you could predict the behavior of a criminal when they're sober, that same person could commit criminal acts against you and your family while under the influence of drugs. Not only can certain drugs unleash a psychotic sense of entitlement, they can also give an individual boundless energy, increased strength, and an elevated pain threshold. Also, some people are simply non responders. That means even in a relaxed, sober state their senses do not register pain in response to injuries that would bring most people to their knees. This can mean defensive maneuvers that rely on pain compliance—such as an arm lock—may prove ineffective. So don't expect to know what an aggressor is thinking or capable of feeling.

Not all non responders are criminals. One of auto racing's most successful champions, Richard Petty, credits much of his success to an ability to get into a race car and concentrate on driving no matter what his physical condition. "For some reason I was fortunate," Petty said in an interview aired as part of *A Racer's Life: Richard Petty* (Speed TV, 2013). "I've got a threshold that pain don't bother me like it does some other people." Petty may or may not be a non responder in the clinical sense, but he was known to have never used Novocain at the dentist. Richard Petty's son, Kyle, explained, "It's just an exercise for him to outthink the pain."

While this should be taken as inspiration for anyone determined to defend home and family, it should also be a warning not to underestimate or try to predict someone's capabilities.

Another common mistake is having too much faith in a particular type or caliber of weapon. Several years ago, I had the privilege of writing an article for *American COP Magazine* that profiled a small municipal police department as it began issuing Springfield Armory 1911s chambered for .45 ACP. Before beginning drills and instruction, we were treated to a demonstration of penetration and expansion of the hollow-point rounds that would be standard issue. The wound canal was impressive and so were the training sessions that followed. Before I left several days later, the assistant chief of police told me a story of a man with a gun who came out of his house, engaged police, and was shot by a .45 ACP round in the torso. The ammunition proved to be a fight stopper but should probably have killed him. After the man was taken into custody, police discovered that he survived because his liver was so hardened by years of consuming alcohol that it acted as a shield. The late Jim Cirillo tells a tale in his book, *Guns, Bullets, and Gunfights: Lessons and Tales from a Modern-Day Gunfighter*, (Paladin Press,1996) about a man he shot in the head at close range with a .38 Special revolver who nevertheless survived. A .38 Special is not renowned as a one-shot fight stopper, but the bullet was fired just inches from the man's forehead and should have proved fatal. Instead, the man was merely knocked unconscious by the impact as the bullet traveled under his scalp, following the circumference of his skull, and exited at the rear of his head.

The point is that whichever method you use to stop an act of aggression, the result is the only thing that matters. Think of your weapon as an automobile speedometer. Say you are on a racetrack and your speedometer reads 140 mph, which is faster than you've ever gone before. Then, another car sails right past you. Now your concept of 140 mph is in perspective. Actually, your concept of speed is irrelevant. At that moment there is no telling how fast is fast enough. You must keep going faster until you pass every car. In terms of a home invasion, let's say you've fired two high-velocity hollow-point rounds of .40 S&W ammunition at close range into the midsection of an intruder, but he continues to race toward you. In your mind, you "know" this should have been enough to stop the fight. To continue the racing analogy, your speedometer is telling you that you are going faster than you've ever

gone before, but you are not catching up to the car in front of you. You expected the aggressor to drop because you thought the shots you fired were enough to stop him, but he's still coming. The question remains: What does it take to stop the aggression? The answer is that you don't know. The point is that nobody knows until it happens. A famous broadcaster at ringside for a heavyweight fight once said of a fighter who was losing on all scorecards, "He needs to stop thinking about punching and just punch."

I will present in this book information garnered from the knowledge, wisdom, and personal experience of outstanding law enforcement personnel and personal protection specialists. But note that self-defense is an art form. It continues to be shaped by experience. This book is not perfect. It does not guarantee. It only seeks to point the reader in the direction of more knowledge and better preparation.

ACKNOWLEDGMENTS

or better or worse, my mind is a Pandora's box. Since beginning my career as a writer with *Gun Games Magazine* in the early 1990s, I've learned that what comes out of it depends not just on the subject but who is asking the questions. In this case, it was Jay Cassell. I'd like to thank him for challenging me to share not just a quantity of knowledge but also a point of view that I feel is timely and so much in need. I'd also like to thank Lindsey Breuer and Nicole Frail for coordinating my efforts in a seamless fashion.

But nothing I have shared would be possible without inspiration from the actions of a few good people. First of all, I would like to thank my wife for not complaining when the alarm clock went off way before any sane person should tolerate being disturbed just so I could bump around in the dark and make my way to the "typewriter" for an extended work day. Her strength and work ethic continues to be an inspiration to me. I would like to thank my two sons and the women they married for being tough, resourceful, and right thinking. I was fortunate enough, lucky really, to acquire them later in life. But as the comedian Gabriel Iglesias likes to say, "I refuse to use the word stepchildren. It sounds too much like I'm renting."

I'd like to thank my first true combat shooting instructor, Michael Quintero. Little known outside a small circle of friends who enjoy shooting tactical pistol matches, Michael somehow instilled in me both the thirst and the ability to learn complex techniques quickly and use them in a fighting scenario.

The popular name for people that put themselves between evil and those less able to defend themselves is that of "Sheepdog." Having lived with some rough-and-tumble herding dogs, I've come to know just what that snap-to "Let's go get 'em!" look means and what kind of controlled mayhem is about to be unleashed. That said, I would like to thank the professionals who took part in making this book real. Texas Ranger Kip Westmoreland is as straight a shooter as can be found. He can ride up front in any era. J.D. Babineaux is a centurion. He lives for the hunt and when he gets his hands on you, you stay got. And they're both Marines, too.

I'd also like to thank Assistant Chief Tom Linnenkugel of the Cypress Volunteer Fire Department. I'm not sure how you thank people who volunteer to fight fires or do it as a profession. I guess you look for ways to help others whenever you can. Or, visit a burn unit whenever you think you've got it rough.

Then there are those who have not just dedicated their lives to teaching, as well as defending, but made it a lifestyle. Damian Halforty went out of his way to provide a looking glass so the reader could see what we'd all be in for if we ever abdicated our sacred right to defend ourselves. Jared Wihongi once described his daily circuit training at his local gym. Somehow it struck me as a microcosm of his life. Jared's mission continues on a truly international basis, yet he always seems to be around when someone needs him. And bad guy (in pictures anyway), good guy, or soldier, Wade Nail is someone you can always depend on.

INTRODUCTION

*Y*our home is your castle, a retreat safe from intrusion or invasion. Riches and bloodline once protected by massive walls, gates, moats, and sentries must now be protected by a lifestyle of preparation and skill.

If the above sounds high and mighty or a touch out-of-date, then you are either not a fan of historical context or you demand striking realism for the world of today. No one can argue that the lessons of history are difficult to escape, but from here on we're going to take a detailed look at what it takes to defend your home in the twenty-first century. No one can be sure when the information following will become obsolete.

I am not quite old enough to remember when people left their doors unlocked day or night. In fact, I spent much of my adult life living in a section of New York City where a majority of the people I knew, myself included, were at one time or another the victim of violent crime. Crime was so rampant that when John Carpenter's science fiction movie *Escape from New York,* starring Kurt Russell, debuted in 1981 many people took it as a sardonic prophecy. Set in 1997, New York City had been walled off and turned into America's one and only federal prison. The projection was that crime in the five boroughs would become so far beyond the possibility of control that rather than continue to patrol the city, it would be more efficient to simply cut it off from society. Why risk personnel when so much of the criminal element was already in one place?

The movie opened on a Friday afternoon, and upon its conclusion my brother and I shared some sarcastic remarks with other members of the audience as we filed out. We took turns laughing nervously about what the future might hold for life in the city if Carpenter's tongue-in-cheek but brutal plot ever became a reality. Living on the Lower East Side, we'd already had a taste of anarchy during the 1977 blackout when mobs roamed the streets unabated, tearing through storefront security gates like hungry locusts. Once the stores were empty, the mobs set upon each other and then us. But after three tense days in the summer heat, power was restored. Ultimately, the city would survive to go through a regeneration of law and order.

The reason the quality of life in New York City was able to make such a dramatic turnaround was the consistent and unwavering application of fundamental procedures and enforcement to the letter of the law under a new administration. In 1994, Rudolph Giuliani, a former federal prosecutor who had successfully gone after organized crime, began his first term as mayor of New York. One of the strategies he employed was to cut back on tickets for minor offenses, such as spitting on the subway or jumping a turnstile. Instead, the offender was brought to the nearest precinct where he was fingerprinted and checked for warrants. What do you know? Many of the same individuals who scoffed at even the least demanding of laws were already wanted in connection with more serious crimes. Giuliani himself, in his 2002 book, *Leadership,* refers to applying the law in this manner as the "broken windows theory."

The broken windows theory holds that a small violation, once tolerated, is an invitation for more trouble. Giuliani writes, "Someone who wouldn't normally throw a rock at an intact building is less reluctant to break a second window in a building that already has one broken. And someone emboldened by all the second broken windows may do even worse damage if he senses that no one is around to prevent lawlessness."

One example of how a violent criminal was apprehended by enforcement under the broken window theory is the case of John Royster, Jr. In New York City on June 4, 1994, Royster went on a rampage that included killing a piano teacher by bashing her head on the ground repeatedly just one hundred feet from a busy playground in Central Park. The next night, Royster attacked a jogger in the same manner but was scared off by the shouts of a passerby before the woman could be fatally injured. No one knows for sure if Royster was guilty of other violent crimes, but on June 11, he beat to death sixty-five-year-old Evelyn Alvarez as she opened her Park Avenue dry cleaning establishment.

Royster was caught because several months earlier, under the broken windows campaign, he had been arrested for jumping a subway turnstile. Instead of merely receiving a summons, he was taken in and fingerprinted. Royster's fingerprints were found at the scene of Mrs. Alvarez's murder. While this book is not about the private citizen taking part in law enforcement, it is, like Mayor Giuliani's strategy, about understanding your environment, paying attention to detail, and never missing the opportunity to discourage or prevent criminal action.

Unfortunately, there will be times when the criminal's actions are too powerful, too thoughtless, and too haphazard to drive them to the next door for an easier target no matter how many alarms sound. The purpose of this book is to supply in-depth information about preparing your home, choosing suitable weaponry, and employing techniques that together should be seen as tools for survival. The task is to adapt these tools specifically for defending our families and the different types of homes in which we live.

The Castle Doctrine: History and Perspective

The tradition of English common law states that a man's home is his "castle" and an individual's sovereignty extends over it. Hence the well-known term Castle Doctrine. Castle Doctrine laws are often confused with Stand Your Ground legislation. Both types of legislation vary from state to state but begin with the same basic concept. That is, you do not have to retreat or run away if someone attacks you. If you reasonably believe your life is in danger or you might be very seriously hurt, you can fight back. The primary difference between the two laws is that the Castle Doctrine applies when the individual is in his or her home. Stand Your Ground laws apply everywhere so long as an individual is not engaged in unlawful activity and has a right to be there.

According to the Bill of Rights Institute, a non profit organization that works to strengthen civic knowledge and values in the next generation of citizens, three separate amendments to the U.S. Constitution or Bill of Rights can be used to support both the Castle Doctrine and Stand Your Ground legislation. They are the Fourth Amendment, the Fifth Amendment, and the Tenth Amendment.

The Fourth Amendment is often interpreted to mean protection of property rights. But its full text reads:

The right of the people to be secure in their persons, houses, papers, and effects, against unreasonable searches and seizures, shall not be violated, and no Warrants shall issue, but upon probable cause, supported by Oath or affirmation, and particularly describing the place to be searched, and the persons or things to be seized.

The Fourth Amendment was born of a struggle that dates back to the seventeenth century and earlier, when Writs of Assistance were issued so the king's agents could break into a home to search for evidence of anything that spoke ill of the monarchy. This is generally considered to be the origin of the celebrated maxim "Every man's home is his castle." An actual case reportedly made famous with this argument is Semayne's Case, decided in 1603. The decision in the case recognized the right of the homeowner to defend his house against unlawful entry, even by the king's agents. This ruling could be considered the original Castle Doctrine, but as law the decision was not

enforceable. As Americans, our right to be secure in our houses is as ironclad as our ability to preserve and protect the constitution.

The Fifth Amendment reads:

No person shall be held to answer for a capital, or otherwise infamous crime, unless on a presentment or indictment of a Grand Jury, except in cases arising in the land or naval forces, or in the Militia, when in actual service in time of War or public danger; nor shall any person be subject for the same offence to be twice put in jeopardy of life or limb; nor shall be compelled in any criminal case to be a witness against himself, nor be deprived of life, liberty, or property, without due process of law; nor shall private property be taken for public use, without just compensation.

It seems reasonable to believe that, in its application to home defense, the most important protection afforded by the Fifth Amendment would be that of not being "compelled in any criminal case to being a witness against himself." This would likely come into play at the conclusion of a home invasion or other assault. Bear in mind that whatever transpires, you may be the only one who can say what happened. Or, it may be your word against the aggressor or aggressors.

The Tenth Amendment reads:

The powers not delegated to the United States by the Constitution, nor prohibited by it to the States, are reserved to the States respectively or to the people.

The complicated meaning of the Tenth Amendment arises from a state application of the law that is not necessarily homogenous. To some extent, each state is free to create, interpret, and apply similar laws through the prism of its own legislature. Simply put, some states afford their citizens the safety of the Castle Doctrine and others do not. Some states go further and believe their citizens should be afforded protection under the Stand Your Ground principal. Furthermore, there are variations in how either law is applied within the individual state. Just like you should know if a right turn on red is permitted in the downtown of your city, you should know how strongly your rights to defend yourself and your home are protected by local laws.

States that do not have a specific law do not necessarily eliminate the use of the Castle Doctrine or Stand Your Ground as a defense. Some states rely on case law instead of specific legislation. This means, in general, if someone else was able to prove they were justified in defending themselves in a similar situation, you may not be arrested or convicted. Or, a jurisdiction may specify an exception to an existing law, such as described by the Legal Information Institute based at the Cornell University Law School. It reads, "An exception to a rule in place in some jurisdictions that requires a defendant to retreat before using deadly force in Self Defense. The Castle Exception states that if a defendant is in his home, he is not required to retreat prior to using deadly force in Self Defense."

Conspicuous in its absence from the Bill of Rights Institute's tutorial regarding Constitutional rights and self-defense is the Second Amendment. The Second Amendment reads:

A well regulated Militia, being necessary to the security of a free state, the right of the people to keep and bear Arms, shall not be infringed.

In the recent landmark case *DC v. Heller,* the Supreme Court reached the decision that the Second Amendment directly affects the ability to defend one's home. Listed in the case brief summary, the holding and rule by Justice Antonin Scalia reads, "The Second Amendment protects an individual right to possess a firearm unconnected with service in a militia, and to use that arm for traditionally lawful purposes, such as self-defense within the home."

Whereas a firearm is not the be-all and end-all for self-defense in any given situation, it does offer a projection of force and destruction unlike any other tool. That is why much of this book will be devoted to how to defend yourself and your home using a firearm.

District of Columbia v. Heller

istrict of Columbia law bans handgun possession by making it a crime to carry an unregistered firearm and prohibiting the registration of handguns; provides separately that no person may carry an unlicensed handgun, but authorizes the police chief to issue one-year licenses; and requires residents to keep lawfully owned firearms unloaded and dissembled or bound by a trigger lock or similar device. Respondent Heller, a D.C. special policeman, applied to register a handgun he wished to keep at home, but the District refused. He filed this suit seeking, on Second Amendment grounds, to enjoin the city from enforcing the bar on handgun registration, the licensing requirement insofar as it prohibits carrying an unlicensed firearm in the home, and the trigger-lock requirement insofar as it prohibits the use of functional firearms in the home. The District Court dismissed the suit, but the D.C. Circuit reversed, holding that the Second Amendment protects an individual's right to possess firearms and that the city's total ban on handguns, as well as its requirement that firearms in the home be kept nonfunctional even when necessary for self-defense, violated that right.

Held:

1. The Second Amendment protects an individual right to possess a firearm unconnected with service in a militia, and to use that arm for traditionally lawful purposes, such as self-defense within the home. Pp. 2–53.

   (a) The Amendment's prefatory clause announces a purpose, but does not limit or expand the scope of the second part, the operative clause. The operative clause's text and history demonstrate that it connotes an individual right to keep and bear arms.

   (b) The prefatory clause comports with the Court's interpretation of the operative clause. The "militia" comprised all males physically capable of acting in concert for the common defense. The Antifederalists feared that the Federal Government would disarm the people in order to disable this citizens' militia, enabling a politicized standing army or a select militia to rule. The response was to deny Congress power to abridge the ancient right of individuals to keep and bear arms, so

that the ideal of a citizens' militia would be preserved.

   (c) The Court's interpretation is confirmed by analogous arms-bearing rights in state constitutions that preceded and immediately followed the Second Amendment.

   (d) The Second Amendment's drafting history, while of dubious interpretive worth, reveals three state Second Amendment proposals that unequivocally referred to an individual right to bear arms.

   (e) Interpretation of the Second Amendment by scholars, courts and legislators, from immediately after its ratification through the late 19th century also supports the Court's conclusion.

   (f) None of the Court's precedents forecloses the Court's interpretation. Neither *United States v. Cruikshank*, 92 U. S. 542 , nor *Presser v. Illinois*, 116 U. S. 252 , refutes the individual-rights interpretation. *United States v. Miller*, 307 U. S. 174, does not limit the right to keep and bear arms to militia purposes, but rather limits the type of weapon to which the right applies to those used by the militia, i.e., those in common use for lawful purposes.

2. Like most rights, the Second Amendment right is not unlimited. It is not a right to keep and carry any weapon whatsoever in any manner whatsoever and for whatever purpose: For example, concealed weapons prohibitions have been upheld under the Amendment or state analogues. The Court's opinion should not be taken to cast doubt on longstanding prohibitions on the possession of firearms by felons and the mentally ill, or laws forbidding the carrying of firearms in sensitive places such as schools and government buildings, or laws imposing conditions and qualifications on the commercial sale of arms. Miller's holding that the sorts of weapons protected are those "in common use at the time" finds support in the historical tradition of prohibiting the carrying of dangerous and unusual weapons.

3. The handgun ban and the trigger-lock requirement (as applied to self-defense) violate the Second Amendment. The District's total ban on handgun possession in the home amounts to a prohibition on an entire class of "arms" that Americans overwhelmingly choose for the lawful purpose of

self-defense. Under any of the standards of scrutiny the Court has applied to enumerated constitutional rights, this prohibition—in the place where the importance of the lawful defense of self, family, and property is most acute—would fail constitutional muster. Similarly, the requirement that any lawful firearm in the home be disassembled or bound by a trigger lock makes it impossible for citizens to use arms for the core lawful purpose of self-defense and is hence unconstitutional. Because Heller conceded at oral argument that the D. C. licensing law is permissible if it is not enforced arbitrarily and capriciously, the Court assumes that a license will satisfy his prayer for relief and does not address the licensing requirement. Assuming he is not disqualified from exercising Second Amendment rights, the District must permit Heller to register his handgun and must issue him a license to carry it in the home.

Through the Eyes of a Texas Ranger

When I was growing up, a neighbor worked as a tow truck driver for a body shop. The side of his tow truck read, "We Meet by Accident." I guess he did repossessions as well, but his bread and butter was towing cars away from crash scenes. By the time I was nine or ten, I'd seen maybe three or four traffic accidents. But he saw more than that every single day. He was more or less an expert, just based on the sheer volume of seeing what happens when things go bad. Police, especially those who have graduated to being investigators, are also experts on when things go bad. But the collisions they respond to can wreck people's lives instead of just cars and trucks.

Given a police officer's training and experience, it is reasonable to believe they see things differently. Much of a police officer's training is developed from what has been learned from prior cases. Once in the field, the education of a policeman never stops. Does the average person need to spend time in the police academy or ride along in a patrol car to learn to be more vigilant? What would we be looking for, anyway? Would seeing our homes or neighborhoods through the eyes of a police officer help make us safer? What if we could see our daily lives through the eyes of a premier law enforcement agency, such as the Texas Rangers?

The Texas Rangers have a long history of being independent men of action. Their first assignments were in the early part of the 1800s, protecting the barbed wire fences that were used to cordon off portions of the vast landscape north of Mexico. This led to a conflict of civilizations between warrior plains Native Americans, Mexican caballeros and vaqueros, and transplants or out runners of the American Frontier known as the Texans. According to Walter Prescott Webb in his book *The Texas Rangers: A Century of Frontier Defense*, the Texas Rangers represented the interest of the Texans. To win against these odds, a Texas Ranger had to combine the fighting qualities of all three races. "In the words of an observer," writes Webb, "the Texas Ranger could ride like a Mexican, trail like an Indian, shoot like a Tennessean, and fight like a Devil."

Through the years, the Texas Rangers have been revered, celebrated, disbanded, and returned to action, sometimes at the whim of the governor. Today, there are approximately one hundred fifty sworn

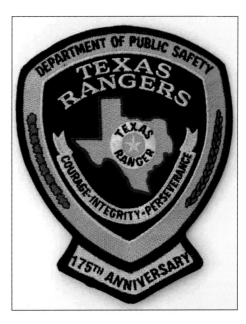

▲ The Texas Rangers began as a small unit of hard riding men that often worked alone. Today, the Rangers operate under the auspices of the Texas Department of Public Safety, lending assistance to smaller law enforcement entities that might not have the equipment or expertise to deal with extraordinary circumstances. According to the Texas Ranger Hall of Fame and Museum in Waco, Stephen F. Austin recorded the first official call to arms in 1823. This commemorative patch must be for rare uniformed occasions because I cannot remember ever seeing a Texas Ranger wearing anything but low key Western wear and an off-white cowboy hat.

Texas Rangers. Much of their duty is investigative in nature, and Rangers offer an extraordinary level of expertise to law enforcement agencies that might not have the resources necessary to solve a complicated crime or turn a cold case. In fact, it was a Texas Ranger, Captain Manuel Trazazas "Lone Wolf" Gonzaullas, who played a sizable role in developing the modern crime lab. Captain Gonzaullas' career began in the era of the horseback Ranger but continued into the twentieth century. The Lone Wolf went on to head the intelligence bureau at the then newly formed Department of Public Safety in 1935, ushering in the modern era of crime fighting, where what is now called forensic science plays a key role.

If we were all Texas Rangers, would we move differently, see people in a different light, or listen more carefully to what they say? Are there any habits in the manner of a second sight we could develop to help spot warning signs? What would our homes look like through the eyes of a Ranger? Would we develop a

▲ The career of Texas Ranger Captain Manuel Trazazas "Lone Wolf" Gonzaullas not only spanned the horseback era to the 1950s, but he was also instrumental in developing forensic science and the modern crime lab. *Photo courtesy of The Texas Ranger Hall of Fame and Museum*

checklist of structural characteristics that we would add to our homes to make them more secure? To learn more about defending the home, I visited with Kip Westmoreland, Sergeant Texas Rangers Company A, based in Richmond.

A Marine Corps veteran, Sergeant Kip Westmoreland spent about nine years in various assignments within the Texas Department of Public Safety, including highway patrol trooper and narcotics investigator, before becoming a Texas Ranger more than five years ago. In the modern era, a Ranger who is commissioned from the Texas DPS ranks must pass a written examination and appear before an interview board. It's not clear how many apply to be Rangers but the Texas DPS is currently made up of about 9,000 commissioned and non commissioned personnel. Expansion from a force of 124 Rangers just a few years ago has been slow and careful, which says a lot about each and every Texas Ranger. Texas Rangers don't wear uniforms per se, just low-key Western wear (aside from a white felt cowboy hat), and a modest silver badge (captains wear a gold badge). According to the Texas Ranger Hall of Fame and Museum in Waco, the current issue badge, engaged in 1962, is not only a replica of the original badges that old-time Rangers carved out of Mexican five-peso silver coins, but is also still made from a Mexican Cinco Peso coin. Asked what other era he would have liked to serve in if he were able, Westmoreland said he would choose the original Frontier era.

I met with Ranger Westmoreland in a suburban restaurant some thirty miles outside of Houston. In the parking lot were two marked sheriff's department units, but none of the other vehicles appeared to belong to law enforcement. Westmoreland had texted me where he would be sitting, but when I walked in the front door all I could see were the two sheriff's deputies in a booth directly to the rear. The Ranger was seated with his back to the wall in the dead center of the restaurant where he could see every table, the front door, and the side door exit next to the takeout register. Yet, I had difficulty finding him. Not having your back to the door, being able to see what is going on around you, and unabridged access to a secondary exit didn't come up in our conversation, but it's good advice. Probably, it is something a Ranger does out of habit.

▲ Like many of today's Texas Rangers, the late Glenn Elliott came up through the ranks of highway patrol with the Texas Department of Public Safety. In total he served the people of Texas for thirty-eight years, including from 1961-1987 as a Ranger attached to Company B. Relentless and fierce, Glen Elliott exemplified the mold of a Texas Ranger. *Photo courtesy of Glenn Elliott*

▲ The original badges worn by Texas Rangers were carved out of Mexican five-peso silver coins. Actual Texas Ranger badges are rare, as there are not many Rangers to begin with. The example on the left is a commemorative collectible but a good example nonetheless. The current Texas Ranger badge is, in fact, still made from a Mexican Cinco Peso coin.

Despite being charged with covering a very large area west of Houston, Texas Ranger Westmoreland said he likes working alone. Being self-sufficient has always been key to a Ranger's personality. But he was quick to add that he also enjoys working with other agencies. To quote Aristotle, "The whole is greater than the sum of its parts," and that is how Westmoreland sees interacting with local sheriffs, city police, constables, and other entities. Westmoreland refused to list a specialty, but most of his cases are homicides and many involve home invasion.

When the subject turned to defending the home, Ranger Westmoreland underscored that most homicides occur between people who already know each other. The cause is typically revenge for something personal, such as infidelity, or a disagreement that leads to a physical confrontation.

But what about home invasions or the types of violent robberies perpetrated by strangers? How do they happen, where do they happen, and who are they most likely to happen to?

Disagreements that lead to a physical confrontation can happen anywhere. But most violent crime occurs in neighborhoods of lower socio economic strata. The adage that poverty causes crime did not come up in our conversation. Ranger Westmoreland simply offered that criminals are generally poorer and live in lower income neighborhoods. Furthermore, the assessment of types of crimes versus types of neighborhoods indicates that higher income neighborhoods tend to experience property crime while lower income neighborhoods suffer more violent crime.

The most likely victims of a home invasion are those who deal in cash or merchandise and are likely to have it in their homes with them. For example, a merchant who regularly brings home the day's cash receipts or the store's change bank to deposit the next morning may unwittingly create a pattern of behavior noticeable to professional criminals. Another example, and this generally feeds back into the incidence of crime in lower income neighborhoods, is the drug dealer or someone who deals in stolen merchandise. Naturally, drug dealing would be an all-cash business. Similarly, someone who deals in stolen merchandise is not likely to seek the protection of the police or have a commercially monitored alarm system. So, anyone planning

to rob from another robber has that much less to be concerned with.

But what about home invasions that happen to law-abiding citizens, no matter what neighborhood they live in? If aggressors know something of value is in the house, how they got this information is often preventable. Letting a stranger, such as a workman, cleaning lady, or houseguest, know that you have a safe, for example, would be a magnet for robbery.

While legitimate small-business owners may make a practice of bringing cash home, thereby creating a pattern of behavior for criminals to spot, the average person may do something similar subconsciously and therefore not be aware of the risk they are taking. For example, one way a criminal would know you have something they want is by following you home from a bank. This can lead to a driveway robbery followed by entry into the home. One of the easiest ways to be marked as having cash would be to complete a transaction at a bank that's located inside a supermarket. This could also happen after leaving a bank that is not housed within another business, but it is easier to spot a potential crook inside the typical standalone bank building. Anyone who comes into the bank just to pick up a deposit slip, for example, might be casing you or the bank. But in a supermarket there is always a large cross section of people coming and going. Someone casing a supermarket bank and its customers can easily appear to be shopping. Bank often personnel have some training to spot a problem and will call the police, while supermarket workers are primarily there to stock shelves, ring up customers, and bag groceries. Furthermore, most shoppers do not associate being in a supermarket with the same level of risk that should go with entering a bank. So the practice of looking out for suspicious characters and alerting supermarket staff or security is less likely. "The best place for a criminal to hide," says Westmoreland, "is in plain sight."

What you put in the trash is another common magnet for thieves, especially around the holidays. A big box from a flat screen television, for example, can invite a robbery. Though flat screen TVs are now commonplace, Westmoreland recommends that boxes for big-ticket items should be cut up and bagged. Some people point out that door-to-door salespeople can also be linked to robbery or home invasion. While

▲ Home invasions and robberies are rarely spontaneous "fishing expeditions." Usually, the invaders include someone who has been in the house or learned from a third party that valuables are stored there. A big safe placed conspicuously in the house would be a tip-off. Another way in which attention can be drawn to your home is if you bring home the daily receipts or change till from a small business. Burglars could just as easily show up when no one is home. If you do have a safe as formidable as this one, the fastest way for the crooks to get inside it is to have you open it and turn off any alarm that may be tripped. *Photo courtesy of Cannon Safes*

it is better to live in a community where soliciting is against regulations or, better yet, a gated community, door-to-door salespeople or a crew that leaves flyers on doors are bound to get in anyway. Asked if flagging, or leaving flyers on doors, was an instrument of would-be robbers, Kip Westmoreland said this is a lesser concern. Do criminals plant fliers, take note of how many flyers are piling up, and, under the assumption that no one is home, choose it for a break-in? This may be true but Westmoreland said, "That's just too much work." A bigger danger would be using the excuse of delivering a flyer to get close to the house and see what's inside or knocking on the door and asking to come inside. In the case of door-to-door salespeople, it is usually a woman or the least threatening member of the crew who tries to gain entry to discuss insurance or give a free estimate on cleaning rugs, painting, or some other offer. The rest of the gang may be lurking out of sight. Westmoreland offered two rules in this case. First, do not open the door to strangers. In addition, "If something doesn't feel right, then it is not right."

Whether you are leaving a store, in the process of parking your car, or just looking outside the window of your house, there are some clues to look for that can help you protect yourself. Be aware of your surroundings. This could mean shopping or getting gas in locations you are familiar with just so you are able to better recognize what might seem out of place. Looking

▲ Placing advertising materials on doorknobs is called flagging. When asked if flagging is used as an indicator of how often the home is vacant, our Texas Ranger said it was unlikely, as it would be way too complicated. But it can be annoying and letting handbills pile up could eventually attract simple breaking and entering.

through the eyes of a Texas Ranger, here are some specifics that should raise a red flag. Anyone who looks different than the usual clientele or anyone getting dropped off and picked up again. Cars with paper license plates or no plates at all. People not dressed consistently with the weather, such as a bulky jacket in August. Oversized clothing can be used to hide a weapon or even a different set of clothes for a quick change of appearance. Wearing a hood up and, of course, a mask or kerchief, are also dangerous signs.

Included with awareness of your surroundings is taking into account the physical structure in which you live. Ranger Westmoreland points out that apartments are much more difficult to defend. In a subdivision of freestanding homes it is not difficult to get to know everyone who lives on your street. If not closely, at least it is possible to know what they look like or what cars they own. Single-family homes don't turn over quickly, so it is relatively easy to be aware of any change in occupancy and remain familiar with what the residents look like, at least in a peripheral sense. Apartment complexes in Texas, for example, usually lease for a period of six months. Given the staggered time periods for each lease, it is possible to see new people come and go from week to week. Another aspect is that most people who live in a suburban subdivision keep a daytime work schedule. Even if the racial makeup of a subdivision is varied, the residents generally share similar behavior in terms of employment and stability. Westmoreland points out that a car showing up in the middle of the night might not be unusual in an apartment complex, while a strange car driving through a quiet neighborhood at night is typically met with alarm.

Obviously the apartment is much less safe than the freestanding house. Let's say a car pulls up in the middle of the night. In an apartment complex, there is no telling if the occupants will approach your door or the one above you. If the apartment complex, or for that matter a subdivision, is protected by a manned gate, this alone can discourage entry. But guards have been fooled by phony delivery services, says Ranger Westmoreland. In these cases, again, the driver who interacts with the guard is typically female or the member of the crew with the least threatening appearance. Merely by appearing normal and not raising suspicion,

such phony delivery services can also be effective in non-gated communities or those that have only a mechanically operated gate.

The position of the home in relation to a road can make it easier or more difficult to attack. What the invaders are looking for is a house in a location that affords a secretive approach and fast get away. Naturally, they prefer to keep their car nearby, so a strange vehicle parked unobtrusively with or without someone inside would be a red flag. For the apartment complex dweller, the red flag would be looking outside at night and seeing a car with the motor running.

Another aspect of defending the home is time. How much time do you have before the aggressor is upon you? According to Westmoreland the amount of time you have may relate to the distance between your house and the ones next door, or the distance the house sits from the street. But once the aggressors are on the property or at the door, the next level of defense is how well your home is fortified.

The primary course of entry begins with the robber knocking on the front door. Once the occupant opens the door, the robbers force their way inside the home. The second most common method of entry would be criminals kicking in either the front or rear doors.

So let's look at the doors themselves. The primary doors (both front and rear), should have a dead bolt extending into the doorframe. The lock should be key-operated on both the interior and exterior sides.

A locking outer door is highly recommended. This door is best fit with a wrought iron grid. Also, the outer door should hinged to open outward, if possible, opposite to the inner door. This buys time, both at the time of a break-in and in a situation where you may have been fooled into opening the inner door.

Anything that slows an intruder down buys you time to access a weapon or escape. The locked double doors not only add precious seconds to your chances, but opening them can generate noise to alert you, such as breaking glass, the prying of a hinge, or just a squeaky hinge. Naturally, an audible alarm system you can monitor is an advantage. But even if the aggressor is not so worried about the alarm bringing police immediately, it does at least provide a warning and hopefully a useful adrenaline rush to the occupants of the house.

▲ Homes that are invaded or burglarized are chosen not only for what they contain, but also their proximity to an easy getaway route. This street is an ideal location for a getaway car or truck. None of the houses face the road, the back wall could be easily scaled, and the trees provide additional cover. Anyone hearing an alarm will likely look out the front of the house and not be able to see the getaway car. The possibility of a home invasion or burglary in broad daylight is a real possibility. People rarely set their alarms when they are at home during the day. Can you spot what is most suspicious about the vehicle, aside from being parked where it is for no obvious reason? The license plate has been obscured.

A fence around the entire property is also effective, but even more so if all the gates are kept locked. Can an intruder climb over the fence or break through the gate? Certainly. But not without (hopefully) making enough noise to wake you up. Think about getting a dog. The majority of criminals do not want to encounter a dog of any description. Even a small dog is an effective noise multiplier. We've all read suggestions about placing thorn bushes by windows to discourage peeping toms, unwanted surveillance, and people waiting in ambush. But when it comes to home invaders, thorn bushes will only discourage the amateur.

Once the invaders are inside the house, if you are not able to mount a resistance you are better off to comply. Of course the purpose of this book is to teach you not to allow the situation to get to this point. But

your life may be an even trade for what they are looking for. Expect to be tied up, probably with a lamp cord, tape, or whatever is already in the house. The invaders will be intimidating, threatening and yelling the names of the specific items they are after. This is a firm indication that the house was targeted and not chosen at random.

Many television programs that deal with protecting the home show the homeowner searching, or clearing, the interior of the house. But in a home invasion such a practice will likely be irrelevant. Since the purpose of most home invasions is to steal something thieves already know is there, the intruders will be moving quickly and looking for you so you can tell them where it is. "In homes that are specifically targeted for the contents of a safe," says Ranger Westmoreland, "the

▲ Having a fence around your home can be a great asset. It does not have to be impenetrable to offer an advantage. Indeed, this gate is not much better than rickety, but whether the trespasser jumps over the fence or pushes though the gate it's going to make a lot of noise.

▲ In a world where all sorts of gadgetry are being peddled as alarm systems, visiting with Texas Ranger Kip Westmoreland was a reality check. According to Ranger Westmoreland, man's best friend is still one of the most effective deterrents to criminal trespass. Do you need a specially trained attack dog? Not necessarily. Canine behavior is unpredictable and even a small dog can make a lot of noise.

criminals typically want the homeowner to be present so that he or she is available to open the safe." One suggestion is if you are going to have a safe, don't make that fact well known. Bolt it to the floor or at a minimum buy one that is too heavy to be easily carried away.

Surprise and speed of attack are what make a home invasion difficult to defend. This also makes it difficult to take advantage of another practice that is commonly recommended, that of having a safe room. Movement to the safe room depends upon whether the way to the safe room crosses the path of the intruder. If it does, the occupants are better off staying put, staying low, and hiding. Above all, there has to be a plan. For example, if there is only one person in the house who has a gun, such as the parent, the other occupants need to stay put so the gunner knows the only people moving around are the bad guys.

If you have had time to arm yourself, you may have a chance to fight or drive out the intruders. This would require ready access to a weapon, preferably a firearm. The first choice, according to Ranger Westmoreland, would be a shotgun. Pinpoint accuracy is not necessary and the force a shotgun can deliver, especially a 12-gauge model, is potent. When asked if he preferred pump action or semi-automatic he showed no preference. But the reliability of the pump shotgun, he noted, is nearly foolproof.

Whether or not the gunner or another family member is tasked with dialing 911, contact needs to be made as soon as it is safe to do so. If one occupant is holed up at the opposite side of the house and needs to stay concealed, it is a good idea to have a cell phone set with ringtones and other sounds turned down so that when it is turned on it doesn't give off an audible sound. Nor should it make any sound while dialing. Today's touch-screen phones need to be visible to be operated. Remember to shield the face of the cell phone so it doesn't throw enough light to be seen. While cell phones may not be ideal, they are, above all, immune to being cut off by an aggressor or burned out in case of fire.

Contact with a 911 operator can be a slightly different experience depending on where you live. I have heard 911 operators answer with, "Where is the emergency?" But I've also heard, "Do you need police, fire,

◀ Home invaders often rely upon deceit rather than brute force to gain entry. Masquerading as law enforcement would be one method. But this can be dangerous for law enforcement personnel, too. While serving a warrant, the appearance of law enforcement clothing and gear can cause some confusion regarding identification. Criminals are more willing to shoot it out with people they think are imposters rather than actual police. The sale, however, of ballistic vests and ID hats was never meant to cause problems for anyone but the bad guys. Security stores sell generic ballistic wear for civilian defense. Hats and faux uniforms are primarily meant to be worn by dummies, or scarecrows, to add an extra layer of protection. *Photos by R. Eckstine courtesy of Central Spy Shop, Houston*

or ambulance?" as the initial greeting. Personally, I prefer the former rather than a multiple-choice question. The latter makes me feel like they're trying to shuffle me off to some other department. In a home invasion, access to the telephone may be limited to seconds. If I were ever involved with an incident that warranted a call to 911, I would just blurt out the problem and location. For example, "1313 Mockingbird Lane, home invasion, send police now." The call is being recorded anyway and if there is time the operator can always ask additional questions. If I were to be cut off at least they would know where I was, why I was calling, and what was needed.

The 911 operator will stay on the line as long as possible. If it was your job to hunker down and call 911 and you were not involved directly with the assault, you will be kept informed of police progress. They will stay with you and tell you when the police are at the door and when it is safe to come out.

There have been reports of intruders posing as police to gain entry. In conversation with Ranger Westmoreland, I learned that this can pose an even greater risk to law enforcement than it does to civilians. For the typical home occupant, it is important to take note of everything each officer is wearing should they approach your home or vehicle. Impostors will generally rely on wearing a partial uniform such as shirt that reads "Police" or some sort of generic body armor—any few items that might convince the unsuspecting eye that they are legitimate law enforcement personnel. Of course, once the robbery is in progress, all pretense would likely be dropped.

For law enforcement, the danger of impostors can involve what could be described as a boomerang effect, something much different from innocents versus intruders. Occupants can sometimes mistake officers approaching the house to serve a legitimate warrant for criminals posing as law enforcement to gain entry. One reason for this may be that often more than one agency or department can be part of the warrant team. This could raise doubts about authenticity simply because all the officers aren't dressed the same. To the skeptical mind the subjects of the warrant may just be using this as an excuse. Most warrants are served without incidence, the increasing number of criminals posing as police has other wanted criminals on the defensive, ready and willing to shoot it out.

Beyond the specific observations offered by Ranger Kip Westmoreland and seeing through the eyes of a Texas Ranger, I'm led to recommend staying in touch with local law enforcement. For example, there was no reason why anyone in the restaurant where we'd met couldn't have come up to Kip or to one of the sheriff's deputies and asked, "Excuse me, officer, can I ask you a question? Should I switch the dead bolt lock on my back door from a twist knob on the inside to key operated?" Or, "Which savings banks are the safest for me to use in this area?" The answer to either one of these questions could end up being of enormous value. It is important to remember that no matter where you live there is an underworld. Your first line of home defense is to raise awareness about the specific threats in your neighborhood that hide in plain sight.

Security Systems and Layers of Defense

A friend of mine named Tony is rather large and imposing. Not a lot of people ask to use his cell phone, for spare change, or what time it is. Aside from a pair of goldfish, he has only one other pet, a Chihuahua named Dropkick. Dropkick is not only his faithful companion but also his primary security system. Tony explains that his dog does not run on batteries, so he never seems to wear out, and he is a light sleeper. "Remember all those big old mastiffs and lion dogs kept by emperors, kings, and queens? They just sleep all the time and they're pretty slow. Of course they can scare the hell out of you, but Dropkick is hyperactive and thinks he gets paid every time he barks. Actually, I guess he does get paid per bark because I give him a treat for sounding off when anybody gets near the house," Tony says.

"Actually, his main job is to wake up the Big Dog. That's me," he adds.

An audible alarm calling attention to an emergency is perhaps the most recognized signal of traditional security systems. This would include the blowing of a cavalry bugle or even the legendary shouting of "To arms!" by Paul Revere. A barking dog is another traditional favorite, but parrots or other birds can also sound an alarm. Even if no one is on the premises, an audible alarm is like the starter's pistol at a track meet. Monitored or not, the trespasser knows his or her time is limited before a neighbor or passerby calls police or a patrol is drawn to the scene.

When it comes to modern electronic security systems, today's homeowners have several options. First of all, just about every new house being built has at least the option to be pre-wired for a security system. This means contact points for each door and window, with keypads at the front and rear entrances, plus inside the master bedroom. The same unit can also react to sound and vibration, which is generally referred to as a glass-break feature. This could be triggered by a window being shattered or just the vibration from an attempt at breaking a window. Doors not actually opened but jarred from an impact will also respond to this feature. Some front doors have a stained glass or decorative center section large enough for an adult to step through. Vibration from the act of breaking through should trigger the alarm, even if the door were not actually opened.

If for some reason forced entry is not detected, movement sensors can also trigger the alarm. Once set, the movement sensor creates an infrared line that, when broken, sets off the alarm. Movement sensors are generally mounted high on the wall so they are out of reach. Also, it should be set up so the trespasser must cross the beam to approach the monitoring unit. It is important to aim the unit's beam so the trespasser sets off the alarm before moving far inside the house.

In addition to responding to entering the house and moving about, today's security systems can also monitor dangerous levels of carbon monoxide—a deadly, colorless, odorless gas—as well as smoke, heat, and the presence of dangerous levels of water in case of flooding. Temperatures can also be monitored on the

▲ Is this a motion detector, camera, or both? This is the type of equipment that stores like Central Spy Shop in Houston specializes in. *Photo by R. Eckstine, courtesy of Central Spy Shop, Houston*

low end to send a warning that pipes are in danger of freezing. Alarms can be monitored by individuals on the premises or remotely by a professional monitoring service.

All of the above is not likely to be news to home owners. But, what's more interesting are options for owner-monitored security systems that utilize digital cameras connected to cellular communication. Cameras mounted inside or outside the house, or both, can relay real-time images to smart phones. In addition, these images can be recorded and stored for up to four weeks or more depending on the size of the hard

drive. Additional features include automatic review and overwrite, which is similar to erase and rewind.

The application, or app, adds value to the system by allowing the user to monitor activity on a cell phone, iPad, personal computer, or through your home network on a monitor or television screen. The screen can also be split to display more than one camera at a time, just like a monitoring agent in a department store. Furthermore, the view from each individual camera can be isolated and enlarged. This viewing can be done from inside the house or anywhere else a cellular signal is available. For example, with the proper app

▲ Security systems with multiple cameras can be monitored from the back bedroom, across town, or across the nation. This means by using an iPad (as shown), cellular telephone, or television screen, you can see who is at your front door and be prepared. *Photo by R. Eckstine, courtesy of Central Spy Shop, Houston*

▲ The picture of the store interior on channel seven is bowed in appearance, indicating a wide-angle lens with the ability to move left and right, sweeping the area. *Photo by R. Eckstine, courtesy of Central Spy Shop Houston*

▲ Monitoring activity on a flat screen digital television is ideal, providing a big canvas on which you can pull event files in the form of a spreadsheet. The blue areas indicate when the motion-activated cameras were recording. Sensitivity to motion is adjustable and so are the areas that each camera is set to cover, all at the click of a mouse. Replays for the typical home system remain available for one month before auto-erasing begins.

you can live in Los Angeles and keep an eye on your house while visiting friends in Chicago.

Naturally, the more intricate the system, the more it will cost. Prices vary depending on how much you shop around and how much of the installation you can do yourself. Upgrading with your current provider is one possible course of action. But, a full system of professionally monitored equipment with video can cost anywhere from $1,500 to several thousand dollars, depending on how many sensors, cameras, and keypads must be installed.

Much of the focus of a monitored security system is on illegal entry, specifically when the home is unoccupied. But let's not forget what we learned in the chapter Through the Eyes of a Ranger. If you have something of significant value in your house or someone thinks you do, you may be targeted for home invasion. And if you do have cash or valuable merchandise, it is probably locked up or hidden somewhere out of view. In this case, the invaders need you to be at home, because the fastest way for the bandits to get what they are looking for is to ask you where it is. While most people do not set their alarm when they are at home unless it is nighttime, the realization that the intruders are being videotaped may in itself act as a deterrent. But if the security system were armed, a monitoring service might be able to respond with appropriate use of force.

With this in mind, perhaps the single most important component a homeowner can install in terms of a security system is a wireless camera offering real-time surveillance of the front door. A second camera view of the rear door, yard, or gate is an excellent idea, too, but here is the point. Whether the cameras

▲ When burglars and home invaders consider a target, they tend to attack in a path of least resistance. As Damian Halforty once said, "I'm not going to stop the guy from robbing. I just want to deflect him to the next house. If he has an alarm, I want to have an alarm and a gate. He has a gate and you don't, you're in trouble. He has a gate and you have a gate and a wall, you're good." Video surveillance is a key advantage in the race to discourage crime. Cameras, both real and decoy, are available at stores such as the Central Spy Shop in Houston. *Photos by R. Eckstine, courtesy of Central Spy Shop Houston*

▲ This is a rotating wide-angle camera capable of covering more space than most other types of equipement. It is ideal for interior corners or exterior overhangs. *Photo by R. Eckstine, courtesy of Central Spy Shop Houston*

are professionally monitored or not, day or night, when someone comes to your door you will not have to leave your position to verify friend or foe. You can view the exterior door from your bedroom, study, a purpose-built safe room, or as you beat it out the back door.

Additional safety features of a wireless- or cell-phone-controlled system include being able to arm or disarm the system. Here how this makes you safer. Alarm system keypads are necessarily located near the very doors they protect. In some cases, the keypad may be visible from outside. For example, a front door with opaque stained glass will invariably have a vertical window to either side. The keypad could easily be visible to anyone at the door, making it possible to witness and record the code as you key it in. This could lead to unauthorized entry immediately or days later when the memory of a brief visit has faded and identifying possible suspects is more difficult. Control by

one touch of a key chain unit or while standing away and using the touch screen of your iPhone can prevent someone from stealing the code.

Being able to remotely arm and disarm a security system can reduce liability all around. Suppose you ask a neighbor to enter your house to, say, feed the dog or turn off some lights. You can let them in or out without revealing the code. This can make them safer and prevent a third party from learning the code.

Additional Levels of Security

How we choose from the wide array of features for a security system is shaped by our expectations and needs based on experience. If you've not had to deal with a high level of crime in the past, then it is more likely that the system you choose will be less extensive than someone who has dealt with break-ins and muggings on a regular basis. So to learn the most we can about security methods and systems, let's go to an extreme and take a look at a specific environment where criminal activity has induced a high level of stress.

In much of suburban America, the friction between groups divided by race, ethnicity, or income is just not that explosive when compared to a place like South Africa. Friction between the classes, which for some time could be considered synonymous with race, was already exacerbating crime when, in the early 1990s, the government began to follow an agenda of disarming the public. This included a "common sense" approach allowing only one handgun, shotgun, and rifle to each citizen. The reality was, however, that each weapon required a separate license and only one such license could be granted per year. Furthermore, there was an 80 percent chance that a license would be denied. Antigun legislation was originally intended to disarm the rich, that is, the white population. But, as more and more black South Africans have prospered, the ill effects of restrictive gun laws are now being felt by every law-abiding citizen, regardless of race.

In a later chapter, Understanding the Stages of Violent Crime, we will meet native South African security specialist Damian Halforty, who runs Four/Zero Firearms and Weapons Specialists out of New Zealand. When asked about security systems, Halforty offered that a home should have five different levels of security features. But when we totaled the number of features built into many South African homes, we were able to list more than twice that amount. "The more levels the better," says Halforty. "More levels increase risk to the attackers."

The overall idea, he suggested, was to have more than the guy next door. "I'm not going to stop the guy from robbing. I just want to deflect him to the next house. If he has an alarm, I want to have an alarm and a gate. He has a gate and you don't, you're in trouble. He has a gate and you have a gate and a wall, you're good."

To some extent, a good security consultant can ride through a neighborhood and tell you the level of crime that goes on in that community. In a high-crime environment, the strength and quality of the walls and doors, for example, can indicate how many crimes take place. If the neighborhood pets are rottweilers rather than poodles, you'll know where you are. With this in mind, here is a list of recommended security levels or layers beginning at the perimeter that can actually be found in an extreme example, the suburbs of Johannesburg, South Africa.

Level 1

Level 1 begins with a perimeter garden featuring a ring of thorn-bearing foliage planted closely to a security wall surrounding the property. Not only will this hinder attempts to scale the wall, but it can also discourage loitering for the purpose of setting an ambush or surveilling the premises. The thorn plant of choice in South Africa is the Devil's Thorn. The touch of the Devil's Thorn is well known to quickly produce an itchy rash.

Level 2

A typical Level 2 structure would be a solid wall in place of a slatted or chain link fence. The purpose is to not only block vision but also create a barrier strong enough to require nothing less than being rammed by a vehicle for it to be breached.

Level 3

In addition to a solid structure, an electric fence is added with the capability to deliver an impressive, if not injurious, shock upon contact. This fence should also be monitored by sensors to respond to breakage and excess vibration.

Level 4

Fully monitored alarm systems are typically standard, but in South African suburbs alarms call an armed response team.

Level 5

Cameras for monitoring all entrances, yards, and gardens with closed-circuit capability on screens inside the house, as well as by a professional security service, are common.

Level 6

Outdoor lighting with motion detectors is a must, but adding floodlights that point away from the house are even better. Floodlights make the interior of house more difficult to see while illuminating the grounds. In addition to motion activation, the lights can be switched on manually from inside the house.

Level 7

Many walled homes have dogs roaming the outside grounds. Often these dogs are professional guards, rented or owned, rather than pets. Most people choose not to endanger their pets because they can easily be poisoned or shot. But keep in mind, if the dogs are shot you should take it as a signal that the trespassers are armed and highly motivated.

Level 8

Homes are fitted with the hardest possible doors, if not steel then solid oak. This includes interior as well as exterior doors. Plus, locks constructed with the hardest metals and dead bolts that pass through a steel frame. Multiple security doors for the same entrance are recommended, hinged to open in opposite directions from one another. The outer door should swing open to the outside. Sliding doors are another good option due to the lack of hinges and better circumferential support.

Level 9

Multiple interior alarm systems that operate independently, so disabling one system will not disable alarms in other parts of the house. Separate alarm systems should monitor different rooms and hallways. In addition, sensors should be placed at the base of each stairwell.

Level 10

There should be security gates located inside the house to block off specific areas or zones. Gates at the bottom of a stairway can be crucial. Many homes feature the construction of a separate caged area or fortified safe room where an attack can be waited out. However, you must have an exit strategy to avoid being trapped in a fire. This is reportedly not dissimilar to what happened to personnel during the attack on the American compound in Benghazi on September 11, 2012 that killed Ambassador Christopher Stevens.

Level 11

One final strategy is to launch gas bombs or a pepper fog as you move away from the threat or retreat to a safe room. Working on the assumption that all family members or other innocents are moving with you, spraying the hall with bullets as you leave might finally convince the invaders that they should reconsider further advance.

Obviously, this list illustrates a very severe level of violent crime that has left South Africans in a desperate situation. You may look at it and say, "I don't live in a home large enough to be sectioned off, let alone surrounded by a wall. Even if I did, I couldn't afford those kinds of hired security services." Then again, you may be in a situation where employing every single one of these methods would be totally plausible, if not completely warranted. In any event, let's take an objective look at each of these levels and see how many can be adapted to your way of life.

Thorn-bearing plants in the United States, for example, may not be as allergenic or harmful as those in Africa, but there are a number of spiky and thorny plants that could be planted at least in front of your windows. As previously noted, this will probably only discourage amateurs, but it might be smart to take every advantage you can get.

Adding a wall to surround your home in the typical subdivision is likely against deed restrictions. But, if it is allowed and you think it fits your needs, then by all means build it. Most houses do, however, come with some sort of fence. But if they are shared with a neighbor you won't be able string barbed wire or electrify it anywhere but on your side, which defeats the purpose of this type of equipment. Gates could, however, be tied to an alarm system. The problem is that, physically, most gates of wood or metal are rarely constructed with enough precision or integrity to prevent the alarm from going off, should a stiff wind push against it. Most people don't padlock their gates, but they should. Remember the advice, "Make them break something." Always make an intruder do something loud.

No matter where you live, a monitored alarm system of one sort or another is going to be available. As for armed response, most people have the luxury of city police or the county sheriff's department. Adding or depending solely on private armed security may be another option. One reason people choose to hire armed private security has to do with economics, an overwhelming increase in crime, or both. For example, a recent headline from Chicago announced that due to the booming murder rate, calling 911 would no longer be an option in the case of nonviolent situations, such as automobile theft. Headlines from other smaller municipalities have spotlighted statements by law enforcement officials that the citizens should arm themselves because police just don't have the manpower to protect everyone all the time.

For example, according to a report by Albuquerque, New Mexico's, Armed Response Team Inc. (ArmedResponseTeam.com), an increase in crime is not always followed by hiring more police. A recent change in the retirement system in the State of New Mexico provided an incentive for veteran police to retire early. This may have saved the state some money, but it ignored and exacerbated the increase in crime.

False alarms, which drain patrol resources, present another obstacle to municipal and county police services. This not only drives up response time but in some cases police have decided to not respond to security alarms at all. This can happen in rural areas as well as cities. Armed Response cites Montgomery County, Maryland, where response by the sheriff's department was curtailed unless they could verify that the alarm was the result of an incident endangering a live person rather than wind, an animal, or mechanical or electrical malfunction.

In fairness to publicly funded law enforcement, it is the duty of anyone who owns or maintains a security system, monitored or otherwise, to keep the system in top shape and maintain the integrity of all connections and sensing points.

One may ask if a private security force would be just as likely to slack off if false alarms begin to pile up. When shopping for a private security company my first question would be, "What is their average response time?" Plus, "How many officers would respond per vehicle?" "What is the average age of the officers and their level of training and experience?"

This is a buyer beware situation and it's best to check with other people who have used the same service or hired private security companies in the past.

Before considering hiring the armed response services of a private company, you should check with a lawyer or your insurance provider for an update on your liability coverage. Then place a call to the management company that services your neighborhood or homeowners association. In some cases, your property management company will be able to supply you with the name of a private security provider with whom they already have a general contract. It's possible you can upgrade to have this same company monitor your specific premises.

If you already have a contract with a monitored security service, be aware of a popular scam that usually takes place in spring or summer, when the weather breaks and there is an increase in door-to-door salespeople entering subdivisions and neighborhoods. Here is how this can affect anyone with a security service contract, active or expired, or even someone with a fake sign propped up in the garden. Let's say, for example, you have a security system that was installed and is currently monitored by 1800DROPKICK (this is a fictitious name), and there is a sign on your lawn and a decal in your window saying so. The scam begins with a salesperson introducing him- or herself by saying they are with 1800DROPKICK security and are offering a free upgrade to their new digital wireless system. Another ploy is saying he or she is from 1800STOMP security (another fictitious name), which he or she claims has bought out 1800DROPKICK. The motivation here is one of two things, or perhaps both. They

then get your money or credit card number by signing you up for a new contract (prorated, of course). If they can't get you to sign up, they can at least have a look at your security system to "verify and analyze" to provide better service or simply "update their records."

What can make these door-to-door sales calls seem legitimate is the apparent sincerity of the salesperson. In some cases, the salesperson may have no connection whatsoever to any criminal activity. The contact person at your door may be a perfectly honest, hard-working person hired temporarily through a posting or classified ad. Naturally, their ignorance makes for a good front. On the other hand, professional scam artists are well prepared. The only way to protect yourself against talented and studied people who play what used to be called the confidence game (because they succeed by gaining your confidence), is to stick with specific protocol no matter what anyone says.

The protocol to protect yourself against being taken in by sales calls include asking for personal identification of the salesperson, a work ID with photo, and a vendor number. Keep in mind that anytime your current security provider intends to call on you, they should provide the name of the representative ahead of time. If you receive a telephone call from your security company other than in response to an alarm, you can ask for the representative's name and call them back. If the caller gives you a number other than the one listed on the security system keypad, be suspicious.

Next on the list are cameras and lighting. As discussed earlier, cameras can save you the trouble of having to go to a door or window to evaluate an unexpected visitor or other situation. Cameras can also alert you to the identity and position of anyone on the premises while you're in a safe room or another location or in a position of tactical advantage. That is, of course, assuming it is daylight, unless you have installed cameras with night vision capability. While the latest cameras may not be capable of night vision, low-light enhanced capabilities have improved markedly and such cameras are widely available.

Lights are essential and can aid surveillance of a situation and identification of a subject, and also act as a deterrent. Lighting makes trespass less safe for the criminal. Problems in keeping a security light system active include maintaining power and protecting them from burning out or being damaged. Lights that suddenly aren't working could indicate they were compromised during daylight hours to make a night-time attack easier. Lights should also be checked for effective positioning. If the lights are mounted just above door height, it won't be difficult for a stalker, for example, to shift the beams of light to create a blind spot. If possible, mark the position of the individual lights after you have adjusted them to the optimum angle. This way they can be checked during daylight hours before leaving the home in darkness becomes a potentially dangerous situation. Any shift in the position of the lights or the destruction thereof should serve as a warning that your property is being surveilled.

Regarding maintaining power, battery backup is usually provided as part of the system. But a separate set of lights may require additional power. For anyone living in an area where hurricanes are common, switching to a generator is standard operating procedure. But a generator system that automatically takes over is not as common. A separate battery backup strictly for emergency lights, such as those found as part of a fire alarm system in commercial buildings, would be a worthwhile option.

Investing in heavier doors and hinges can get expensive if you intend to replace every door in the house. One inexpensive but effective product is the NightLock. The NightLock provides a vertical block mounted into the floor to prevent the door from swinging inward. The base of the unit is bolted into the floor and the vertical piece slides into place from either side. While the construction is heavy steel, the components are nicely finished and somewhat visually appealing, if not decorative. The NightLock is often applied to the back door where an intruder can work with less possibility of detection.

Certainly, an upgraded two-door system at the front entrance is a must. The standard front door is wood

▲ Whether outdoor security lights are manually operated or motion activated, they need to be checked regularly to make sure they continue to illuminate entry ways and blind spots. One easy way to make sure they are not tampered with is to tighten them into position and mark the connecting hardware. Note how all three of the lines are broken, rather than continuous. Both of these lights have been tampered with and the beams have been redirected.

▲ The NightLock, available from installers such as Door Refinishing Company of Houston, is a clever, simple, and strong way to prevent doors from being pushed inward. The base plate bolts directly into the slab. The vertical piece is not only removable for daytime access, but it's reversible, too. In one position it serves to bridge the gap above a step plate (as shown). Slide it out and turn it around, and it fits flush against an interior door. The NightLock is made from heavy steel and treated to an electro-chemically applied finish in colors gold, silver, or black. *Photo by R. Eckstine, courtesy of Door Refinishing Company*

with decorative carving, a pattern of leaded glass, or both. A thumb-operated latch, rather than twist knob, with a separate dead bolt lock is also standard. The first upgrade, if necessary, should be to replace the twist-turn mechanism that sets the dead bolt from the inside with a cylinder that requires key operation from both the interior and the exterior. In addition, the channel into which the dead bolt feeds, or the strike, should be extended and braced well into the door frame with products like the Tuff Strike.

The next upgrade should be to add a second outer door that also features a two-way deadbolt. Most people avoid installing an outer door to the front entrance primarily for appearance as well as cost. The wood and leaded glass front door is universally appealing. No one wants to spoil the looks of their house with a metal screen door or ugly burglar bars. Clear glass pane doors allow for the decorative value of a front door to show through but obviously doesn't seem much like a security upgrade. However, today's advancements in glass technology offer a remarkable layer of security.

KeepSafe glass from Monsanto is an example of a window barrier consisting of a clear plastic laminated between two layers of glass. The layers are bonded under heat and pressure so the glass shares the elasticity of the plastic without losing clarity. Struck repeatedly, the glass outer layers will indeed break. But they stay in place against the plastic layer so no shards of glass separate and become hazardous and the glass panel remains almost impenetrable.

For anyone concerned about appearance, the KeepSafe glass is clear and tough enough that a single panel can be used from top to bottom, allowing for nearly a full view of the decorative front door. Companies such as Larson Door offer a variety of designs using KeepSafe glass, which include single-pane designs offering an unobstructed view to door frames that are enhanced with a variety of designer grill work.

One of the reasons doors such as the Larson products succeed as a barrier to break-ins is that the glass is set in a steel frame. Even products such as KeepSafe glass

▼ Dead bolt locks are a must. However, they are only as strong as the striker plate mounted on the door jam. Most dead bolts simply pass through a small plate held with two ½-inch wood screws. The Tuff Strike from HappyDoors.com consists of a hardened steel faceplate and pegs that sink more than three inches deep into the studs that support the door frame. *Photo by R. Eckstine, courtesy of HappyDoors.com*

▲ High-crime areas demand high tech locks. The Ultimate Lock offers a unique level of durability and design with hardened steel components and internal crush zones that compress under the force of most attacks, spoiling the attempt before the primary components can be affected. The striker plate consists of specially hardened steel and is screwed into the jam at a 45-degree angle. Professional installation of The Ultimate Lock is recommended. *Photo by R. Eckstine, courtesy of Door Refinishing Company*

would be worthless if they popped out of their frames during impact, no matter how difficult it was to break. For anyone considering bulletproof or bullet-resistant laminates on home windows, consider the following important points. First, out of the many law enforcement personnel interviewed for this book, virtually all agreed that the primary focus of home defense is to prevent forced entry. That being said, anyone considering installing bulletproof glass, a bullet-resistant type of glazing, or stick-on laminate must keep in mind how the glass pane itself is secured. The ability of different products to stop projectiles tends to vary. Some laminates advertise that installation as easy as applying window tint. One problem that could occur is that while the windowpane itself may be able to withstand ballistic impact, it could get pushed out of the frame altogether, leaving a gaping hole. The wooden frames

in your windows may have to be replaced by steel frames or even more elaborate interface with the home construction. Professional installation is recommended.

But what if you are a renter? In an apartment complex you can always ask for an upgrade, but don't necessarily expect one. In high-rise apartments the front doors tend to be heavier for fire protection because of stricter codes for multi-unit dwellings. One upgrade you should be able to do yourself in any house or apartment is to install a heavier door to a specific room. The bedroom is usually the farthest room from the front door and the place where you spend the most time in your most vulnerable state. So, installing a heavy locking door to the bedroom would be a worthwhile security upgrade. Access to the bedroom, or any other room you would choose

▲ The Larson Door is a steel frame door system originally developed to withstand the impact of debris hurled by hurricane force winds. The glass section is actually three layers. The layers are bonded under heat and pressure so the glass shares the elasticity of the plastic without losing clarity. Struck repeatedly, the glass outer layers will indeed break. However, they stay in place against the plastic layer so no shards of glass separate and become hazardous. And the glass panel remains almost impenetrable.

▲ The Larson door system includes a proprietary steel frame for its claw-like bolts to lock into. Two heavy steel claws are located on the edge of the door and the locking mechanism is double locked. First, by a turn bolt at the central strike point and again by setting the door handle upward.

as a safe room, is an important point. For example, if you have a choice between rooms to sleep in, pick one at the end of a hallway. The goal is to stop more than one person from arriving at the door side by side. Taking on intruders one at a time can cut the odds drastically in your favor. Furthermore if intruders must approach more or less single file, a shot that misses the first intruder has a good chance of striking the second or third person in line.

Secondary alarm systems that protect different parts of the house and respond independently are a great idea. But not everyone lives in a home so large that portions of the house can be cordoned off. Nor are these separate areas necessarily far enough away from a main bedroom or living area so the intruders can't cover the ground before the occupants have an oppor-

tunity to react. But suppose you are at home asleep or wide awake concentrating on writing a book on home defense, for example. Anything that sounds an alarm is helpful. While it's just as easy to set an alarm for daytime activity as it is at night, we don't always choose to do so. In this case, any mechanism that produces an advanced warning and may even serve to locate an intruder is going to be welcome.

Here is a hypothetical situation related to advance warning: The occupants at home in a quiet house are awakened by the sound of someone breaking in. No alarm sounds. The robber is making his way slowly about the house and the occupants recognize a squeaking board and realize the intruder is at the base of the stairs. Could this happen? Yes, but it doesn't fit a very popular narrative.

Let's say it is daytime and the alarm system has not been armed or you do not have one at all. Furthermore, let's say you are positioned far away from either the front or rear doors. A mechanically triggered alarm could easily provide early warning. Devices such as a door-stop alarm, which fits like a wedge beneath the door, will sound when the door is opened. Selling for less than $20 each, these alarms would be one way to provide independently operated alarm systems that not only guard separate areas of the house but also locate the point of entry. Will the intruder hear the alarm and decide entering the house is not as safe for them as they hoped and leave? There is no way of telling, but if you respond immediately to the alert and have ready access to a weapon, your chances of survival are increased dramatically.

The strategy outlined in the eleventh level of home defense could certainly be viable if it weren't for some obvious pitfalls. First of all, the use of gas as a deterrent is probably at best going to be only a temporary distraction, and decontamination can be a problem. In addition, there is always the likelihood that gas can have as much effect on the home occupant as the attackers. If you are prepared to use OS gas (tear gas), you'll need masks for each occupant of the house.

▲ People living in ultra-high crime cities like Johannesburg, South Africa install caged interiors, safe rooms, and separate alarm systems for different parts of the house. You may not need to turn you home into a series of cells, but you can easily dedicate an alarm system to different parts of your home. The inexpensive Doorstop Alarm can be moved easily from room to room. Take it anywhere. It would seem to be a must for roadside motels. The Doorstop Alarm is also a viable option for apartment dwellers where alarm systems are typically not supplied. The Doorstop Alarm is equipped with three levels of sensitivity for its compression switch, but the unit was switched to off for the photo session. After accidentally setting off its 120-decibel alarm, we were convinced that this unit is a most capable, if not shocking, system of warning. *Photo by R. Eckstine, courtesy of Central Spy Shop, Houston*

The problem with firing as you retreat is that every bullet will land somewhere. If it could be assured that each shot fired was going to either hit an attacker or be contained in the walls of the house, then unleashing a spray of bullets to suppress an attack is a viable option. If this is part of your defensive plans, make sure your guns are loaded with frangible ammunition that is more likely to break up and not penetrate the interior walls of the house. This is not a guarantee that a stray round will not find a window and continue its flight next door or into the street. But, it is a precaution worth taking.

If some of the above seems too radical, feel free to pick and choose those methods or tools that might suit your needs. But don't be too eager to eliminate a method or a piece of equipment that seems impossible or unnecessary. Remember to always go one better than the other people on your block. When it comes to equipping your home for security, don't just keep up with the Joneses. Let the Joneses keep up with you.

Panic Proofing

No matter how well someone thinks they are prepared for an emergency, the sound of a fire alarm or break-in can leave them foundering—shocked and confused. You may sleep with the comfort of knowing your security system is armed and feel supremely confident in your ability to deploy the weapons hidden at your bedside, but the sheer impact and shock of the alarms is a rare experience that can cause you to wake up completely disoriented.

Imagine making all the preparations you can think of but finding yourself frozen and unable to take action when your security alarm blares in the middle of the night. Even if the delay is just seconds, the result can be the difference between successfully defending the home or being overrun by intruders. Is there any way of assuring the sound of the alarm will prompt you to action rather than cause you to freeze?

Fear of loud noises is common. Many anthropologists and psychologists consider fear of loud noises to be innate or built-in to the species. Yet some people are more susceptible than others. Perhaps it is just the way people are made up, just as some people are better at one sport or another, or their inability to tolerate loud noise was somehow learned.

The common name for the fear of loud noises is phonophobia. But the actual clinical term is ligyrophobia. Symptoms include nausea, fainting, and sweating, but at the top of the list is the desire to flee. As defenders of the home, this is a symptom we wish on the bad guys rather than ourselves.

Within the typical household, each member of the family is likely going to be a different age and have a different set of experiences to draw from. Some ears may be more sensitive and suffer physical pain from the sound of the alarm. Loud noises can even trigger a migraine headache. As a result, migraine sufferers have been known to develop a phobia of loud noises stemming from the fear of suffering a migraine episode. Still others may be affected emotionally due, perhaps, to forms of post traumatic stress disorder (PTSD). No matter what the cause is of what sometimes referred to as a "sound intolerance phenomena," it needs to be overcome so each member of the family can perform as planned in the event of an emergency.

If the result of the sound intolerance produces a physical reaction or disruptive emotional distress to the point where it interferes with performance, clinical treatment may be necessary. One type of therapy would be cognitive behavioral therapy or CBT. Recognized as being highly successful in treating anxiety disorders, CBT attacks the problem by trying to change the patient's perspective through education, thought challenging, and exposure and response prevention. A more direct method of treatment is referred to as exposure therapy. Exposure therapy could be described as an inoculation. Smaller doses of the offending stimuli are applied to the subject in the hope that with increased dosages the patient will develop greater tolerance for increasingly louder sounds.

For anyone seeking therapy for phonophobia, ligyrophobia, or PTSD, the following may not be suitable. But it should be helpful to anyone motivated to overcome levels of fear that hinder, or prevent them entirely, from taking action in an emergency. Let's look at what can be done to not necessarily cure anyone but nevertheless enhance their ability to concentrate and perform throughout the sudden wailing of an alarm.

First of all, let's change, or rather adjust, our perspective on fear by focusing on the following. Fear can stop good people from acting solely out of shame. But experiencing fear is nothing to be ashamed of. Everyone experiences fear, just as even the very best drivers are nervous before a race. If someone tells you that they never experience fear, they are lying. In all likelihood their greatest fear is for that lie to be exposed. Once you realize there is no shame in experiencing fear, you are free to act.

My personal opinion, based on experience, is when you focus on what is right versus what is wrong you take yourself out of the equation. Once you care more about what happens to someone other than yourself, you are free to act. This applies even when it is only you being attacked. If fear is crippling you, think about the next victim of the person attacking you. Or think about all the victims you will leave behind, such as your loved ones and family members who depend on you.

The most direct method of developing tolerance for the sound of an alarm is to experience it full blast. But, like methods found in the exposure therapy process, it may be helpful, if not downright safer, to develop tolerance in a series of increments. While it may not be possible to simulate the suddenness of an alarm sounding in the middle of the night (unless you have an unusually prankish housemate), exposure to its sound without surprise is a valuable learning experience. Before setting off the alarm in training, be sure to contact the monitoring service and tell them you're going to be testing the system.

The first phase of such a practice should focus strictly on developing sound tolerance to enhance your ability to think and move while under the pressure of a blaring alarm. Have a housemate hide something—perhaps something new you haven't seen before so you are forced to visualize, look for it, and move things around while the alarm sounds. Make it a competition. Time how long it takes to find the hidden object just for the additional motivation. Once you've become accustomed to operating with the alarm constantly sounding, you can move on to developing a planned protocol for exactly what you would do in an actual emergency.

Ultimately, you'll want to be able to tolerate the alarm at its loudest. But you can effectively lower the volume to begin your tolerance training by wearing earplugs stuffed tightly into place. Gradually loosen the seal so more sound waves can enter the ear canal. Or you can simply start your drills in a room farther from the source of the alarm. In fact, you should practice responding to the alarm while in different parts of the house. In each room or in each situation it is necessary to know what you will do next. Will you hide or move toward a weapon? Will you move to cover or can you escape?

Hearing the alarm sound from different rooms can present different challenges. Two rooms in the house typically find the occupant at their most vulnerable. In the bathroom try exiting the shower. Note which way the door opens. Where would you go next? Obviously, response from sleeping quarters is especially important. Practice here should begin from the prone position. This includes beginning the drill lying on your back, then while lying on your stomach. Also, while lying on one side then the other. Covering up with a blanket is another potential obstacle that should be integrated into the drills. It is recommended that your

first reaction after hearing the alarm is to not sit straight up. Instead, roll off the side of the bed. Staying low will not only make you a smaller target but more difficult to see, as well. In the event of a fire, staying close to the floor will make you less susceptible to breathing superheated air, which can collapse your lungs.

Before practicing the roll-out drill, take stock of the floor space immediately to either side of your bed. Is the floor bare wood or tile? If so, a frantic roll-out is going to hurt. Adding a small rug to the floor around your bed can make exiting not only more comfortable but safer. You don't want to begin an escape attempt injured and you certainly do not want to get hurt practicing. Keep in mind that even after padding the floor area, an emergency landing can still be rough. One way to prevent injury is to add a step to your roll-out maneuver that will help to improve your coordination. When the alarm goes off take a moment to cue your thought process by consciously breathing in deeply and letting it out in one unforced blast. Think of how a competitive weight lifter approaches the bar. Breathe, visualize the move, and go. If this sounds like it will slow you down, don't worry. Once it is habit, the protocol will pass by automatically and positively.

Once you are on the floor, you need to rehearse what you are going to do next. In fact, each scenario based on where you might be at the time of emergency should be practiced as part of a series of Immediate Action Drills (IADs). According to personal security consultant Damian Halforty, each IAD requires approximately thirty repetitions before the response becomes automatic.

A flashlight and cell phone should always be next to the bed. Preferably, you should also have a weapon within immediate reach of the practiced roll-out position. Take care to place all such necessary items in the same spot each night before you retire. If there are children in the house who are not properly trained, you might want to consider a quick-opening safe. Touchpad-operated safes are small enough to fit inside a drawer and pop open when the code is entered. This will slow down access to the weapon, but elapsed time can be minimized if you choose a safe with a five key index that follows the outline of the hand. In this configuration the keypad need not be visible. In complete darkness the code can be entered merely by touch.

◄ Effective weapons storage in the home or on your person, is a balance of both security and availability. Once out of your briefcase or handbag, or unstrapped from a holster, no one should have access to your gun but you. This could mean a burglar, houseguest, or child. But in the middle of the night you must be able to take up arms quickly. One of the best ways to balance security and proximity for your weapons is a drawer safe that requires only coarse motor skills to open. The door of this GunVault safe springs open when the proper sequence is keyed in. What makes it panic proof is the natural accommodation of the hand, rather than demanding fine dexterity to key in numbers or spin a dial. This design also makes the safe easier to open in the dark. There is also a key override with several other configurations available for car or home. Top of the line safes in the GunVault catalog include biometric technology so that fingerprint recognition is required for opening. *Photo courtesy of GunVault*

▼ If you are going to store weapons in a night table or other drawer, be sure to designate the proper amount of space and keep it clear. Off to one side in a corner is best so if other items shift toward your gun and gear, it is only coming from one side and clearing it away means a single sweep in one direction. Place the gun so the strong side of the gun is face up. This means the right hand side of the gun for the right-handed shooter. When practicing opening the drawer and taking up the gun, make sure it is unloaded and deactivated with a chamber flag or pull tie that arrests the cylinder, hammer, or stifles the chamber.

▲ Affixing a holster to furniture is a good alternative to keeping the gun in a drawer. Think about what it might be like to retrieve a gun from the nightstand drawer under great stress. Do you grab the drawer handle with the same hand you will shoot with or the opposite hand? How will you first pick up the gun and acquire a shooting grip? Not having to worry about what may shift and fall on the gun when the drawer is opened hurriedly is a big advantage. With the gun fixed in one dependable position, you will be better able to train and develop the focus necessary to avoid panic.

If you intend to access a firearm in the course of your emergency protocol and wish to add it to your alarm drill, make sure it is empty. Place all ammunition and spare magazines in another room altogether. Disabling the gun by inserting a brightly colored piece of rope, wire, or pull-tie into the chamber is a good way to ensure the gun can be handled safely.

Many people keep a loaded gun inside a drawer next to the bed, hence the term nightstand gun. One danger or complication to this plan is that the gun is likely not in the drawer by itself and might move around when you open the drawer. Any time a gun is kept inside a drawer of any type, it is best to locate it away from other objects and brace it in some manner to reduce the probability of its shifting anytime the drawer is opened. Position the gun with the muzzle facing away from you and anyone else in the room. If you are right-handed, place the gun with the right side of the grip facing up. A better choice is to access it from a fixed position beneath the bed or behind the headboard. If you can safely grip the weapon before exiting the bed then so much the better but, as always, keep your finger off the trigger until the sights are on an identified threat.

No matter where you are in the house, you must have a plan. Is it better to hide, necessary to engage, or possible to escape from any given location? Do you have access to a trail of improvised weapons leading to the exit or where a firearm is hidden? Can you call 911 or communicate effectively with your security provider's dispatch? It all begins with being able to function calmly and coherently as the alarm system continues to sound its harsh and intimidating alert. Are you up to the task?

Fire: The Ultimate Home Invasion

There are, in reality, very few answers to the question of how to defend the home from fire. The more important question is how to defend or prevent you or your family from being injured or killed by a fire in the home. Common causes of fire are faulty wiring, an abundance of flammable chemicals stored near heat sources or readily combustible materials, careless management of an open flame or willful experimentation with fire, accidental contact with the heating element or the flame of a poorly designed heating unit, or arson.

The fact is, most fires are caused by accident. Accidents can and will always happen. Prepare all you might, there is always a chance that a fire can start by means no one could predict. Commonsense preventive measures include having working smoke detectors in every room and not letting trash or flammable liquids accumulate inside your house. Stacking wood, building materials, or collecting any type of combustible material outside and close to the house can provide an open invitation to a pyromaniac or amateur thrill seeker.

The most sinister cause of fire in the home or workplace is arson. Arson is the practice of starting a fire with malicious intent to destroy someone's property or net worth, or to hurt, injure, or kill the occupants. The two most common reasons given for this heinous crime are either financial gain or revenge. This is a terrifying proposition because not even the most experienced arsonist can fully predict the result.

If you think arson is limited to the urban landscape, consider the following. If someone were holding a grudge against someone else living in a rural location, they could start a fire upwind of the house and let nature do the rest. It is much more difficult to prove or even trace arson involving wildfires than in subdivisions or improved land.

Whether or not a fire is accidental or set intentionally, taking steps, such as those offered by organizations like Firewise.org, can save your home or minimize damage. The focus of Firewise.org is centered primarily on defense against wildfires, but homeowners in any setting can benefit from their advice.

If you are building a new home or renovating an older one, Firewise.org has numerous recommendations regarding construction and location. But no

▲ Homes are in danger of catching fire from burning embers carried by the wind. These embers are called firebrands. Eaves do need to be ventilated but holes in the overhangs should be no more than 1/8th inch wide.

matter where you own or rent, there are quite a few details to be aware of, large and small, that can help make your home safer from the rapid onslaught of fire.

Location can be a key aspect. Housing on level ground is generally less susceptible to spreading flame than a structure at the top of a slope. Even a small incline can cause rising heat to dry the media in front of a structure and make it more likely to burn. In addition, burning embers, often referred to as firebrands, can ride in the wind, especially if terrain offers a natural wind channel. Maintaining a distance of at least thirty feet from the house to wooded landscape can enhance safety from spreading fire. In a rural setting, make sure access roads are large enough to accommodate emergency vehicles. Fire trucks generally need a twelve-foot wide access road with about fifteen feet of vertical clearance to enter a property and set up operation. If firefighters cannot access or position themselves properly, they may be forced to fight the spread of the fire without being able to save the structure.

Whenever we hear of wild fires gutting neighborhoods and landscapes, some houses nevertheless remain intact. These homes may benefit from location, but another characteristic that can determine survival is building materials. Bear in mind that homes are susceptible to fire from contact with the roof, penetration into the interior, and contact at or just above ground level.

Flammable roofing is perhaps the most dangerous structural component. Stretching across the entire house, a burning roof offers access across the entire length of the structure. A fire-resistant sub-roof, tiles, or nonflammable synthetics that can look like the more traditional wood shingling are safer choices. Skylights should have tempered glass rather than plastic. Another point of entry for burning embers is from beneath the overhang or eaves of the roof. Sealed eaves with 1/8-inch screened venting are one valuable precaution. Closing off or boxing the soffits is another. Gutters should be cleaned regularly to prevent the accumulation of leaves and other debris.

Protecting the home's interior from embers also means the application of flame-resistant siding, stone, or stucco. HardiePlank, for example, is a fiber-cement product that is not only fire-resistant but also an excellent source of insulation. Windows are more vulnerable points of entry, and plate glass windows are the most likely to break under heat or impact. Smaller panes of plate glass are stronger, but tempered safety glass or, better yet, double-pane windows are the best choice. An exterior screen can also be effective in preventing firebrands from entering the house. Again, all types of venting should be covered with 1/8-inch screen.

Whether you're renting, renovating, or building an entirely new structure, protecting the home from the ground level is where you may have the most impact and flexibility. Key points within your control are shrubbery, accumulation of debris at or near the slab or basement wall, and the manner in which ancillary structures are connected to the house.

Undergrowth needs to be kept at a minimum and small trees should be trimmed to hang at least four feet from the ground. And keep an eye out for any tree limbs that could reach power lines. Plants and shrubs that thrive with on high water content are favored and can actually present a natural fire break. Bedding next to the foundation is better covered with gravel or small stones rather than mulch. The base of any type of elevation, such as a porch or deck, should be sealed or screened off to prevent leaves or other flammable debris from collecting beneath. The support or stand for heating-oil tanks, which in themselves may not pose a threat, should be regularly inspected for accumulation of flammable debris.

Any structure directly attached to the house can become a fuel bridge across which flames can travel. This includes wooden fencing. Naturally, metal fences are fire resistant. Nevertheless, by replacing the final few feet of wood with metal fencing or a cement post,

▲ Take a good look at this. Have you ever seen one before? Sure, you have. Maybe so many times it has become invisible in your own home. According to statistics, the number one reason for death due to home fire is the lack of a smoke detector or the lack of power to run one. With all the happenstance that can possibly start a fire, you and your loved ones, survival may depend on a single nine-volt battery. Change batteries and check smoke detectors every six months. Try reminding yourself with the time changes in the Spring and Fall.

▲ Bridging is when fire from one structure travels across a combustible media to ignite a second structure. This fence is in danger of spreading a fire from one building to the other. It is recommended that the final few feet of fencing that leads to the next structure be composed of metal or other flameproof material.

for example, the danger of creating a fire bridge can be reduced. Other examples of fire magnets are trellises, the aforementioned deck, or a section of roofing that connects the house with the garage.

If you do have a fire, the sooner you know about it, the better. One traditional early-warning system is a pet that barks. Another is birds, which are particularly sensitive to changes in air temperature and composition. It wasn't that long ago that miners took canaries with them underground to detect odorless gas that could prove deadly. When the canary stopped singing or keeled over, they knew it was time to get out. But what's needed for home occupants is an audible warning loud enough to wake a sound sleeper. Today's modern smoke-detection devices also monitor heat and can be hard wired into the burglar alarm system. According to the National Fire Protection Association (NFPA), "Almost two-thirds of home fire deaths in 2005-2009 resulted from fires in homes with no smoke alarms or not working smoke alarms." The typical smoke alarm is powered by a single nine-volt battery, and each unit operates independently. Making sure fresh batteries are in place is a necessity. The NFPA says that almost one quarter of smoke alarm failures are due to dead batteries.

Fighting a fire is not like fighting an individual, armed or unarmed. In hand-to-hand combat or a close-quarters battle, it is easy to locate your opponent somewhere in front of you. Fire, though, can be deceptive. Not only can fire jump with the wind, but a swift rise in ambient temperature or a sudden rush of air can cause ignition in one place and another across a smoldering room. Superheated air can cause your lungs to collapse, and fumes from anything burning or merely smoldering can smother your breathing or cause disorientation. In the event of fire, whether it's arson or accidental, the only goal should be to survive. And the key to surviving can be encapsulated by two words: Get out.

Escape from a fire for a family or group should be planned—even if the plan is a simple as "Everyone go out the nearest door or window." You might try some fire drills to find out how easily a window can be opened and the screen popped out. If exiting in an emergency requires breaking glass or is blocked by permanent security bars, make the appropriate changes immediately. If your exit is to the roof, add-

▲ The best way to survive a fire is to get out. Think of the fire extinguisher as a gun in the event of two madmen running loose in the house. They are wearing body armor and firing high capacity carbines, but all you have is a five-shot revolver. It's not a fair fight. Rather than choosing to confront the shooters, take the revolver with you for your protection as you make your escape.

ing a fixed or folding ladder, is a good idea. Be sure to make locating and deploying any auxiliary equipment, such as the ladder part of your fire drill.

It is not necessary for occupants to meet up at a given location before exiting the house; it's better to meet outside afterward so everyone can be accounted for. If you've gone out into the backyard and are physically able, plan to circle around away from the burning structure to the street so you can meet up and do a head count. This will also put you in touch with first responders when they arrive or neighbors who can call 911. If there is one thing to remember about escaping a burning building, it is once you are out do not go back inside. The condition of the interior and the stage of the fire never remains the same. It only gets worse.

If there is any fighting to be done it should not be to fight the fire but to fight your way out. One good tool to have is a portable fire extinguisher. The purpose of the fire extinguisher is not necessarily to stop the fire from destroying your home. It can protect you as you move to an exit. In this regard, fighting your way out of a fire may be similar to surviving an active shooter situation. If you are at work in a warehouse or office complex, for example, a good tool to have with you is a gun. Having a gun should not necessarily embolden you to go after the shooter. Instead, it can be used to protect you as you move toward an exit.

Every home should have at least two fire extinguishers within reach. One fire extinguisher should be in the kitchen area where an open flame or multiple heating elements are regularly used. It is not being suggested that a kitchen fire be fought rather than ran away from. Most freestanding homes have a door leading from the kitchen directly outside. But suppose the exit door was blocked by fire. Or you need to go to the aid of a baby, small child, or someone who is bedridden or requires assistance. The fire extinguisher may be used to ensure a clear path to safety.

Fire extinguishers should also be placed in every bedroom. The bedroom is where people are at their most vulnerable both physically and mentally. It's not difficult to hide a fire extinguisher within reach of the bed and still keep the decor.

Before going further, a couple of other precautions bear mentioning. It is also a good idea to keep a set of outerwear, including shoes, near the bed. Pajamas or less make one vulnerable to injuries commonly suf-

▲ The bedroom is where we are most vulnerable to emergency. Being able to slip easily and quickly into some heavy denim pants and a solid pair of boots is better protection from fire and the inevitable broken glass than most garments. The pants are Wranglers with an extra layer of thorn proof cloth for Upland bird hunting. Man or woman, hunter or not, buy a pair and leave them by the bed. The fire extinguisher can be used to clear a path, break open a window, or smash through a locked door on the way to escape.

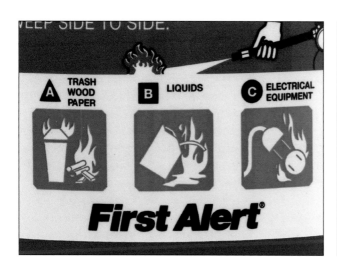

▲ A-, B-, and C-rated fire extinguishers should be adequate for the typical home. But if you have a workshop on the premises with metals that can burn or commercial use chemicals, you probably need to shop for a D-rated unit with greater capability than can be found at the local hardware store.

▲ Fire extinguishers do have a generous but limited shelf life. Check the date when you buy one and replace it every few years. In the mean time, suppressant capacity should be checked on a regular basis.

fered as a result fire, such as cuts from broken glass and burns. I could share the experience of two friends who were both seriously burned in a fire that destroyed their home. The only portions of their lower bodies that were not seriously burned was the skin beneath their denim shorts. Based on this, it doesn't seem like keeping a pair of heavy denim jeans and a pair of boots that can be slipped on quickly would be a bad idea. But above all, only do this if time permits. In addition, you should already have a flashlight within reach of the bed. Today's flashlights need not be larger than a roll of coins to be capable of delivering a piercing beam of light.

Choosing the correct fire extinguisher requires understanding how they are rated. According to an Occupational Safety and Health Administration (OSHA) memo, OSHA fire extinguishers are labeled to indicate the class of fire (based primarily on what is burning) and the relative size of fire it can be expected to handle. A Class A designation inside a triangle indicates ordinary combustibles—paper, cloth, wood, etc. Class B inside a square indicates better effectiveness for flammable liquids, such as grease, or gases. Class C in a circle means the extinguisher may be used on fires involving energized electrical equipment. The letter D inside a star is for use on metal fires. But the agent inside a Class D-rated extinguisher may only have been tested for effectiveness against the combus-

tion of specific metals, which should also be listed on the faceplate.

Fire extinguishers capable of putting out more than one type of fire should display multiple letter designations. But no extinguisher is awarded a Class C designation without receiving a Class A and/or Class B certification. Class A- and B-rated extinguishers are also rated with a number to indicate how much fire the unit is able of putting out. For example, an extinguisher rated 4-A should be able to put out twice the fire as a 2-A unit. Ratings for Class B extinguishers can be listed as high as 640-B. Class C- and D-rated extinguishers are not rated for additional levels of effectiveness. The chemical agents used in fire extinguishers are perishable, so be sure to replace them as necessary.

Operation of the fire extinguisher, according to fire prevention services supplied by the University of Texas, can be encapsulated in the acronym, PASS:

P—Pull the pin that locks the operating handle.
A—Aim the extinguisher low at the base of the fire.
S—Squeeze the lever on the extinguisher to discharge the agent.
S—Sweep the nozzle or hose from side to side, and continue to sweep the extinguisher back and forth at the base of the flames until the fire is out or the fire extinguisher is empty.

With a fire extinguisher leading the way, you'll have a better chance of escape. Pitfalls to look out for are superheated air and lack of oxygen. Stay low to the floor. Crawl if necessary. Firefighters are equipped with breathing apparatuses not just to prevent smoke inhalation, but also because fire produces massive amounts of carbon dioxide and hydrogen cyanide while sucking in oxygen to feed its flames. Carbon dioxide is odorless and colorless so it is impossible to trace. Poisons from the burning of hazardous material may be just as untraceable.

Common wisdom says you should make sure you have a reliable escape route. Position yourself between the fire and the exit door. But what if you are trapped in a room while the rest of the house is filled with fire and smoke? In some cases the interior of the home can be hot enough to burn but no flames are visible. Furniture or other combustibles may be giving off noxious fumes, but a limited oxygen supply may be delaying full combustion. You may want to make sure your door is tightly closed. If time allows, place bedding, towels, clothing, or anything else in the crack beneath the door to seal off the room. This can reduce your exposure to smoke and temporarily deny additional oxygen to the fire.

Exiting through a window presents its own set of problems. When opening a window during a fire, there is a chance of the fire gaining intensity thanks to the sudden dose of oxygen. The result may even

▲ Sealing off the door behind you as you make your escape may be necessary, especially if you are going to take some time to open a door or break a window. Jamming bedding or towels into the cracks can limit the amount of oxygen that will suddenly become available to the fire and hopefully stifle an explosion or prevent a sudden burst of flame.

▲ Apartment security gates that border the fire escape should not be locked by combination or key. The shielded area to the right is where an instant release lever is located, making it nearly impossible to be reached from the outside. Once the latch is opened, the unit compresses from left to right and opens inward. Note the hinges along the left side of the window. Actually, the most common way apartment window gates are defeated is by using a pipe to grab hold and pry from the bottommost hinge, creating a space just large enough to crawl through. The raised area along the bottom track was added to prevent this. Egressing with stolen goods is usually via the front door.

be explosive, sometimes referred to as flashover. The International Organization for Standards (ISO) 13943, which covers fire, defines flashover as "transition to a state of total surface involvement in a fire of combustible materials within an enclosure." This is more likely to occur when a superheated room with smoldering material receives large amounts of oxygen in a short time. If the outer rooms are already aflame and being fed by open windows on the opposite side of the house, the sudden opening of a window could create a crosswind and blow the door to your room open. Try not to let the hot air at your back distract you from getting out.

If you are on the ground floor and the window opens easily without the encumbrance of fixed screenwork, you are practically home free. But what if you have installed burglar bars or decorative grille work? Make sure the grille work or the bars are hinged with a release that is available only from the inside. Do not install a key- or combination-operated locking system on the bars, whether it is integrated with the bars or in the form of a padlock.

Fire department approved burglar bars or security gates designed for ground-level apartments or access to a laddered escape system (commonly referred to as fire escapes) have several distinct features. One popular design does not swing outward but opens right to left, folding in a scissor-like motion. The latch lever is moved upward to release but hidden from view, usually inside a box that is either shielded visually or enclosed with trapdoor access. The important aspect of this design—and one to look for in other gates—is that the latch is not lockable but physically impossible to access from the outside. In terms of security, similar designs were found to be vulnerable by using a pipe or other lever to bend back the grid from the bottom. This problem was corrected by mounting a steel, U-shaped well to surround the bottom of the unit and put it out of reach.

Escaping from a room located more than two floors above the ground typically requires passing through a window onto a fire escape that scales along the outside of the building down to the street or onto a section of the roof. For anyone who lives in a two- or even three-story house or apartment, window-anchoring escape ladders are available from companies such as Kidde or online retailers that specialize in child safety, such as Onestepahead.com. Naturally, such products are a worthwhile alternative to suffering through a fall or succumbing to smoke before you can make up your mind to jump.

In some cases the windows are not easily opened. Using a heavy object like a chair, lamp, or small television to breach the window is a possibility. Having a heavy-duty steel tank fire extinguisher is the best idea, so it can be used as a ram as well as for fire suppression.

Sometimes the window unit can be driven out in one piece or slid upwards or aside, exposing a screen that needs to be pushed away. If the window is plate glass, take care to break away all the glass you can down to the edges of the frame. If you live in a mobile home or prefabricated house, the windows may not have been installed with the intention of being opened or removed. This is likely a violation of code, but that does not mean the problem doesn't exist. In this case, the ability to swing a hefty fire extinguisher can be a godsend. No matter what kind of windows you have, now would be a good time to evaluate what would be required to break through to the outside if you needed to make a sudden escape.

Construction Safety and Health
Outreach Program

U.S. Department of Labor
OSHA Office of Training and Education
May 1996

Portable fire extinguishers are classified to indicate their ability to handle specific classes and sizes of fires. Labels on extinguishers indicate the class and relative size of fire that they can be expected to handle.

Class A extinguishers are used on fires involving ordinary combustibles, such as wood, cloth, and paper. Class B extinguishers are used on fires involving liquids, greases, and gases. Class C extinguishers are used on fires involving energized electrical equipment. Class D extinguishers are used on fires involving metals such as magnesium, titanium, zirconium, sodium, and potassium.

The recommended marking system to indicate the extinguisher suitability according to class of fire is a pictorial concept that combines the uses and non-uses of extinguishers on a single label. This system is illustrated in the accompanying figure. The first set (row) of symbols illustrated in the figure is a label for use on a Class A extinguisher. The symbol at the left (which depicts a Class A fire) is blue. Since the extinguisher is not recommended for use on Class B or C fires, the remaining two symbols (which depict Class B and Class C fires) are black, with a diagonal red line through them. The second set (row) of symbols illustrated in the figure is a label for use on a Class A/B extinguisher. The two left symbols are blue. Since the extinguisher is not recommended for use on Class C fires, the symbol on the far right (which depicts a Class C fire) is black, with a diagonal red line through it. The third set of symbols is a label for use on Class B/C extinguishers. The two right symbols are blue. Since the extinguisher is not recommended for use on Class A fires, this symbol is black, with a diagonal red line through it. The fourth set of symbols is a label for use on Class A/B/C extinguishers. All symbols on this label are blue.

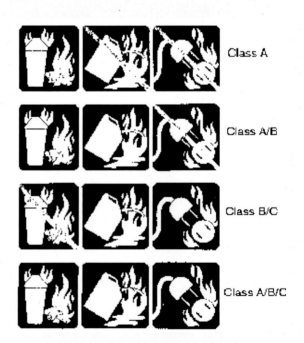

Letter-shaped symbol markings are also used to indicate extinguisher suitability according to class of fire.

Extinguishers suitable for Class A fires should be identified by a triangle containing the letter "A." If colored, the triangle should be green.

Extinguishers suitable for Class B fires should be identified by a square containing the letter "B." If colored, the square shall be colored red.

Extinguishers suitable for Class C fires should be identified by a circle containing the letter "C." If colored, the circle should be colored blue.

Extinguishers suitable for fires involving metals should be identified by a five-pointed star containing the letter "D." If colored, the star shall be colored yellow.

Extinguishers suitable for more than one class of fire should be identified by multiple symbols placed in a horizontal sequence.

Class A and Class B extinguishers carry a numerical rating to indicate how large a fire an experienced person can put out with the extinguisher. The ratings are based on reproducible physical tests conducted by Underwriters' Laboratories, Inc. Class C extinguishers have only a letter rating because there is no readily measurable quantity for Class C fires which are essentially Class A or B fires involving energized electrical equipment. Class D extinguishers likewise do not have a numerical rating. Their effectiveness is described on the faceplate.

Class A Ratings

An extinguisher for Class A fires could have any one of the following ratings: 1-A, 2-A, 3-A, 4-A, 6-A, 10-A, 20-A, 30-A, and 40-A. A 4-A extinguisher, for example, should extinguish about twice as much fire as a 2-A extinguisher.

Class B Ratings

An extinguisher for Class B fires could have any one of the following ratings: 1-B, 2-B, 5-B, 10-B, 20-B, 30-B, 40-B, and up to 640-B.

Class C Ratings

Extinguishers rated for Class C fires are tested only for electrical conductivity. However, no extin-guisher gets a Class C rating without a Class A and/or Class B rating.

Class D Ratings

Class D extinguishers are tested on metal fires. The agent used depends on the metal for which the extinguisher was designed. Check the extinguisher faceplate for the unit's effectiveness on specific metals.

ORDINARY

COMBUSTIBLES

FLAMMABLE

LIQUIDS

ELECTRICAL

EQUIPMENT

COMBUSTIBLE

METALS

Understanding the Stages of Violent Crime, or Countering the Violent Encounter

Whenever a stranger knocks on your door, your first reaction and every thought thereafter should be one of skepticism. In a time where we have both landline and cellular telephones, fax, email, the United States Postal Service, text messaging, and social networking sites, anyone who wants to contact you has too many other methods of doing so at their disposal to justify knocking on your door. If their car is broken down, let them call on their cell phone. If they really need a drink of water, let them go someplace else. If they claim to have a medical emergency, you are not a doctor and you do not drive an ambulance. Whether the knock on the door is the opening scene of a crime or just a random sales call, the purpose of showing up unexpectedly is to catch you off guard.

As we learned from Texas Ranger Kip Westmoreland, home invasions are more often targeted rather than random. Is there anything in your house that would draw the attention of a robber or robbery crew? Do you or someone in your family regularly bring home cash or merchandise from a business? Do you have a safe that is conspicuous or large enough to raise an eyebrow? Have you had strangers in your house recently painting, cleaning, or putting down carpet? If so, you should be all the more suspicious and ready to engage with a defensive mindset.

The key to building a defensive mindset is being aware of certain information and protocol. But recognizing key signs of trouble takes experience. The problem is that most people, prior to being a victim of violent crime, have no relevant information to go on. Indeed, most people, have never been in a physical confrontation of any type and do not like to argue. Other than scrapping with siblings or tussling in a schoolyard, most people have had little preparation for sudden violence. Even karate students at the typical modern dojo are able to obtain advanced belt rankings without ever being challenged in a sparring session driven by any real urgency or malicious intent. The point is, there is more going on during a criminal act than greed, sociopathic behavior, or blind rage—and the so-called average person simply may not have the capacity or experience to act with the knowledge or insight necessary to deal with the

situation. But in the worlds of private security and law enforcement, certain studies have been developed to help cope with the progression of a violent crime.

One such study that deals specifically with the progression of violent crime is one of the most widely recognized matrices in law enforcement. According to Mark MacYoung (nononsenseselfdefense.com), "The Five Stages of Violent Crime is an internationally recognized system to identify if, and determine when and if, you are being set up for a crime of violence." The five stages are widely recognized as:

1. Intent
2. Interview
3. Positioning
4. Attack
5. Reaction

The Five Stages of Violent Crime may not be a topic of conversation among the general public, but it has been available in books and on the internet for quite some time. The following is a brief interpretation of what each stage entails.

Intent

Intent is not to be confused with the mere thought process of an individual as they work up to committing a violent act. Rather, it is often defined as discernible physiological manifestations that a person ready to commit violence will display. Some forms of intent may be described as body language, such as clenching fists.

Unfortunately, the most dangerous criminals are those who have learned to mask intent. For example, Donald Bess, a dangerously violent sex offender standing about 6 feet 6 inches tall and weighing more than 275 pounds, was able to make himself appear so nonthreatening that he gained entry into the apartment of a Houston, Texas woman in 1977 just by asking for a drink of water. Once inside the apartment, Bess raped her. The woman survived and pressed charges, resulting in a conviction. Paroled after serving just seven years of a twenty-five-year sentence, he used the same ploy again after his release, this time murdering his victim.

Interview

The criminal attack differs from interpersonal violence, where anger, emotion, or pride can short circuit the assailant's reasoning. Criminal violence is, in a sense, more professional, requiring a conscious decision. During the interview phase, the criminal decides if you are a suitable victim and makes up his or her mind whether to attack based on what they recognize as an assurance of their own personal safety.

Positioning

Criminals do not want to fight for what they get. They'd rather overwhelm their victims. Positioning is the process wherein they put themselves in the position of best advantage so the victim can be defeated quickly. Being able to recognize movement to a strategic position by a possible assailant is key to recognizing the protocol being used to set you up. Like the interview, there are several types of positioning.

Attack

The attack is when the criminal commits to using violence or the threat of force.

Reaction

Reaction is how criminals feel about what they have done. Reaction can be made more complicated by the fact that the victim's reaction is a contributing factor.

To better understand how violent crimes escalate, I sought out a security specialist who has credentials and a wealth of actual experience. We met Damian Halforty, proprietor of Four/Zero Firearms and Weapons Specialists, earlier in discussing levels of security. Now based in New Zealand and serving primarily New Zealand, Australia, and the South Pacific, much of Halforty's on the job experience has taken place in his native South Africa, where there is no shortage of opportunity to fight violent crime. Due to a mix of racial unrest with class warfare and corruption, home invasion and carjacking are crimes perpetrated on such a large scale that violent crime might be described as a separate economy altogether.

▲ Damian Halforty's experience as a protection specialist in Johannesburg, South Africa led him to develop one of the most complete studies of carjacking published to date. *Carjacking Countermeasures* outlines not just the history and the culture of the carjacking industry but also profiles and debriefs specific incidents using methods that instruct the reader so they can go about their lives in greater safety. The South African government has effectively disarmed its public and seemingly spends more effort penalizing the average citizen than prosecuting its underworld. Now based in New Zealand, Halforty's Four/Zero Firearms and Weapons Specialists contract throughout Australia, New Zealand, and the South Pacific. *Photo courtesy of Damian Halforty*

The numbers for violent crime in South Africa are astounding. The figures alone, as outlined in Halforty's landmark book, *Carjacking Countermeasures,* reflect as many as 20,000 carjackings per year in a country of only about 40 million people. In an effort to stem the tide of rising crime, the government of South Africa instituted greater restrictions on the sale and possession of firearms by the civilian population. Much of South Africa's current firearms laws closely resemble recently proposed or enacted legislation restricting the private use of firearms in the United States. A brief overview of firearms laws and restrictions that have done nothing to contribute to the prevention of violent crime is as follows.

According to *Guns in South Africa*, a study by Philip Alpers and Marcus Wilson, here are some highlights of current gun laws in South Africa: As per the Firearms Control Act of 2000 and the Firearms Control Regulations of 2004, guns are regulated by the National Commissioner and Registrar of Firearms. The right to ownership of firearms in South Africa is not guaranteed by law. Civilians are not allowed to possess semi-automatic firearms without special endorsement. Private possession of fully automatic weapons is prohibited. In South Africa, only licensed gun owners (with competency certificate) may lawfully acquire, possess or transfer a firearm or ammunition. An applicant for a firearm license in South Africa must pass background checks, which consider criminal, mental, medical, domestic violence, addiction, employment, and previous firearm license records. Furthermore, where a past history or apprehended likelihood of family violence exists, the law in South Africa stipulates that a gun license should be denied or revoked. In South Africa, third-party character references for each gun license applicant are required. Licensed firearm owners in South Africa are permitted to possess only one firearm per firearm license.

Could such harsh regulation in the United States provide a breeding ground for the same level of chaos found in South Africa? Following is the result of my own experience and discussion with Damian Halforty.

Having lived through the downward spiral of both firearms restrictions and violent crime in South Africa, Halforty, who has planned and executed more than 700 security missions, was sure to have keen insight garnered from a wealth of test cases. According to Halforty, body language is indeed an example of intent. Hidden hands, baseball cap down on the face. Eyes with blood seemingly drained, the blatant stare. These can both disguise an assailant and intimidate a victim, but in reality doing so creates a sort of Catch 22 for the actor. "Don't be afraid to take clothing literally," says Halforty. In covert surveillance you look for the opposite of bland. To some extent, you might compare

it to a male bird in mating season showing off his feathers. Someone in the throes of intent may be wearing a tough guy outfit like Sons of Anarchy gear. They want to have the advantages of dressing tough but doing so gives away their intent.

Intent often begins with the criminal surveillance of you and your residence. While this might be obvious and alarming in a rural neighborhood or subdivision, inside the gates of an apartment complex where many people come and go on different schedules, it may be less so. Another course of behavior that can be a part of intent is the sales pitch. For example, a precursor to carjacking that Damian witnessed several times was a man approaching with a bag of merchandise asking if his targets wanted to buy this or that, but no goods were shown. In this case, the bag invariably held a weapon. When this same action was tried on Damian as he sat at a stoplight, he already had his pistol drawn and made sure the "salesman" was able to see the muzzle without raising alarm to others around them. "Yes, boss," was the would-be carjacker's reply as he slinked away.

The key to breaking off a progression to the next stage of violent crime is to mess up the aggressor's programming. Do something they don't expect, or say something they don't want to hear. But act as soon as you can, because the longer you wait the longer they have to develop their nerve, finalize a plan, and gain a

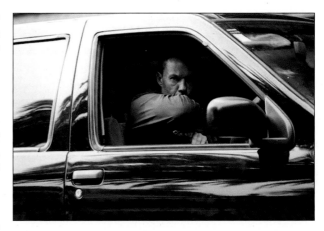

▲ We've all been approached on the street by a stranger asking us what time it is or trying to sell us something. In South Africa, this is a typical precursor to a car jacking. Approached by a man holding a bag, which undoubtedly contained a weapon instead of the goods he was hawking, Halforty made sure the man could see the gun he was holding beneath his arm pointed directly at him. *Photo courtesy of Damian Halforty*

position of advantage. Show them something in terms of behavior that tells them you are not an easy target. It is important to remember that they are looking for assurance their plan will work 100 percent.

One of the best examples of a would-be victim messing up the program of an aggressor was told to me by an acquaintance who had recently opened a small resale shop located in a somewhat ragtag lower income neighborhood in Boston. On this day, I found him quite agitated, worked up, and sweating. The store sold a hodgepodge of items, and he made a meager living buying and selling knick knacks, small appliances, and furniture—basically anything he could get in the door. The problem for the shop owner was that resale shops, such as his, fit the profile of a typical fencing operation where stolen merchandise is bought at a wholesale price illegally and re-sold ostensibly on the opposite or legal side of the fence. But the owner was honest and all transactions were completely aboveboard. Nevertheless, there was an element in the neighborhood that was willing to put his store into the stolen goods business and provide protection. Knowing that his shop was ripe for this sort of solicitation, he had been on the lookout for such a visit from the first day he opened.

The strongarm guys weren't difficult to spot. Not worried about being obvious, one man was in a suit and appeared to be older. The suit was perhaps supposed to be an indication that he was connected to a larger underworld entity. His accomplice was younger and bigger, wearing an untucked shirt, hooded sweatshirt and jeans. Spotting the pair from about fifty feet away, the shopkeeper immediately changed his demeanor. Stomping back and forth across the store, he began picking up merchandise and throwing it down, violently raving about being broken into again the previous night. Complaining he couldn't get any justice and if he could just get his hands on the thieves . . . spit flew from his mouth as he launched further into a tirade of gibberish and profanity. Seeing this behavior, the two would-be extortionists left the store and to my knowledge never returned.

What happened was the extortionists realized that he wasn't a suitable victim. But let's backtrack and break down what happened from within the framework of the Five Stages of Violent Crime. First, as Damian Halforty pointed out, the subject of the extortion was surveilled and the store itself was sized up to meet their needs. Next, it was seen that just one person ran the store. The proprietor seemed to have a rapport with his neighbors and was always smiling whether someone made a purchase or not. The extortionists saw him as being a nice guy.

More than likely the extortionists thought the storeowner was a soft target. This fed into their intent because they made up their minds that it was going to be easy. All they had to do was show up in their usual tough-guy mode with a touch of arrogance that was meant to say "You wouldn't dare mess with us." The older man's suit was out of place in the bohemian neighborhood and the larger younger man was much more rough and aggressive looking than the college students who rented apartments nearby. They were to some extent depending on their appearance to intimidate the shopkeeper, but all it did was send up red flags of intent.

In this episode, the interview stage was short circuited. Well, actually not. Let's just say that the shopkeeper failed the interview and wasn't hired on as a victim. Perhaps the more accurate way of looking at the situation was that the intended victim had actually interviewed them. In fact, the entire situation had been turned around. The victim had done his own surveillance and picked out two people who did not belong on his street based on their appearance and demeanor. He was waiting for such an overture based coolly on his awareness of who he was, where he was, and what he was doing. Then, when it came time to be interviewed for suitability, he acted not only in a dangerous manner but crazy and unpredictable, as well.

The line between the stages of intent and interview can often be blurred. If the period of intent is allowed to continue for too long, the interview may already be blending in with positioning. If, for example, the person or persons walking in front of you are changing their physical position in relation to you, such as circling, it may be too late to stop an attack. But let's backtrack and see if we can more clearly describe the interview stage.

A key component to any type of interview is misdirection. Just like a magician's first objective is to make the audience pay attention to an action that seems to be important while moving the more critical items into position. The goal of misdirection may be to discover information or create a distraction while they move into a position that leaves you physically vulnerable. For example, a clever interviewer might be able to get you to say something like, "I'd have to ask my husband." You've just told them that the man of the house is not home. If they follow up with, "When will he return?" and you answer, you could be in real danger—not necessarily that day, but that is important intelligence for their cause. Women who live alone have been known to say things such as this and follow up with, "He'll be right back." But this, too, can be a dangerous ploy. If you have already been surveilled and they know you live alone, this can be taken as a sign of fear and weakness.

Misdirection can also be used to move you around physically. For example, someone who comes to the door might fake illness to get you to come outside and leave the door open. This is like a sucker punch that caps off an argument or even a seemingly harmless conversation. You think the episode is at an end. But when the person you are speaking with turns to leave they wheel around and deliver a punch. The body language was "All through, all clear, lower your guard," but that would be all that was needed for you to be defeated.

There are actually several types of interviews, but they may not take place in any particular order. You need to look for them independently. If one type of interview changes into a different type of interview, you had better recognize it because it rarely changes a second time before moving to the attack stage. For example, all attacks begin with surveillance. This could be as simple as "I need a lady with a purse." There's one that's seems totally oblivious and progression to the attack stage is immediate.

The first type of interview to be discussed is the silent interview. This is another form of surveillance. If you recognize that someone is watching you closely, you are experiencing intent. It may be as simple as the aforementioned blatant stare. If the person watching you makes sure that you know he is watching you, this is a test to see how you will react. If you ignore this, they may conclude that your attitude about crime

is that it can't be happening to you. This is a sign that you are probably a good target who will present little risk to the attacker.

One other type of surveillance or silent interview that bears mentioning is the prolonged interview, also known as stalking. Stalking can take or weeks or months or a relatively short period. The problem is that stalking may not be apparent until the stalker does something to let the person know what they are doing. Most people think of stalking as being perpetrated by admirers. In this case, the stalker makes his or her presence or identity known in hopes of approval. But contact can also be made for the purpose of intimidation. How you react helps the stalker rate your suitability as a target.

Another way a stalker can be discovered is by regularly checking your premises for tampering. Suspicious that she was being followed, a neighbor of mine began to notice little things that didn't look right in and around her house. In the evening the grounds seemed darker than usual. Her suspicions that something was wrong were confirmed when a neighbor's dog wandered onto the property and triggered the motion activated spotlights positioned to illuminate the driveway and backyard. She noticed that critical spots that should have been illuminated remained dark. It turned out that some of the bulbs had been unscrewed and other units redirected, both actions taken in an attempt to create blind spots. The stalker was watching from the darkened positions.

In the weeks that followed, this woman actually saw the stalker and so did neighbors who chased him to the car he was using, which was parked at the other side of a field adjacent to the subdivision. In one episode, the woman fired a 20-gauge shotgun at him as he climbed over her back fence and escaped unharmed. The stalker's luck ran out when sheriff's deputies matched his description to an offender coincidentally being walked into the county jail on an unrelated offense. Being aware of her surroundings interrupted his silent interview and allowed her to confront and eventually stop progression to the next stage of violent crime.

A silent or prolonged interviews, such as the example above, could also be used to gather intelligence about your premises. Important information to be gathered would include when you are there and when no one is at home. Is there actually anything in the house worth the risk to obtain, and where might it be stored? Looking inside through a window during the time when you are not at home and few, if any, neighbors are about might also reveal how to best gain entry into the house.

The two most obvious forms of interview are the escalating interview and the hot interview. Both involve the aggressor asking a question or a making a command. The escalating interview typically begins with "Do you have the time?" or "Do you want to buy . . . ?" How you react is the first test of how hard your defenses are. Anyone who comes to your door is likely to begin with a soft question that seems appropriate or harmless. The introduction, "I'm so and so and we're doing a survey" sounds innocuous and typical, but this is simply buying time to evaluate the situation. If your first thought was to ask, "Who is 'We'?" then you're on the right track. If the person's eyes are shifting right and left, you might think about arming yourself or getting away from the door immediately. The "We" are about to appear.

It has come to my attention that some police departments are asking homeowners to be aware of people who knock on their door and step back. The fear is that once the least-threatening member of the robbery crew has brought you to the open door, they are stepping back to let their more aggressive partners rush past them into the house. But this is also what many legitimate solicitation crews are being taught. Ring or knock and then step back. Being cautious is to be skeptical of the necessity for anyone to be at your door. Armed or not, it is best to stay back from the door and call out if you feel you must answer. Shifting to one side to put a corner or at least some furniture between you and the door is also a good idea.

The escalating interview will continue for as long as it takes for the interviewer to decide whether or not you are a target who will not offer too much risk. All the time they are talking about their product or their mission, they are actually probing to see if you are armed, alone, have an armed alarm system, and what it would take to get you to open the door.

If you have a deadbolt lock on the door that requires a key, don't leave the key in the lock for the sake of convenience. Yes, you should have a key nearby so you can get out in case of an emergency, but it should be well hidden. A couple different ploys can be related to key-operated interior locks. If you find yourself surprised and already by the front door, find an excuse to get away from the door. While not recommended, some people will say, "I have to get a key for this door," or, "I have to turn off the alarm." While both of these ploys play into the desire of the possible intruder to take the least amount of risk, these plans are weak and have liabilities of their own. However, any excuse to get you away from the door and put them off for a few seconds might permit you to go to another keypad and set the alarm that should already have been on and take up arms and a cell phone. Bear in mind that any time you leave them alone at your front door, they are most likely going do one of two things. They will either go away because they don't trust where you've gone and what you're doing, or they will proceed to smash in your door. The opportunist may be more likely to go next door. But if they have had you under surveillance and determined that there is something of value inside, specifically if it is hidden or inside a safe, they're probably coming in. Remember, they might need you to quickly find a hiding place or open a safe. But if they don't need you to find what they're looking for, they'll more likely come back when no one is home.

A hot interview is what some people refer to as a gorilla act. This is generally performed in the street or as part of a carjacking. At the home site, it could be part of a follow-home driveway robbery, but it could also take place from the doorstep if they thought they could scare you enough to open the door. The hot interview entails being shouted at and threatened. It's a crazy act to make you back down. The gorilla act is a favorite with pimps and thieves. Once they establish dominance, much like a dominant male gorilla, there may not be the need for violence.

Don't think a gorilla act or any other display meant to cower a subject has not been rehearsed. Hopefully, by this point in the book you have come to the realization that the majority of violent crimes are perpetrated by repeat offenders who have already spent time in prison. And what do you think they talk about and practice when they're serving time? Leading the list are fighting, acting tough, comparing notes on interviews they've done in the past, techniques of misdirection, and positioning (along with how to get over on the guards). Another group that has been showing up on the arrest rolls in increasing numbers is young people performing a crime as a gang initiation or established gang members seeking a promotion. Just like the inmate population, the gang serves as a clearinghouse for all sorts of knowledge that can be used in criminal enterprises.

It's not just criminals who have trained themselves to be intimidating. A married couple I've known for many years had long careers teaching in public schools, each of them retiring from the position of assistant principal at different schools. (In some districts the assistant principals are referred to as the "Deans of Discipline".) They had passed along to me several stories of chastisement where they had really "gotten them good that time." Did they mean corporal punishment? No, but the trepidation they could instill in a student was legendary. They took great fun in describing the entire machination of how the student was called into the office, sat down, and lectured in a most cunning fashion. Then they would relate how they were on the verge of bursting out laughing throughout the entire ordeal. Before you go about seeking an injunction or filing a lawsuit against such behavior, I must add that I have personally met more than a dozen of their past students, mostly from poor and middle-class families, and they count their former assistant principals among the most positive influences in their lives.

Professional actors also learn to fake all sorts of emotions. Few actors are anything like the characters they portray. When it comes to having an act or alter ego that is capable of launching fear or at least doubt in the mind of a would-be assailant, remember that if they can do it, you can do it.

Even if you are highly trained in the use of weapons and martial arts, you might be able to save yourself a lot of trouble if you can short circuit the five stages and avoid bloodshed by adding an effective front to your defensive repertoire. Even if you don't appear to be physically imposing, one of the fastest ways to change the way other people respond to you is to use a commanding voice.

As you know, we speak by forcing air past our vocal chords. Most people push the air by contracting their chest cavity. Just like holding a blade of grass between the hands and blowing through it, the size and intensity of the air stream determines the amount of vibration and the sound it makes. Imagine an actress playing a shy retiring schoolteacher and then playing someone like the "Iron Lady" Margaret Thatcher. One has a determined, directive voice. The other a wispy and almost apologetic voice, sounding as if she wanted to immediately take back every word. When playing Margaret Thatcher, the actress is pushing a column of air in an entirely different manner from the way she is speaking as the shy and retiring schoolmarm.

Actors and, whether they know it or not, many people who regularly practice intimidation have learned to project their voices. This doesn't necessarily mean loud. A good Shakespearian actor, for example, can whisper the slightest detail and hear his or her words reverberate off of the farthest wall. The key is to open the chest cavity as wide as possible and support a column of air with the diaphragm. The action of exhaling becomes an upward push rather than a constriction from the walls of the chest. The easiest way to train yourself to breathe in this manner is to consciously inhale, beginning with expansion of what appears to be the stomach. Try it lying down and see if your stomach doesn't move first. Watch a powerful singer and his or her chest may barely heave but the stomach appears to be working overtime.

It might seem odd that a chapter on violent crime should morph into instruction on how to project like a trained actor. But whether your encounter progresses from the interview stage to positioning and attack depends not just on actions but on how you present yourself verbally. One of the tenets of verbal judo, a school of thought devoted to using words as a defensive option, argues that "rhetorical skill is partially the ability to make oneself into what it has to be in order to handle a situation." You can't instantly get bigger like the Hulk or turn into Superman, but you can approach the encounter with a commanding voice and generate doubt in the mind of the interviewer.

With or without surveillance, a criminal can skip interview altogether and gain a large advantage by using the element of surprise. For many criminals, ambush is their specialty. They find a location that fits their needs and set up shop. For example, they might wait by the mouth of an alley, where they or a partner can block your path on the sidewalk so you must turn away from the curb and pass closer to the alley where you are pulled out of the mainstream and behind a dumpster. But the criminal knows how to catch you off guard at home, as well. Such as when relaxing in the evening. If it is dark outside and you have lights on inside the house, anyone surveilling the house from the sidewalk can watch you as clearly as watching a television screen. Come nightfall, close your shades, pull the curtains together, or close the blinds.

If you have to take out the garbage or you forgot something inside your car parked on the street or in the driveway, take a weapon or a second set of eyes, or both. Have someone watch from the window or take along a dog. Their protective nature will at least be able to provide a warning. Ambushing you while you go to your car in the morning is another key time. Parking in a locked garage is much better than being parked in the driveway or at the curb. If the car is outdoors, make a habit of approaching the car in an arc rather than moving directly toward it. Keep your distance so you can get a look at the blind side of the car. This way, you can get a head start in getting away if you see anyone hiding behind it. If you have parked in the driveway and the garbage cans have been placed nearby, they could also be used by an assailant as a place to lie in wait.

The above examples of setups or ambush are a type of positioning. One way to counter ambush position-ing is to be aware of your surroundings. Know your own terrain. Learn to recognize possible points of attack on your own property. You are the one who puts out the garbage cans and parks your car. Position items such as these so you can see all the way around them. Be careful not to create a blind spot where someone can hide. If you park on the street in front of your building or condominium, you might give it a good look from across the street before approaching. Before leaving the house, look outside to see who is walking down the street or just hanging around. How are other pedestrians acting as they walk down the street? Do they seem to be nervous or avoiding someone? If any-one is crossing the street in the middle of the block, is there a reason for this you should beware of? In a quiet subdivision do you see any cars that you've never seen before? If a car is stationary but the engine is running, watch what happens before going outside.

Once you are in the habit of looking for and know-ing how to recognize possible points of ambush on your own property and neighborhood, apply this same keen eye to when you visit friends in other environ-ments. I recall one day during the New York City blackout of 1977 saying that before we left a friend's apartment building and entered the street that I would "Go outside and scan the perimeter." My companion, a good-natured street thug who, by the way, was also the neighborhood Casanova, asked me if I had been in the military. My answer was "No, but I've learned that much."

▲ This row of trash containers looks neatly squared away. But, they also provide effective cover for anyone wishing to ambush the homeowner.

▲ Placing trash containers tightly against the fence should make it impossible for anyone to hide behind them without being noticed.

▲ Knowing how to position yourself to limit vulnerability turns the table on attackers seeking to do the same thing to you. *Photo courtesy of Damian Halforty*

One difference between an ambush and a positioning that evolves is that in an ambush, rather than being steered during the course of an interview, your path alone brought you into the danger zone. You may have been surveilled and judged not only to have what the criminal wants (the car or entry into the house), but you have suddenly provided your own trap, such as leaving your car in the driveway with the lights on. Realizing you'll probably be coming back to the car soon and likely in a careless state of mind, the opportunistic criminal lies in wait to see if his instincts are correct. No further interview is necessary because the criminal feels with just the element of surprise on his side, he's going to be able to pull off the crime at little or no danger to himself.

▼ By, approaching a victim literally with hat in hand, peasant carry is a form of deception wherein an armed assailant feigns submissive behavior. But this same tactic can be used when confronting a trespasser or anyone else that may present a threat.

Even when a confrontation progresses slowly with the criminal seeing you, working up his nerve and intent, and then interviewing to see if you are a safe enough target to rob, the next step is similar to an ambush. In short, it is to put you in a position that is safer for him than it is for you. If the interviewer or the interviewer's partner(s) can get behind you, that is a win for the perpetrator. Nighttime works in the favor of a perpetrator. So does blocking your escape or steering your path of escape into a place where neighbors or passersby will not be able to see what is going on.

Anytime an aggressor can attain a position of advantage, it lends greater encouragement for them to attack. The next time you watch a boxing match, pay careful attention. The most likely moment in which punches will be thrown is when one boxer has cornered the other. So what is it that you can do to prevent being steered into position and set up for attack? Do some positioning of your own.

If someone comes to your door, stay back from the door and stand to one side. If possible, only expose a portion of your body from around a corner or the edge of an inner doorway. If you can conceal the right side of your body, have a gun in your right hand. But don't tense your arm and keep your finger off the trigger. Hold your trigger finger straight, hugging the side of the frame. If you are concealing the left side of your body and you are right handed, keep the gun concealed by other means. When no cover is available, concealing the gun with a hat, for example, is effective because it appears to be a harmless, even humble gesture. Actually, this is a favorite ploy of robbers in South America referred to as peasant carry.

When you engage from behind the door, the speaker is trying to get you to open it. Should the door be opened, the position stage has ended and the attack stage is free to begin. In the meantime, speaking through the door without giving up a position of cover is a battle of wits and will decide who will give up position first.

The purpose of this book is to help prevent situations from reaching the attack stage. If we were to think of the five stages as a pyramid, as you move upwards towards the fifth stage the number of ways to avoid becoming a victim lessen. Preventing progression

beyond the intent stage might be as easy as running away. But it is not hyperbole to say that once in the attack stage, actions may be as grave as do or die.

The goal of the attack is to take from or take control of someone by force—the threat of force or violent attack without warning. Without warning might be described as without being asked whether or not you would like to comply instead of being shot, stabbed, bludgeoned, or something else. You will have to gauge whether the intensity of the attack is violent action or only a threat. What makes the attack stage so difficult to analyze is the unpredictability from both the attacking side and the target.

Some robberies can be achieved simply by a bullying approach, threatening without display of a weapon. This may include a violent outburst or demonstration. This is primarily a psychological game, so its success depends on the weak mindset of the victim. Responding with your own verbal assault might work in your favor or just as easily escalate the situation. Let's, for example, say that you struck back. This might complicate things for you, not the perpetrator. If you haven't seen a weapon or been struck in the head (which is in many jurisdictions is considered in itself lethal force), there may be enough legal jeopardy to put you in trouble. The standard for violent action in most jurisdictions is, did you fear that your life or the life of another was in danger of suffering death or serious bodily harm.

Display of a weapon or an immediate violent attack usually results in compliance by the victim. But there is never a guarantee that the actions of the perpetrator will cease when they get what they are after. Letting you go after taking your valuables would be a rational course of action, but rational thought and behavior on behalf of a criminal is impossible to depend on.

Perhaps the number one reason that people come under attack is that they didn't see the trap coming. Their first mistake was poor counter surveillance. Let's say that when you looked down from your third-story window, you didn't see the three men standing on the corner in front of your building. You didn't notice that each time the city bus came and went they didn't get onboard. They are dressed with hats and coats despite it being a warm day. They seem to be looking certain pedestrians up and down, then talking briefly among themselves. You go back to the table to finish your morning coffee. When you return to the window they are still there watching the passersby without saying a word, then talking again. They are standing across the street from where you have parked your car.

Let's say you noticed the men but didn't think anything of it. This mistake in itself may not be your undoing. But when you crossed the street to get to your car they crossed the street as well. Not noticing their movement, which is often referred to as closing, can be fatal.

Counter surveillance is looking to see who is surveilling you. It begins with seeing people or things such as vehicles that appear out of place. Take a good look at where you live, your property and the surrounding property, at your street, and what typically goes on in and around it. You should be more familiar with your surroundings than anyone who comes from another part of town, either for legitimate purposes or to commit a crime. If you can develop the habit of looking for changes in your local landscape, you will begin to apply to same skills of observation wherever you go. When you take in your surroundings, imagine you are the director of a high school play. The street scene outside your window including neighboring homes, cars and people on the street are each props that should be in designated places according to a script that you should know better than anyone else. Is there someone on stage that is not normally in the cast? Is there a broken window that's not supposed to be there? If you can develop the habit of looking for changes in your local landscape, you will begin to apply the same skills of observation where ever you go.

The result of poor counter surveillance is surprise attack. Or at least a confrontation that catches you off guard. The added danger is that, when caught off guard, you may forget to apply some key strategy. Ideally, you should engage with a commanding voice if speaking is called for. Keep an eye toward an escape route, position your hands toward your face for defense or move one hand within close proximity of a weapon.

To review the final stage, reaction is how the criminal feels about what he or she has done. Reaction can be made more complicated by the fact that the victim's reaction is a contributing factor.

The two sentences above represent a very complex interaction. The first sentence more strongly implies that the crime was carried out successfully. The victim was overwhelmed or acquiesced after putting up little or no struggle. At this point, it might depend on why the criminal chose to commit the crime. Was it strictly professional, as in stealing for the cash value or as part of a job they were paid to do, or was it to fill an inner need?

If it was professional, then the survival of the victim is likely unless the criminal feels they are in danger of being identified or the victim is capable of bringing some form of revenge. If the crime was to satisfy some personal lust, getting through the fifth stage without severe injury or death is less likely. One popular theory is that criminals, especially rapists, are looking for a sense of empowerment. If somehow the commission of the crime fails to bring them the desired sense of empowerment, they might choose to take it out on the victim. As such, a simple robbery or a rape can result in homicide. In either case, the end result is never assured until the attacker has left the scene.

If the intended victim is able to access a weapon, it is usually a surprise to the attacker. This is the ultimate way to short circuit a criminal's plans. Success depends on the skill of the defender but not necessarily the skill of the attacker. Some criminals are very proud of their fighting prowess with or without a weapon, and the commission of a crime provides a thrill ride for the attacker, as well as possible monetary gain. But some criminals have never actually fired the gun they carry and know little about its operation. In either case, fighting back challenges the will of the attacker to continue. This is an important point because the likely reason you were attacked was that you seemed to pose little threat to the criminal. Finding out they were wrong can be a shock they may not want to deal with and they will abort the crime. But until the attacker has been rendered unable to continue the assault or simply left the scene, the attack stage remains an unpredictable situation.

Improvised Weapons

The best time to suffer a break-in or home invasion is when standing well behind a bolted front door shielded by a steel beam with shotgun in hand, high-capacity pistol on your hip, and a cell phone in your breast pocket with a hands-free device in your ear just shooting the breeze with your friendly neighborhood 911 operator. But if that's not the case, you may have to improvise.

The fact is, you may own every possible piece of equipment for home defense but not have them with you at the moment of attack. One of the methods that any good thief or violent criminal depends on is surprise and catching people off guard. But, what if your lack of preparedness was just a bad case of Murphy's Law? Look around you. Is there anything at your disposal that can help you defend the home?

Improvised weapons are sometimes hidden by an article's original intended purpose. For example, the common ashtray has shown up in more than one B-movie as a bludgeon. During the Hungarian Revolution in 1956, one of the weapons used by the resistance was glass bottles filled with gasoline, the proverbial Molotov cocktail.

Not every improvised weapon is one you can pick up and swing at an opponent. Sometimes, it's just a matter of quick thinking. In one very clever episode of the TV sitcom *All in The Family* entitled "Edith's 50th Birthday," the ordinarily dim-witted Edith Bunker, played by the brilliant actress Jean Stapleton, was threatened by a sexual predator in the family home. But the man was in her kitchen, not his. The predator had gained entry into the house masquerading as a police detective. She continues to spurn his advances while she turns to put a cake into the oven. I couldn't help but notice something unusual about her actions as she shut the oven door. Something additional or extraneous seemed out of place. Naturally, she was alarmed, but I couldn't figure out what I had just seen aside from her fearful mannerisms, such as widened eyes and shaking hands. The man continues his verbal overture and just when he grabs her and they begin to struggle, smoke begins pouring from the oven. Edith screams out 'Fire, fire' and pushes the man aside as his grip weakens in the confusion. She pulls the burning cake from the oven and shoves it into the man's face, making way for her escape. What I had seen but had not been able to identify was Edith turning the flame all the way up as she closed the oven door.

But when people think of improvised weapons they tend to think of the type made by prisoners during incarceration. For example, the Gillette bayonet is a razor on a stick fashioned from a popular disposable razor that works with a small blade set into a plastic handle. Reconfigured as a weapon, the blade is repositioned to expose much more of the sharp edge. Prison shivs, or puncturing weapons, are fashioned by sharpening a screwdriver, nail, spring, or metal rod that might be removed from a bunk bed. But each of these weapons takes a great deal of time to make. When looking for an improvised weapon for home defense, you need an item that can be pressed into service without modification. It has to be fully formed and readily within reach.

The Molotov cocktail and Edith Bunkers' home-baked distraction are examples of improvisations drawn from history and fantasy. For a more realistic and contemporary discussion of improvised weaponry and their possible applications for defending the home, I turned to internationally recognized consultant Jared Wihongi of Salt Lake City. Wihongi trains police and special forces soldiers in hand-to-hand combat, as well as being one of the driving forces behind the Black Label Tactical division at Browning Arms. You may recognize his name from a Spike TV episode of *The Deadliest Warrior,* but having portrayed a Maori warrior (the birthright of his father, in fact) you might not recognize him in person. Jared Wihongi is also one of the few practitioners of Pekiti-Tirsia Kali (the Filipino art of fighting with blades) to have earned a bona fide master ranking and the revered title of Tuhon.

That Jared Wihongi remains fascinated by improvised weapons is not completely separate from his immersion with Pekiti-Tirsia. Sometimes referred to as a combat technology, "Pekiti-Tirsia," explains Jared, "is an art that focuses on developing the speed, timing, power, and precision of slashing and thrusting angles aimed at the destruction of specific targets on the body. This is universal regardless of what kind of weapon is in your hand (edged or impact) and even translates to the empty-hand fighting subsystem of Pekiti-Tirsia. This makes Pekiti-Tirsia the perfect art for the application of improvised weaponry."

◀ Jared Wihongi, a SWAT operator and internationally renowned instructor of Pekitit-Tirsia Kali, is uniquely qualified to consult in the application of improvised weapons. Pekiti-Tirsia Kali is often referred to as a combat technology rather than a fighting art because its system has, for generations, proven both versatile and effective no matter what weapon was employed. The primary weapon in Pektiti-Tirsia Kali is the blade. But throughout history Pekiti-Tirsia Kali has suffered periods of secretive practice when edge weapons were banned among the populace in a prohibition similar to what some parties wish for today in relation to the private ownership of firearms. In response, practitioners continued development but with sticks and anything else that could be improvised to substitute for the edge of a blade. *Photos courtesy of Jared Wihongi and Browning Black Label Tactical*

Our discussion began with a clarification regarding the situation in which you might have an opportunity to prevent criminal entrance to the home. In the earlier chapter Through the Eyes of a Ranger, we established that most home invasions are targeted deployments by criminals hoping to steal cash or specific items they knew or suspected through surveillance were inside the house. Home invasions are typically planned to take place when the occupants are at home so the occupants are available to show where valuables are hidden or to unlock a security cabinet or safe. Furthermore, if the occupants are home the chance of a security system being armed and ready may be reduced, especially if the invasion takes place during normal waking hours. Lastly, the amount of force implicit in the number of invaders and their aggressive demeanor is designed to overwhelm. All these factors lend confidence to the invaders and give them a sense of security, not to mention that they might have taken drugs that can dull pain and increase their natural level of aggression. Against these odds, the occupant or occupants are more than likely going to acquiesce and hope for the best.

Unless you are ready for a home invasion on the scale described above with a solid plan involving enhanced security doors (interior as well as exterior) and quick access to high-capacity firearms, improvised weapons are probably not going to come into play. But not all home invasions are well planned. "Most home intrusions are burglaries," says Wihongi, who is also a SWAT operator and former property crimes detective. "The intruders will likely be surprised that anyone is home and try to flee. If they randomly stumble upon an apparently soft (and surprised) target, they may decide to overwhelm the target and the crime may evolve from there (kidnapping, sexual assault, etc.). Generally they won't want to escalate things that far. But there is always an element of unpredictability when dealing with drug addicts. Most burglars are looking to make money to buy drugs."

In the case of a single attacker, such as a sexual predator, the use of improvised weapons can be key to survival.

One of the first things to consider when choosing items that could be used as weapons is that any fighting is going to take place in the close-quarter confines

▲ Anyone entering the home would recognize this domestic furnishing and not be suspicious or intimidated. What, if any, combative potential do you see? The umbrella or the walking stick could be used for poking, striking, or blocking. So could the entire coat rack for that matter. Swing a purse or a briefcase? How about the bug spray? It is just as likely that ants could be invading the home as someone more dangerous who might need to be sprayed in lieu of mace. But, is there more here than it seems?

of a home. "Longer weapons that would require room to swing, like a broom or mop, or flexible weapons, like a belt or chain, may not be the best choices," advised Wihongi. "It is important to remember that if you aren't able to force an intruder to flee, then you will have to neutralize the imminent threat. And in many cases that means physical incapacitation, which means the more effective (i.e. deadly) the weapon that you choose the better."

Wihongi suggested that improvised weapons can be divided into three categories. Designated weapons, planned improvised weapons, and truly improvised weapons.

Designated weapons would be items that were in fact designed specifically for protection. This would include defensive knives, firearms, pepper spray, civilian tasers, batons, and the like. What makes them improvised weapons is their hidden, strategic placement, such as by a front door or inside a den,

bathroom—anywhere you are likely to be caught off guard. Designated weapons, however, require a certain amount of concealment, especially if children are present. A purse, laptop, or iPad case may offer a separate weapons compartment that is low profile, and the fewer people who know about it, the better. A can of pepper spray behind a bottle of aspirin inside a medicine cabinet might provide enough cover and yet offer instant access. And we've all seen clocks and books with false compartments that can be placed on a shelf without drawing suspicion.

Planned improvised weapons are for people who don't want designated weapons spread around the house, especially if children are present. Planned improvised weapons require a beauty-is-in-the-eye-of-the-beholder outlook. This means that a baseball bat could be left in a corner ostensibly because you are a baseball fan. You may have a gas-burning fireplace with ceramic logs, but to make it look more

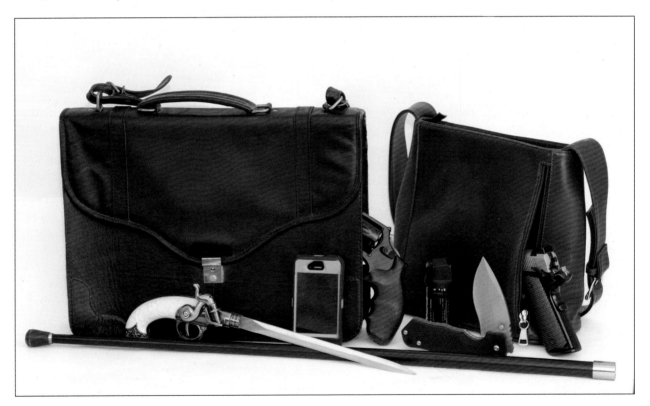

▲ Here are six or seven items of self-defense you did not see on the coat rack by the front door. Both the briefcase and the Galco purse were armed and ready. The briefcase can also accommodate a ballistic plate or Kevlar partition that could be used to shield vital organs. The raincoat had a can of mace, with a safety catch by the way, in one pocket and the intimidating Grayman SATU folding knife in the other. The flintlock pistol grip may have been faux but the double-edged half-sword is not. The stainless steel capped shank of the walking stick should not be trifled with either. Not to mention the ever-present cell phone, for good measure. Welcome home.

▲ When it comes time to defend your home, hideout gun safes, such as this handsome clock from Central Spy Shop in Houston, can make your day. *Photo courtesy of Central Spy Shop, Houston*

planned improvised weapons. During a March 2013 rampage through Chicago's Magnificent Mile, teenagers bludgeoned people with heavy items, such as padlocks slung inside the end of a sock. At one time, these weapons could have been considered truly improvised and used for defensive purposes. What it comes down to is that anything you pick up can be a force multiplier more devastating than a bare hand. This could include car keys, a statuette, or a ballpoint pen.

Another way to categorize weapons is by their action or effect, like edged weapons (including a purely puncturing weapon like a screwdriver), impact weapons, and distraction weapons. "Distraction weapons would be something like bug spray or oven cleaner," says Wihongi. "Anything (car keys, ash tray) that can

traditional and authentic you keep a poker by the hearth. A can of ant spray by the front or rear doors could merely signal that your war with ants is ongoing. Under the cloak of normal reasoning, none of these items would be seen as being out of place. But in a tight spot the baseball bat becomes a devastating weapon, the poker a vicious tool, and the ant spray a substitute for mace. But bear in mind that any airborne chemical can also splash back at you as well. And chemicals other than mace or pepper spray can cause permanent damage instead of just temporary discomfort. But in places where guns are, for all practical purposes, utterly banned, you have to continuously think over what the best candidates for using as a weapon are, where to place them, and constantly devise plans to deploy them.

Truly improvised weapons, or perceiving common objects as weapons, may be just as much an exercise for the imagination as they are for the hands. "Truly improvised weapons," says Wihongi, "are things that happen to be available when you need them." The trick is how to recognize them. While living in New York's Lower East Side during the 1970s, I discovered that hurling unopened cans of baked beans was one way to get a would-be burglar away from a window and off the fire escape. The first time the cans were used as a weapon, they were truly improvised weapons. But once it was decided to keep a supply of baked beans on hand strictly for their ability to be used as weapons, you might then be able to recategorize them as

▲ Fighting with empty hands or any type of weapon should begin with only one mindset: To fight until the threat is stopped. Fighting with improvised weapons requires an additional mental process, that of visualization. First, you must be able to see things for their potential. A can of soup or beans is heavy, hard, and has relatively sharp edges. Note the finger over the top to apply downward force. What are the chances a fight can be finished with only a can of beans? Probably not, because it will likely end up being dropped or thrown. This means you will have to reload with whatever you can pick up next on your way to escape or to where a more potent weapon is stored.

be thrown in the face of the intruder that distracts them and creates an opening for your next move. I even consider pepper spray as a distraction, because it cannot be relied upon to incapacitate a subject. Sometimes it will drop someone, which is best-case scenario, and in many other cases it will just distract an individual momentarily and then have no lingering effect, if any effect at all. I've seen that many times personally. Throwing a chair or a vase at someone can be both a distraction and an impact projectile weapon."

Regarding the use of gas, I wanted Jared's opinion on some of the tear gas (CS) dispensers that can be mounted on the wall and triggered along with audible alarms. Another ploy sometimes heard around the bar circuit is heaving a canister of flea-and-tick bomb into a room between the intruders and yourself inside a safe room for escape, or to take up a position with firearms. "Tear gas booby trap is a bad idea in my book. This would be more for a hardcore place like Joberg (Johannesburg), South Africa, or Rio De Janeiro, Brazil. I'm very experienced with tear gas (CS) as it's a staple tool in SWAT Teams. CS is more effective than OC spray [pepper spray], but it would require a large concentration to be effective. And without knowing where in the house the intruders would be, it would require placement throughout the whole house. This would also require coordinated efforts by the home occupants to get gas masks on, and the aftermath would require a lengthy decontamination process for the house. Great concept in theory but fairly impractical. If you are looking for a chemical spray that reduces cross contamination, try one of the foam type

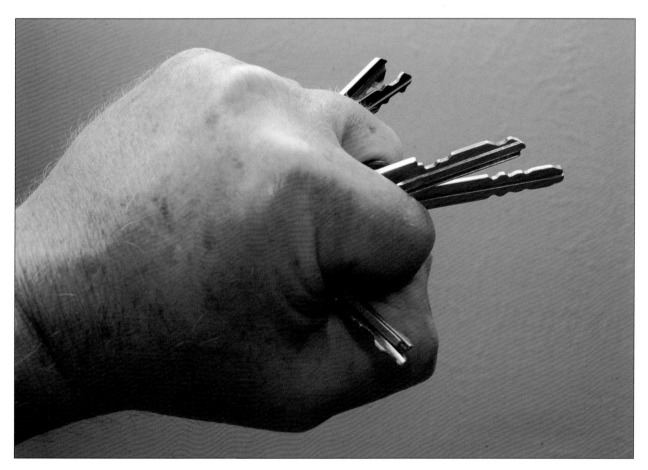

▲ Above all, fighting and defending takes a never-give-up attitude. Chances are, if you have nothing else with which to project or multiply force, there are always your car and house keys. Split between your fingers, a rake of the eyes by a very small person can be as powerful as a blow struck by a giant. Some people have iron jaws and others have washboard abdominal muscles, but we all have the same vulnerable eyes.

sprays that doesn't mist into the air as much as others. Even then there will be some cross contamination, though, if things turn into a hand-to-hand fight."

It is important to be reminded that when using an improvised weapon, especially one that is not generally recognized as being capable of delivering lethal force, your counterattack may just be stage one of the fight. Hopefully, the intruder will be discouraged and leave to find an easier target. That the aggressor has suffered a physical blow, no matter how hard you think you've hit them, may not be enough to change their mind about continuing the attack. Adding conviction and attitude to your delivery can be an important ingredient.

"In any self-defense scenario, aggression counts. Aggression can tip the scale in your favor even if you are smaller than your assailant. Make *him* choose flight over fight. Make yourself big and loud, and counterattack like your life depends on it because it probably does in a home invasion scenario. The difference between us and the bad guys is we need to have controlled aggression, something I would try and train in police recruits when I was a police academy drill instructor. But be able to switch it off when the imminent threat is neutralized."

But you can't just throw an offensive move at someone, then stop and look to see your attacker's reaction. If you have scored a blow that offers you the opportunity to flee, you may now have two options. "In most situations," says Wihongi, "the option to flee is going to be the best option if it's viable. I like to call it a tactical disengagement. We all know the adage, 'He who fights and runs away, lives to fight another day.' Don't risk your life to protect replaceable property. But sometimes fleeing isn't a viable option. You may have to fight to defend your family who may not be able to flee with you."

If you choose to stay and fight, any viable opening could be seen as an opportunity to access a weapon from the next level in your arsenal. Having a protocol or progression, such as disperse ant spray (distraction), hit with a vase (impact), and run to where you have a firearm, could be a winning combination. I've heard some hardened fighters say all they want is to be able to fight their way over to their AR15 propped up behind a door.

Since Jared Wihongi's edged weapon skills operate at an extremely sophisticated level, I wanted to know more about his perspective on the use of knives. Naturally, the knife has several advantages over a variety of weapons, even firearms. For example, while some weapons will likely be stationed in one place or another inside the home, the combat knife, folding or fixed blade, can be easily carried with you wherever you go. It can be carried concealed, which helps safeguard the knife from being taken from you.

But when it comes to a situation where you are literally at arm's length from your attacker, perhaps a winning strategy would be to do something to make your attacker use both their hands while you use only one. Then the free hand acquires the knife and cuts, stabs, or slashes. Could this mean throwing an object to serve the purpose of occupying both of the attacker's hands? Or perhaps their hands could be drawn to their eyes by the delivery of a chemical substance like mace or pepper spray, opening an opportunity to attack with a knife.

If you thought the answer would be "No, that's just in the movies," you'd be wrong. Improvised weapons can be lethal but in many cases their primary function is to buy time. Just as a boxer fakes throwing a punch or feints left or right to make their opponent flinch and leave an opening in their defense, improvised weapons are often relied on to create an opening during which a transition is made to a more effective weapon. But this is where the triumvirate of distance, proximity, and opportunity comes into play. For example, if you can access a firearm before an attacker can close the distance and capture you, it may be a waste of time to continue swinging a baseball bat any more times than was necessary to create an opening to run to where the gun is kept.

At some point in any confrontation you will probably have to decide between the urges of fight or flight. Knowing when to strike and when to run are decisions made in a split second. That the effect of an improvised weapon such as throwing a potted plant or even slashing with a knife is most likely going to be temporary begs us to learn more about the mechanics and inner workings of violent confrontations.

One of the most widely quoted studies of how a mind works in battle (or, in more clinical terms, the process by which we respond to stimulus) was developed by United States Air Force fighter pilot Colonel John Boyd. Colonel Boyd's motivation was to find ways that pilots

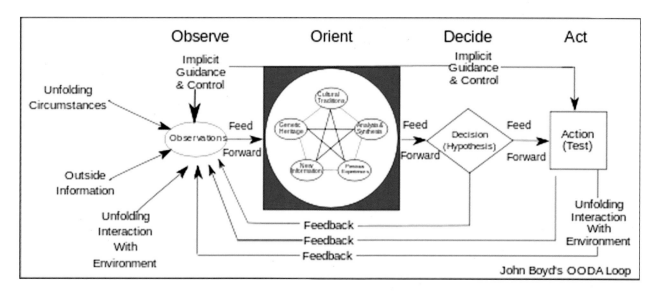

Observe · Orient · Decide · Act

Implicit Guidance & Control

Unfolding Circumstances

Observations — Feed Forward

Cultural Traditions
Genetic Heritage
Analysis & Synthesis
New Information
Previous Experience

Feed Forward — Decision (Hypothesis) — Feed Forward — Action (Test)

Implicit Guidance & Control

Outside Information

Unfolding Interaction With Environment

Feedback
Feedback
Feedback

Unfolding Interaction With Environment

John Boyd's OODA Loop

could win engagements with the enemy even when the odds were stacked against them. He developed a chain of definitions for how the human mind responds, which to this day is referred to as the OODA Loop.

OODA stands for Observe, Orient (recognize the possibilities based on your training and experience), Decide what to do in response, and take Action. Because, each of the four processes feeds back into the others continuously, it is referred to as a loop. The OODA Loop takes place inside the mind for every decision no matter if it is of trivial concern or of life or death. What this teaches us is that no matter how different people are in stature or strength, our minds work through the decision making process in the same manner. Therefore, no matter how big and bad your attacker appears to be, he or she is just as susceptible to being momentarily distracted, stunned, or confused as you are.

Colonel Boyd suggests that knowing details of his opponent's background and culture, as well as his capabilities and his armament, could form a basis for attacking them mentally. In layman terms to "get into their heads." Perhaps anger them, anything to short circuit their reasoning and interrupt the cycle of their OODA Loop. For the home occupant suddenly attacked, it doesn't seem likely that a psychological approach would be appropriate or effective even if you did have the time to speak with your adversary. But a physical intervention, such as the deployment of an

improvised weapon, could serve the same purpose in at least delaying their advance.

Improvised weapons may or may not enable you to end a violent confrontation. Whether or not your counterattack stops the fight is ultimately up to your attacker. As in all defensive situations, you must repeat the application of force or increase the amount of force until the threat has stopped. Your unexpected violent response may create doubt and indecision within the mind of your attacker. Or it might just make them more determined. In either case, an improvised weapon can serve as a force multiplier as either an end or as a tool to move to a location of tactical advantage, access a more lethal weapon, or escape altogether. In short, the use of improvised weapons can help you create a series of further opportunities to survive the encounter.

Look around you. Your home and the possessions it contains are more familiar to you than anyone else. Don't be afraid to visualize a connection between common objects and effective weaponry. Plan emergency home defense decisions with family members or cohabitants to quickly recognize the weapons around the home, both improvised and designated. Experiment with the possibilities and techniques for putting them into action. Familiarity, recognition, and preparation will help you process your OODA Loop faster and afford you precious seconds, which could mean the difference between life and death.

A High-Capacity Point of View

Whenever cries for more gun control fly into a rage, the debate typically centers on how many rounds of ammunition a civilian needs. Or how many rounds should each individual firearm be able to fire before reloading? I like to think of maximum capacity in a different way altogether. That is, how many chances should be given to law-abiding citizens to allow them to survive an attack?

I am always mystified by the willingness of anyone to tell me how many rounds of ammunition it takes to stop even one aggressor. So instead of dealing in the theoretical, let's analyze an actual event and see if we can calculate the proper number of rounds, or opportunities to survive, that should be available to the civilian before it is necessary to reload. The following incident was reported by a number of different news organizations including WSB-TV, ABC News, and the *Walton* (Georgia) *Tribune* on television, print, and the internet.

Synopsis:

At around 1 p.m. on Friday, January 4, 2013, a woman in Loganville, Georgia, was at home working in her upstairs office. She was also minding her nine-year-old twin boy and girl when she spotted a man outside a window. The woman, Melinda Herman, called her husband, who instructed her to grab her gun and take the kids upstairs to hide in what has been described as a crawl space. According to the *Walton Tribune* report, the man rang the doorbell before prying it open with a crowbar.

The man searched the house and finally made his way upstairs. All this time, Mrs. Herman was on the telephone with her husband, Donnie, who in turn was on the telephone with the Walton County Sheriff's Department. When the intruder found Melinda and her children, she fired all five shots from her revolver as he moved toward them. On a recording of the 911 call, Mr. Herman's direction and encouragement to shoot repeatedly can actually be heard. According

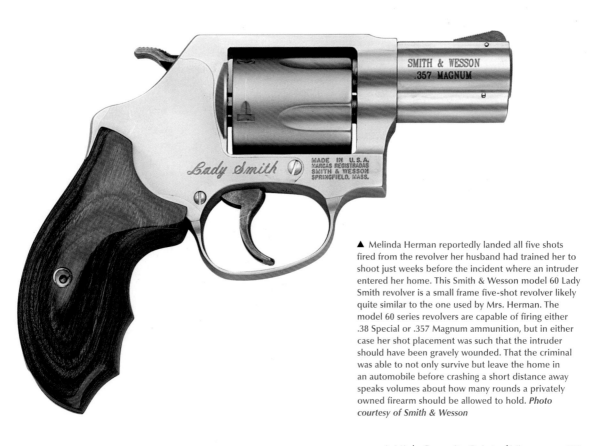

▲ Melinda Herman reportedly landed all five shots fired from the revolver her husband had trained her to shoot just weeks before the incident where an intruder entered her home. This Smith & Wesson model 60 Lady Smith revolver is a small frame five-shot revolver likely quite similar to the one used by Mrs. Herman. The model 60 series revolvers are capable of firing either .38 Special or .357 Magnum ammunition, but in either case her shot placement was such that the intruder should have been gravely wounded. That the criminal was able to not only survive but leave the home in an automobile before crashing a short distance away speaks volumes about how many rounds a privately owned firearm should be allowed to hold. *Photo courtesy of Smith & Wesson*

to an interview with the 911 operator, the intruder could be heard pleading not to be shot again. Melinda Herman was smart enough to play upon his fear and threatened to continue shooting even though she knew she was out of ammunition.

The intruder was hit with all five shots from Melinda Herman's .38 caliber revolver. WSB-TV reported that the intruder suffered injuries to his head, face, and neck. Nevertheless, the intruder was able to exit the house, get in his car, and drive off. But he didn't get far. For reasons that are unclear, perhaps due to his injuries, he lost control of his car and crashed into a tree, finally stopping in a neighbor's yard.

When the police arrived, the intruder was arrested and taken to a nearby hospital. He was identified as 32-year-old Atlanta resident Paul Slater. WSB-TV reported that, according to the Gwinnett County Sheriff's Office, Slater had been arrested six other times in the county since 2008, including an arrest for simple battery as recently as February 2012. The assault on the Herman residence resulted in Slater being charged with burglary. Slater was released from the hospital within one week and appeared in court. A plea for bond was denied.

The above incident presents several key points, each more remarkable than the next. First of all, Mrs. Herman took refuge in an attempt to hide from the intruder. This forced the intruder to find her and her children. Even though the intruder was successful in locating the hiding place, he was immediately at a disadvantage because he was fully exposed to an opponent who was both prepared and waiting for him. The intended victim fired every round she possibly could. Furthermore, even when she knew the gun was empty she prolonged the threat to her opponent by means of deception. She accomplished all of this with only minimal training. In fact, her five-shot revolver was purportedly her first gun and she had only recently been trained to use it by her husband. Yet, she was able to land every shot she fired.

It's difficult to convey just how unusual it is for someone to hit their assailant with every shot they fire. Take, for example, the February 2013 pursuit of former Los Angeles police officer Christopher Dorner. Of all the rounds fired at him by trained police officers with modern high-capacity weaponry, Dorner, according

to the coroner, died of a single self-inflicted gunshot wound to his head.

In the Herman case, it was sheer preparation by the intended victim and the lack of preparation by the intruder that determined the outcome. That the house was not reported as ransacked for valuables could indicate that Slater was specifically looking to rape Mrs. Herman, kidnap the children, or both. If Melinda Herman had not been armed, she would have been overpowered. Her fate and the fate of her children would have been in the hands of a career criminal who would have had to consider killing each of them to prevent being identified. "She protected the kids. She did what she was supposed to do as a responsible, prepared gun owner," said her husband.

Despite initial reports of shots to the head and neck, it was later reported that Slater was placed on a ventilator suffering from punctured lungs, a punctured liver, and a punctured stomach. The Walton County Sheriff reported that Slater had four distinct exit wounds yet was able to survive. If Slater had also been armed with a gun, Melinda Herman would probably not have been able to fire, let alone land all of her shots. Since it is doubtful that Slater can legally buy or possess a gun, the motive for the attempted burglary might have been to steal one. If we were to assume that he did indeed prefer to find Mrs. Slater at home rather than merely searching for valuables, maybe Slater was hoping she would be able to open a gun safe or show him where anything of value might be. But all the guns in the house were either secured, well hidden, or in the owner's hands. Based on the fact that Slater survived being hit with five rounds at close range and his opponent was out of ammunition, it is reasonable to assume that if Slater had arrived armed or found a loaded gun prior to locating Mrs. Herman and her children, all three of them might have been killed or seriously wounded.

For the purpose of our discussion of how many rounds of ammunition a civilian-owned firearm should be allowed to fire without interruption, the fact that the intruder did not have a weapon himself is irrelevant. The fact that the intruder survived all five shots and managed to go down stairs, open a car door, start the engine, and drive, albeit a short distance, is much more telling and germane to the debate.

▲ When Melinda Herman ran out of bullets, she kept her cool and didn't let on that the gun was empty. The only thing that kept the intruder from advancing on Mrs. Herman and her two children was the threat of being shot again. But what if there had been more than one assailant? If she had been armed with an eighteen-round Smith & Wesson M&P 9mm pistol, she could have made good on her threats. *Photo courtesy of Smith & Wesson*

Based on reports, there was no mention of whether or not Slater approached the crawl space with the crowbar that was used to force open the front door. If we had to answer the question "How many rounds of ammunition does it take to kill an unarmed man?" we would have to say, "We do not know." We could, however, say that in this instance it took five rounds to stop an attack by a man without a firearm. But what if there had been two unarmed men? Then are we to believe that all that is required to stop an attack by two unarmed men would be ten rounds of ammunition? No, because there is no guarantee that all ten shots will hit the intruders or inflict enough damage to stop the attack.

Suppose Paul Slater had been armed or had with him multiple armed accomplices? If you were the subject of their assault, how many rounds of ammunition do you think you would need to survive?

Choosing a Firearm for Home Defense

Firearms: An Overview

The firearm is the most effective advancement in personal defense ever invented. Why? Because a firearm can be used to project force well beyond arm's length, meaning that any person can deliver a blow of meaningful impact no matter how small they are or how big and strong their attacker. This means that a firearm can be used to defend yourself without having to push, pull, wrestle, or otherwise physically engage your attacker.

According to Webster's dictionary, the definition of the word firearm is surprisingly short: "noun: a weapon from which a shot is discharged by gunpowder. Usually used only of small arms."

"Small arms" means a firearm or gun that can be held in one or two hands, such as a pistol or revolver. Or it can mean a firearm that requires the use of both hands with a section of the firearm supported by a third point of contact with the body, usually the shoulder. Common terminology for such weapons includes shouldered weapon, long gun, or rifle. A rifle with a shorter overall length may also be referred to as a carbine. The shotgun is also a shouldered firearm but gets its name from its primary purpose of propelling multiple projectiles, or shot, rather than a solid bullet. But shotguns can also be loaded to fire large single mass projectiles referred to as slugs.

The propulsion of bullets, slugs, or shot is the result of igniting gunpowder and controlling the direction of the blast. Each round of modern ammunition is composed of a self-contained unit of a projectile (or projectiles), gunpowder, and a primer. The primer serves as the fuse. To light the fuse, the primer is struck rather than touched with an open flame. Once the gunpowder is ignited, it becomes gas expanding toward the path of least resistance. With the back of the ammunition case firmly against a wall (the breechface), the expanding gases push the projectile free of the case and keeps pushing against it until the gases escape through the open end of the barrel (at the muzzle). The linear direction of the barrel at the precise moment when the bullet exits into space determines its path.

Perspectives on Handgun Power

The two most important considerations in choosing a firearm are the amount of force the firearm can project and the ease with which the operator can deliver the projectile to the desired point of impact. In short, power and accuracy.

The amount of power available from a given firearm is traditionally viewed as synonymous with the caliber of ammunition it is chambered for. But there is more than one way of looking at it. Expressing the amount of power from an individual round of ammunition is a lot simpler concept to understand than determining the power of a specific firearm. The concept that the power of a handgun should be determined by adding together the power of each individual round was brought to my attention by Bill Davison, an expert in VIP security and a former British Royal Marine who owns and operates Tac Pro Shooting Center in Mingus, Texas. One reason higher capacity is important in security work is because it offers a greater ability to expend rounds to cover teammates, which is sometimes just as important as making a one-shot stop. The relationship between higher capacity and caliber is

▲ No one can argue that a single round of 9mm ammunition (foreground), is as powerful as one round of .44 Remington Magnum ammunition (background). But here is a different way of looking at caliber choice, or rather the power of an individual handgun, as suggested by one Bill Davison, former Royal Marine, VIP protection specialist and owner/proprietor of Tac Pro Shooting Center in Mingus, Texas. When choosing a gun for defensive applications, it is necessary to consider the power available not just from a single round of ammunition but also from the sum total of all the rounds it can hold. Is 9mm ammunition more powerful than .44 Magnum? No. Is an eighteen-round capacity 9mm pistol more powerful than a six-shot .44 Mag revolver? Yes.

this: Ammunition topped with larger diameter bullets, such as .45 ACP or .44 Magnum, produce more power per shot than ammunition that drives smaller diameter bullets, such as 9mm. But, since the larger caliber ammunition takes up more space, the 9mm pistol is able to store more rounds.

Using a common formula for muzzle energy (velocity squared divided by a constant of 450,000, multiplied by bullet weight measured in grains), we can compute the power of a single round of ammunition to present a value in foot-pounds of energy. Black Hills Ammunition lists its most powerful 115-grain hollow point 9mm ammunition as leaving the muzzle at a velocity of 1300 feet per second (fps). This equates to approximately 432 ft.-lbs. of muzzle energy. Black Hills also lists two different rounds of .44 Magnum that deliver as much as 848 ft.-lbs. of energy. But a .44 Magnum revolver would run dry after delivering a maximum of six shots or, a total of about 5088 ft.-lbs. A typical full-sized 9mm pistol can store sixteen rounds or more. This means the 9mm is ultimately the more powerful weapon system capable of delivering almost 7000 ft.-lbs. of energy. In addition, the 9mm high-capacity pistol offers greater potential to reengage a target or take on more than one attacker.

The power of a firearm can also play a role in accuracy and rate of fire. For every action there is a reaction, and the recoil from each shot is bound to cause the gun to move off target with every shot. The more powerful the ammunition, the more recoil. The more difficult a firearm is to control, the longer time it takes to regain the proper aim for the next shot. If the gun is not properly controlled, the blast from a single round can disturb aim even before the bullet leaves the barrel.

The value of accuracy is that a shot of nearly any size or power properly placed will stop an aggressor. The term bull's-eye is meant to refer to hitting a fearsome animal at its most vulnerable point. But in a home invasion or other attack, the chaos, the lighting, the sound, and the element of surprise are likely to be so distracting that judging one's marksmanship solely by what can be achieved on a Sunday afternoon at your favorite shooting range will probably preclude relying on perfect shot placement.

Choosing the Best Gun

It has been said, and rightly so, that under stress, we revert or default to our lowest perfected course of muscle memory. That's why if you already own a firearm, the best gun for home defense may be the one you know best.

So far, our approach to choosing a firearm has been as though we have yet to purchase a gun for home defense. We have established that we need a balance of power, accuracy, and enough capacity to deal with more than one attacker. But what if you already own firearms? Even if you do not own a high-capacity assault weapon (either by infringement of your Second Amendment rights or from sheer lack of availability), let's focus on the combative potential of several popular platforms.

Single-Action Revolver

When it comes to personal or home defense in this day and age, the single-action revolver is probably the last weapon that comes to mind. But single-action revolvers were deadly in their heyday and are formidable now, too. Whether you choose a large-caliber revolver or a smaller-caliber model, most single-action revolvers still chamber six rounds. This means choosing a powerful cartridge topped with a big bullet will not mean a further compromise in capacity. Modern single-action revolvers, such as the Ruger Vaquero, are safer than ever. In traditional single-action revolver design, the firing pin (sometimes called a nose pin) was attached directly to the face of the hammer. The danger was that accidental impact to the spur or thumb piece of the hammer could cause the firing pin to impact the primer and set off a round unintentionally. Modern single-action revolvers include a firing pin block or a hammer block so the old-time practice of carrying the gun with the hammer down on an empty chamber for enhanced safety is unnecessary.

Can single-action revolvers be fired quickly and accurately? Certainly. If you have any doubt, go watch a local match staged by SASS (Single Action Shooting Society). The downside of the single-action revolvers is that it would be impossible to reload without taking so much time that you would be at risk. A single-action revolver requires that each chamber be unloaded and reloaded individually and the manipulation required is

Double-Action Revolver

The double-action revolver is far more flexible than its single-action counterpart. The gun can be fired without changing the shooting grip, and movement of the trigger finger forward and back can keep the gun ready to fire without interruption. Or it, too, can be fired in single action by manually pulling back the hammer. That is, until the ammunition is spent. At this point, there are two options. One, drop the gun and pick up a second revolver. Or two, reload. The cylinder that contains the ammunition is positioned on a hinged yoke. The double-action revolver can be reloaded by releasing the cylinder so it swings outward from the frame. The ejector rod is pressed and empty cases fall away. Rounds can be inserted one at a time or better yet all at once if they are held in a speed loading device that holds them in alignment to the cylinder.

A really fast reload takes only about one and a half seconds or less. But that's if everything goes right. The spent cases need to fall clear and the fresh rounds have to go in smoothly. Frankly, this is a complicated process made much more difficult by any manner of awkward position, such a kneeling down behind cover. Thankfully, revolvers of seven- and even eight-round capacity are available in effective rounds, such as .357 Magnum.

▲ Single-action revolvers might not be the first choice in a modern firearm, but they are as deadly now as they were in the old West. The Ruger Vaquero with Bird's Head grip (and case-hardened finish) could be considered something of a concealed carry piece due to its low drag grip. The Vaquero SASS, named for the Single Action Shooting Society, is a favorite among lightning quick competitors because it is not only rugged and well-made, but safer than old style single action revolvers, as well. In days gone by, safe carry meant with the hammer down on an empty chamber, relegating maximum capacity to only five rounds. With the Vaquero's transfer bar mechanism, instead of a firing pin mounted directly on the hammer, there is no longer any danger of incidental impact to the hammer transferring energy to the primer of a loaded round. So, the operator can safely load all six chambers. *Photos courtesy of Sturm, Ruger, & Co.*

tricky and time consuming. Even after a confrontation appears to be over, you'll want to be ready to fire again while scanning for more aggressors. The answer for the single-action devotee is, just like in the old west, to have two guns at your disposal for a total of twelve shots maximum.

What single-action revolvers lack in capacity they can make up for in accuracy. And for defending a home surrounded by plenty of space, an accurate long-range shot might be what's called for. An example of single-action capability would be NRA Hunter's Pistol Silhouette competition. Revolvers fired single action only are used to knock down steel silhouette likenesses of small animals at distances to one hundred meters.

▲ Revolvers need not be limited to five- or six-round capacity. The Smith & Wesson N-frame model 627 revolvers chamber eight rounds of .38 Special or .357 Magnum ammunition. Smith & Wesson's slightly smaller L-frame model 686+ packs seven rounds. The 627s can be reloaded quickly, thanks to full moon clips as standard equipment and chamber mouths that are angled, or chamfered, to help funnel the rounds into place. HKS makes seven-round speedloaders available aftermarket.

Another example of the flexibility of the revolver is that it does not rely on ammunition to load its next round. While a semi-automatic pistol may not reliably feed one round or another due to a slight variation in overall length or the profile of the bullet, any round that fits inside a revolver chamber is going to function. This includes miniature shot shells filled with small BBs for killing snakes and rats or any type of hollow point. This includes rounds like MagSafe, which features hollow-point bullets packed with BBs held in place with epoxy filler.

A good quality double-action revolver should offer an easy to pull trigger for consistent motion both rearward and forward upon release. For anyone with lesser hand strength or manual dexterity compromised by arthritis, a revolver rather than a semi-automatic pistol can be a very good choice. Loading the chamber (or clearing a malfunction) does not require pulling the slide to the rear against the resistance of the recoil spring. In addition, a lack of strength in the shooter's grip does not endanger the reliable function of a revolver. Cycling is completely mechanical, based on the actions of the shooter rather than depending on a system of ignition versus inertia.

Double-Barrel Shotgun

The double-barrel shotgun is a downright scary weapon. Just ask anyone who has had one pointed at them. The configuration most favored for self-defense places two 12-gauge barrels side by side. The shotgun is hinged between the barrels and the butt stock so it breaks open, exposing the chambers for loading. Some shotguns automatically eject the spent hulls, but

▲ Coach guns, (named for accompanying stage coach drivers on their dangerous journeys) may only hold two rounds of 20- or 12-gauge ammunition, but they are fast, easy to use, and the results are devastating. Some people refer to coach guns as back door guns meant to deliver an opening salvo stopping or stunning the attacker while transitioning to another weapon of higher capacity. This coach gun from Cimarron Firearms in historic Fredericksburg, Texas operates with two separate hammers that can be cocked independently. *Photo courtesy of Cimarron Firearms*

reloading is still a time consuming one round at a time. Trigger operation varies and may or may not require manually retracting a separate hammer for each barrel. Some double-barrel shotguns place two separate triggers, one ahead of the other. A third design features a single trigger that once pressed returns to operation, set to release the firing pin inside the chamber of the opposite barrel.

Double-barrel shotguns with a short overall length are generally referred to as coach guns, so named for their usage by stagecoach drivers. Light, short, and easily handled, the coach gun can be fired with one hand while still holding the reins as they drive off from an ambush. The bore of each barrel is typically more open than hunting guns, which are constricted to better project the shot in a tighter formation over a longer distance. The open barrels present wider patterns within a closer range.

Kept loaded, the double-barrel shotgun can be put into action very quickly. A sheriff I know in West Texas refers to his double-barrel shotgun as a back door gun. He carries a 1911 style .45 ACP pistol but doesn't keep it on his person inside the house or when he sleeps (I think). The double-barrel shotgun only offers two shots, but he feels that is enough to stop or put off a surprise attack long enough for him to retrieve a higher-capacity weapon.

Pump Shotgun

The pump shotgun can serve as a primary weapon or, like the coach gun, to deliver an opening salvo and cover while transitioning to another weapon. The advantage of a pump shotgun over the double-barrel design is higher capacity. Additional rounds are held in a tubular magazine supported directly beneath the barrel. The foregrip unlocks after each shot. Pumping

▲ Pump shotguns are valued for their reliability and power. This Mossberg 590A1 comes from the factory with a powerful Insight Technologies light integrated into the sliding fore end. Note the thumb-operated safety. The simplicity of the bead sight produces a near zero differential between line of sight and line of fire. This minimizes the possibility of finding a clear sight picture but firing with the muzzle obstructed by barriers of cover or concealment. *Photo courtesy of Mossberg & Sons*

it toward you and then toward the muzzle replaces the spent shell with a fresh round of ammunition.

The standard chambering for defensive shotguns is 12-gauge ammunition. But 20-gauge pump shotguns might be a better choice for shooters who are sensitive to recoil. A third choice, the .410-gauge shotgun, is much less effective and generally reserved for pest control, such as dispatching snakes and rats. But, the .410 can be an effective defensive tool when loaded with aggressive ammunition. It is also a lot of fun to shoot and can serve as a training device.

Most 12-gauge pump shotguns are sold with a magazine tube that holds four or five rounds. After buying one, you will often find a device inside the magazine to limit capacity to two rounds. This is so the shotgun meets legal requirements for hunting that make it illegal to load more than two rounds at one time. This can be easily removed if the shotgun is going to be used for purposes other than hunting.

Pump shotguns are generally longer, heavier, and more unwieldy than the double barrel. This is due primarily to the added bulk of the receiver and the mechanism required to move rounds from the magazine to the chamber. The minimum legal barrel length for civilian shotguns is eighteen inches. But the overall length of a pump shotgun can be reduced by replacing the shoulder stock with a pistol grip. The tradeoff, however, is less control.

The pump shotgun with pistol grip is more difficult to aim, pump, and aim again. Without being braced against the shoulder, the hands tend to want to push in opposite directions, dancing the muzzle left and right. One method that has proved successful is a push-pull technique. The hand on the pistol grip pulls rearward and the hand on the fore end slide pushes forward. This guarantees that the slide is locked and keeps the gun straight.

Some people like the pump shotgun merely for its intimidating appearance and reputation. They recommend racking the shotgun for dramatic effect, thinking that the sound alone is enough to scare off an attacker. No one can say this would never work. But it could also work against you by giving away your position.

The maximum capacity of a typical eighteen-inch barrel shotgun with tubular magazine is eight rounds of 2¾-inch shot shells, plus one additional carried inside the chamber. Some shotguns are sold with a seven- or eight-round magazines already in place, but standard-capacity shotguns can be modified by attaching an extended magazine tube. Magazine extension kits are available from supply houses like Brownells.com.

The tradeoff of higher capacity is more weight, but the result is a devastating and reliable weapon. Additional rounds can be carried in loops alongside the receiver or on the butt stock. Of the three different gauge shotguns, the 12-gauge models are easiest to reload both to the magazine and directly into the chamber because the points of access are larger. In addition, .410-gauge and 20-gauge shells are long, thin, and rectangular. In comparison, 12-gauge shells are short, round, and easier to insert.

Magazine Fed Semi-automatic Shotgun

The magazine-fed semi-automatic shotgun is an improvement over the pump shotgun primarily because the shooter is no longer tasked with having to manually move stored ammunition from the magazine into the chamber. If, for example, working the pump is a hardship due to a lack of strength or arthritic condition, the semi-automatic is a good choice. Some people point out that the semi-automatic shotgun offers a faster rate

▲ The .410-gauge Mossberg Cruiser might not be as powerful as its 20- or 12-gauge brothers, but it can nonetheless be useful. Traditionally used on snakes, rats, and small game, the latest editions of .410-gauge ammunition are more formidable than ever. It does take practice to fire a pistol-grip shotgun accurately, regardless of caliber, and learning on a .410 Cruiser is the best course of action. *Photo courtesy of Mossberg & Sons*

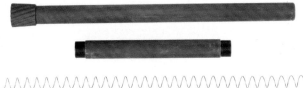

▲ Most popular shotguns, semi auto or pump, feed from what amounts to a tube or pipe. Aftermarket catalogs, such as Brownells, offer several good options for extending any tubular shotgun magazine to as many as eight rounds. *Photo courtesy of Brownells, Inc.*

▲ Today's semi-automatic shotguns are as reliable as pump-driven models. This Mossberg Special Purpose not only has a heat shield but a stand off muzzle for striking or literally blowing the hinges off doors. Still used today in the Middle Eastern campaigns, such guns are often referred to as skeleton keys. *Photo courtesy of Mossberg & Sons*

of fire than a pump-action model. The potential for faster follow-up shots is inherent in a semi-automatic shotgun, but since the shooter still needs to account for the return of an acceptable sight picture after experiencing a substantial amount of recoil, rate of fire is somewhat dependent on the ability of the shooter.

We make the distinction of magazine-fed semi-automatic shotguns because multiple barrel shotguns with a single trigger that releases multiple firing pins in succession may also be referred to as being semi-automatic. But, going forward, we will refer to magazine-fed semi-automatic shotguns simply as being semi-automatic and multiple barrel shotguns as being double barrel, side by side, or over-under.

The magazine capacity of today's semi-automatic shotguns is a product of magazine tube length and may be modified with the same type of kits referred to in the pump-action section. In both cases, the quality, strength, and efficiency of the magazine tube, spring, and follower have a direct connection to reliability. Suffice it to say that extended-magazine systems should be checked regularly for function.

The key ingredient to getting the full potential from any shotgun is how it fits the shooter. Fit means the ease in which the shotgun is held on target and the efficiency with which the eye can look straight down the barrel. A shotgun tailored for defensive needs must also be fast handling. This begins with acquisition, the ability to pick it up from on the floor, off of a rack, or from standing upright. The shotgun should have a working safety, which can be operated without changing hand position from the shooting grip.

Most shotguns, pump or semi-automatic, are delivered to suit an average size body structure, usually someone about five feet ten inches tall. But a shotgun intended for home defense should fit everyone in the house capable of shooting. The most important mea-

surement is the distance from the face of the trigger rearward to the surface of the recoil pad or, length of pull (LOP). Shortening the stock can result in faster overall handling and a more comfortable head position that makes it easier to shoot with the eyes level over the top of the barrel. Some compromise may have to be made depending on the size of the different shooters. But it is easier for a larger person to adapt to a slightly shorter length of pull than it is for a smaller person to mount a shotgun that is decidedly too long.

Shotguns advertised with the model designation Home Defense or Defensive are typically built on synthetic stocks (polymer or fiberglass reinforced plastic). To solve the problem of adjusting length of pull, multiple spacers and recoil pads may be included. The synthetic stock may also be shortened, but this often requires a professional to cut and re-attach the recoil pad. One alternative that can end up costing less is to choose a standard model shotgun with an old fashioned wooden stock that can be easily cut and modified. An increase in capacity can be achieved by applying an aftermarket magazine tube extension and more powerful magazine spring.

One additional advantage that a semi-automatic shotgun has over a pump is its facility for attaching weapon lights and lasers. This is due to the fact that the fore end of a semi-automatic shotgun is typically longer than one found on a pump shotgun, and it is fixed in place. This provides a stable platform for mounting both the accessory and the necessary controls. Mounting accessories on a fore end that must be free to slide forward and back is inherently more challenging.

Lever-Action Rifle

The lever-action rifle could be considered one of the first mass-produced practical rifles. As late as the 1990s, the term practical was a buzzword used to describe a weapon or a methodology that implied enhanced readiness and overall capability suitable for defensive situations. Today, the word tactical has taken its place in many instances. Does this mean that the lever-action rifle is still a viable tactical option?

The lever-action rifle is slim in profile and capable of carrying extra rounds that can be rapidly cycled

▲ Lever-action rifles and carbines have a long history synonymous with winning the West, and they're not through yet. Lever action carbines are nimble and strong, capable of chambering formidable loads, including .45-70 Government. The big loop on this Tactical model from Grizzly Custom in Montana makes lever action smooth and fast, and there's plenty of room to mount lights, lasers, or your choice of scope. Note the enlarged loading gate. *Photo courtesy of Grizzly Custom*

through the action by working the lever in about a sixty-degree arc. Rate of fire is enhanced because the beginning hand position and the end of each stroke places the hand in the proper grip for firing. The magazine is tubular and, like the pump-action shotgun, is mounted directly below and parallel to the barrel. The amount of extra rounds is dictated by the length of the magazine tube versus the length of each individual cartridge.

The lever-action rifle became a truly practical weapon when its barrel was shortened for added mobility. The resulting carbine configuration made it possible for cowboys to carry their lever-action with them next to the saddle. The practice of carrying a revolver (or two) on the hip plus the lever-action carbine offered plenty of options especially if both the handguns and the carbine fired the same caliber.

Today's lever-action rifles and carbines include models designed specifically for self defense. But the lines between a hunting model and a tactical design are easy to cross. Conversions offering accessory rails and greater overall efficiency are available from specialty shops, such as Grizzly Custom. Just like the previous discussion of shotguns, the key ingredients to a tactical weapon are rapid acquisition, mount, and magazine capacity.

Lever-action rifles and carbines are available in both centerfire and rimfire chamberings. Handgun calibers include .38 Special, .357 Magnum, .44 Special, .44 Magnum, and .45 Long Colt. Rifle calibers include the classic .30-30 Winchester and .45-70 Government. In addition, there are some proprietary calibers, such as .338 Marlin Express.

Rifle-caliber lever-action rifles or carbines would be best for longer-range applications. This could be necessary for defending a home on larger plots or in rural settings. Rifles are also a better choice for defending against feral animals that can wander on to property and threaten livestock. Like all rifle and carbines, lever-action models can be fit with optical scopes offering magnification, an illuminated reticle, or both. By using a scope, the shooter can more easily take advantage of the long gun's ability to strike a more distant target. Or simply make a more precise shot at a near target.

Carbine lever-action rifles with barrels between sixteen and twenty inches long offer the most versatility for defensive applications. Whereas rifle-caliber carbines may be limited in capacity due to overall length, a carbine chambered for handgun rounds may pack as many as ten extra rounds of ammunition. Please note that all of the handgun calibers are specific to revolver cartridges. So if you were going to match up a side arm with your lever-action carbine, your handgun would

▲ Eotech developed a holographic projection sighting system with several unique features for competitive shooters and the military. For one, the reticle or aiming graphic is virtually parallax free. This means the reticle need not be in the center of the screen. From behind cover or in any awkward position tilting or canting the gun diagonally has little or no effect on point of impact. This means you do not have wait for the gun to be perfectly lined up before taking a shot. The outer circle is for rapid acquisition at near distances and the dots are for precise aim. Brownells catalog now sells this mil-spec product to civilians, including its protective canopy and a two-dot reticle for holding above the target. This means aiming with the lower of the two dots raises elevation and allows the shooter to impact targets that are substantially further away. *Photo by R. Eckstine courtesy of Brownells, Inc.*

need to be a revolver. Spare ammunition for the lever-action is typically from loops placed along the butt stock opposite the shooter's cheek.

Just as it was described in our conversation with a Texas Ranger, the distance to your adversary equates to the amount of time you have to make ready or reload. Like the shotgun, the reloading method is one round at a time placed into the magazine or directly into the chamber with the lever in the open position. Once the lever action is empty and with the intruder closer than say fifty to one hundred yards, your best chance of staying in the fight would be to transition to another gun that was already loaded.

Bolt-Action Rifle

Bolt-action rifles are commonly used for tactical situations where a precise, accurate shot must be taken. Great distance may or may not be a factor. While we hear of extremely long-distance shots performed by military snipers, their police counterparts usually perform at distances less than one hundred yards. The difference is that for the police, the desired point of impact may be very small, such as the eye socket of someone holding a hostage close to their body. Or access to the target may be limited to a small void in cover. In rare cases, the target may be the adversary's very own weapon.

The advantage of a bolt-action rifle is its simplicity of design in regards to producing a precise mechanical device. The primary disadvantages are low capacity and relatively slow operation. Working the bolt quickly in its intricate pattern of up, back, forward, and down can interfere with maintaining an adequate

▲ Bolt-action rifles are generally considered to be accurate long-range weapons rather than for close quarters battle. There are plenty of highly priced tactical or sniper precision rifles available, but for defending acreage from both four- and two-legged predators, almost any hunting rifle will do. Browning's X-Bolt Hog Stalker (chambered for either .223 Remington or .308 Winchester ammunition) ships with a twenty-inch longbarrel pre-threaded for a suppressor. Adding a sound suppressor is a good idea because in an emergency you may not be able to quickly access hearing protection. The Hog Stalkers feed from four- and five-round magazines for .223 and .308, respectively. *Photo courtesy of Browning*

sight picture and delay the next shot. Bear in mind that the same hand that works the bolt is needed to work the trigger. Even a right-handed shooter who chooses to work a left-side mounted bolt to avoid having to release his or her shooting grip between shots must temporarily give up support of the rifle. However fast an expert can run a bolt-action rifle, its strength is still accuracy rather than rate of fire.

The problem of capacity can at least be partially solved by choosing a bolt-action rifle designed to feed from a removable magazine. Top-loaded internal magazines are reloaded one shot at a time and seating the individual rounds can be slow and clumsy. The disadvantage when compared to a removable magazine is obvious. Grabbing an extra loaded magazine and putting it inside a pocket as you pick up your rifle is one way to ensure you'll have all the rounds you need and the means to quickly reload. Nevertheless, rifle magazines can be bulky and awkward so the process of inserting a fresh magazine is not always as fast as on that of a pistol.

The problem of how much time a bolt-action shooter may need for follow-up shots is not always a problem for military or police. The police sniper is on the scene and set up as part of a team. A military sniper at long range may also be backed by other soldiers or even air support. At the very least the sniper's partner, the spotter, is usually equipped with a high-capacity fully automatic or select-fire rifle or carbine.

There are a few short bolt-action carbines with removable magazines that might be suitable for fighting at moderate distances where a more rapid rate of fire is an asset. But the primary use of a bolt-action rifle or carbine for home defense would be on a rural property or oversized lot where the extended effective range of a rifle can be used to engage an obvious threat where accuracy and power at distance or the need for an extremely precise shot is necessary.

Semi-automatic Rifle: Traditional

The semi-automatic rifle can offer every advantage of a bolt-action rifle, but they are usually heavier and more expensive. Heavier because extra machinery is needed to cycle ammunition through the action and more expensive for the same reason. However, the benefit of increased rate of fire should far outweigh

▲ Springfield Armory's M1A based SOCOM II fires .308 Winchester from a 16.5 inch long barrel. This is one of the few semi-automatics designed specifically for .30 caliber ammunition. Other variations of Springfield Armory M1A are for High Power competition and long-distance precision shooting. But the versatile SOCOM II is perhaps the most powerful carbine with a removable magazine you can buy. *Photo courtesy of Springfield Armory*

these concerns. In addition, semi-automatic rifles are magazine fed, making them easier to reload. More often than not, higher capacity magazines are available.

There actually aren't that many semi-automatic rifles available in traditional form. By traditional, I mean a straight stock without the profile of a true vertical pistol grip. The most popular semi-automatic rifles in this configuration are the Springfield Armory M1A series and the Browning BAR.

The Springfield Armory M1A is a direct descendant of the M14 military rifle chambered for 7.63X51mm NATO ammunition or .308 Winchester. The M1A is a semi-automatic rifle that feeds from ten- or twenty-round removable box magazines. Configurations range from standard models with wood stocks and iron sights to highly accurized models with twenty-two-inch-long match-quality barrels and a special scope mount. The most battle-worthy in the modern tactical sense is the highly maneuverable 16.25-inch barreled Springfield Armory SOCOM II that features multiple rails for lights or lasers.

The Browning BAR shares its acronym with a legendary military weapon the Browning Automatic Rifle. But this is actually a different design. The current BARs focus on hunting and are available chambered for popular hunting calibers ranging from .243 Winchester to hard-hitting rounds such as .300 Winchester Magnum. One model that might be of particular interest for home defense is the .308 Winchester Short-Trac Hog Stalker. This model differs from the other currently available BARs because its twenty-inch barrel (the shortest in the BAR lineup) makes it more maneuverable. In addition, the Hog Stalker loads from a ten-round removable box magazine, rather than an internal magazine with a

hinged floorplate. Scope mounts and a rail for accessories are mounted on the fore end. What is ostensibly the same rifle but with a plain gray stock is available from FNH USA, the American arm of the Belgium manufacturer Fabrique Nationale. This would be the FNAR series of rifles.

Each of the rifles chambered for .308 Winchester or greater are devastating weapons. But their power could easily lead to over-penetration at close range. This could disqualify it for use inside an apartment, where the rounds might injure someone in the next room or apartment. One plus to this level of power is the possibility to defeat body armor worn by an assailant. Nevertheless, big-bore semi-automatic rifles with removable higher-capacity magazines are formidable weapons, especially for defending freestanding homes on sizeable plots of land.

High-Capacity Carbines

Popular high-capacity carbines include the AR15, Ruger's Mini 14 and Mini Thirty, and the Kalashnikov AK-47. Each of these weapons, save the Ruger Minis, was designed for military use. The primary difference between the military versions and the civilian weapons is the quantity of rounds capable of being released with a single press of the trigger. Military weapons can be adjusted for fully automatic or select fire. Fully automatic means that as long as the trigger is pressed, rounds will continue to be ignited and cycled from the magazine into the barrel chamber until the ammunition supply runs out. Select fire means the weapon can

▲ The AK-47 platform is renowned for its rugged reliability. While not as accurate as some people would prefer, it is nevertheless an effective weapon with which to counter an assault. Century Arms offers many different variations with both fixed and folding stocks. This is the WASR-10 chambered for 7.62X39, and it features a special scope mount. Note how high both the electronic dot scope and the iron front sight ride over the barrel. *Photo courtesy of Todd Woodard*

▲ The AR15 is currently the most popular carbine in America. Modular in design, the AR15 can be built and rebuilt to offer a variety of features. The muzzle of this Carry handle model from DPMS has been upgraded from a flash hider to a recoil compensator by Tac-Grip. Other additions include a tail cap controlled flashlight by Safariland and a Genesis green strobe laser from LaserMax. The laser unit can be controlled by switches found on either side of the unit or by a pressure pad mounted on the fore end. Like the AK-47, AR15 sights sit tall above the barrel and need to be accounted for when firing from behind cover. The scope, in this case, is a fixed ten-power design, but the iron sights are still visible thanks to a see-through lower channel. Lock washers, sometimes overlooked in mounting, make sure that the mount does not come loose. Note the oversized charging handle.

▲ The Ruger Mini 14 and Mini Thirty carbines are, in effect, lightweight versions of the M1A. Originally referred to as a Ranch or handy rifle, they are available built on wood or synthetic stocks with magazines capable of carrying up to thirty rounds of .223 or twenty rounds of 6.8 SPC or 7.62X39 ammunition. *Photo courtesy of Sturm, Ruger, & Co.*

be set to fire one round at a time, a limited amount of multiple shots per trigger press (usually three rounds), or fully automatic. Civilian versions of these weapons are semi-automatic, limited to firing one shot at a time per each press of the trigger.

The very designation AR15 means that this Armalite Rifle is semi-automatic rather than select fire like its military M16 counterpart. The design of the AR15 platform is modular and highly adaptable. Several variations in sighting options, barrel contours, and caliber are available. The most popular chambering for the AR15 is 5.56mm NATO or .223 Remington. A slightly larger but less popular version, the AR10, chambers 7.62mmX51 NATO or .308 Winchester ammunition.

What makes the AR15 so attractive is its power, ease of operation and maintenance, versatility regarding

sight configurations, and potential for high capacity. It can be used effectively both in close quarters and from long range. Like a shotgun, it can be quickly made easier to mount and shoot by changing length of pull (the distance between the shoulder and the trigger) thanks to a six-position adjustable stock. This also enhances maneuverability and makes the AR15 quickly adaptable to shooters of different physical size. The vertical pistol grip offers superior control and the operator has immediate access to the thumb operated safety, the trigger, and the magazine release. The magazine well is large enough that a magazine can be inserted quickly. Magazine capacity (5.56/.223) in the original vertical staggered column magazine ranges from five rounds to ten, twenty, and thirty rounds. Surefire offers two different oversized, staggered column magazines, with one capable of packing forty rounds and another that can hold one hundred.

Sighting options on AR15 rifles depend on configuration. Even the earliest design offers a choice of rear sight apertures for accuracy in different circumstances. The latest A4 design can accommodate a variety of open sights, electronic sights, or traditional tubular sights with magnification. The AR15 can be set up with all three types of sights in place so that speed and accuracy can be achieved in almost every situation.

Ruger's 5.56mm/.223 caliber Mini 14 and 7.62X39, .30-caliber Mini Thirty carbines are in many ways a lightweight version of the M14 design. Available barrel lengths for both calibers range from 16.12 to 18.5 inches. Designed as an all-around light rifle for the ranch, these weapons were never produced for the military so no fully automatic version (legally) exists. But they are somewhat popular with police. The basic configuration is solid stock with relatively short length of pull. The Minis can also be purchased with the AR15 adjustable butt stock.

Maximum capacity for factory magazines tops out at twenty rounds for both Minis. But, thirty-round magazines are available aftermarket from Brownells. A ninety-round drum magazine for the .223 model is also in production from a company called MWG. When it comes to oversized magazines for any semi-automatic rifle or pistol, you have to make a decision based on two principles. First, all the magazines have to be completely reliable and not play any part in a possible malfunction. Second, you have to consider its added bulk and weight of the loaded magazine. You have to ask, "Will it work? And will it make shooting more difficult?"

It is difficult to beat the AR15 platform for delivery of 5.56mm or .223 Remington. In its AR10 configuration for launching .30 caliber bullets, this platform has proved not nearly as popular. Advancements for the AR10 are ongoing but in the meantime the Ruger Mini Thirty matches up well with 7.62x39, .30 caliber ammunition.

The benefits of the lower powered 7.62X39 round is lower cost per round and an increased bullet width that produces a larger wound canal with less expended energy. The fact that 7.62X39 is not as powerful as .308 Winchester can also be a plus. Lower velocity reduces the potential for over-penetration. One drawback to the Mini 14 and Thirty carbines is a lack of flexibility in terms of sight packages. The supplied sights are indeed adequate, but accommodations for adding a scope, optical or electronic, are limited.

Another weapon chambered for 7.62X39 is the Kalashnikov designed AK-47. This, too, is available to civilians as a semi-automatic weapon only. Buying an AK made in America is almost impossible but there are several shops, including Colorado Shooting Sports and TroMix of Oklahoma, that specialize in refining imported weapons. Supply is bound to be scarce as laws tightening up on the import of high-capacity weapons may cause owners to reconsider even taking them to the range. The strength of this weapon is its reliability earned by its performance in the Middle East where sand can wreak havoc with any machine.

Portability of the AK-47 is enhanced by a hinged folding stock that is a popular optional feature. Capacity is typically thirty rounds but drum magazines that hold up to seventy-five rounds are available. Standard sights are tough and accurate for shorter distances but may not be as refined as today's shooters have come to expect. The AK-47 was never designed as a target rifle and standard design relies heavily on its use as a fully automatic rifle that can spray and suppress oncoming soldiers, as well as take them down one by one. Some of the popular upgrades available aftermarket are enhanced sights, a scope mount or rail system, ambidextrous (bolt) charging handle, and a

safety lever that can be operated by the trigger finger without changing grip.

The AK-47 and its variants are a lot of fun to shoot but quality can vary. For example, while a particular run of AKs out of Bulgaria might be good, another run from a different country might require a lot of aftermarket work just to function. Contacting a shop that specializes in AKs may be the best way to find out what to buy and what imports to avoid. Once proofed, the AK platform is an effective high-capacity close quarters weapon.

High-Capacity Handguns

The high-capacity handgun may be the all-around best choice for home defense. While all handguns are relatively inexpensive and easy to store, the high capacity handgun is the better choice. Here is why: Every round after the first shot is another chance to stay alive.

In terms of the amount of available second chances, it is possible to house as many as nineteen rounds of ammunition in the magazine of a 9mm pistol. Given that larger caliber ammunition takes up more space, it is still possible to have twelve or more rounds of .40 S&W, .357Sig, or .45 ACP at your disposal. Setting

▲ Driven by the will to win, competitors in the sport of practical shooting have developed many useful upgrades, including extended magazine basepads that increase capacity by as many as five extra rounds. This means the owner of this Glock model G34 may have as many as twenty-three chances to deliver 9mm ordnance in the event of an attack. Basepads applied to the seventeen-round magazines are left to right, from Taylor Freelance and Dawson Precision.

aside any discussion of the effectiveness of one caliber over another, the point is that the shooter can concentrate on shooting for only as long as the ammunition stream remains constant.

High-capacity handguns are an excellent choice for home defense because they are highly maneuverable. They can be turned quickly to point one direction after another. They can also be operated easily with one hand should the other hand become injured or unavailable due to a struggle or simply performing a chore like opening or closing a door.

A handgun of any type is easier to defend against a takeaway. To begin with, half the surface area (or more) of a handgun is locked inside the hand. A long gun offers a greater amount of area to defend and in a struggle becomes a source of leverage that can work for or against you. It is more likely for your opponent to have exactly the same amount of leverage when fighting over a long gun than when struggling over a handgun, which is dominated by the first person to grip it properly. The grip of a handgun is the safest point of contact. Most of what is left exposed on a handgun—the muzzle and the ejection port, or on a revolver the cylinder gap (the gap between the cylinder and the opening to the barrel)—is dangerous to your attacker.

The natural length and extension of a long gun makes moving muzzle-forward through a doorway or other blind advance, no matter how momentary, more dangerous than with a handgun. A handgun can be retracted and held close to the body. This makes it easier to lead with your eyes. Furthermore, one hand may be extended to defend while the other hand holds the gun, as long as you keep your free hand out of line with the muzzle.

When shooting a handgun around a point of cover or concealment, it is easier to account for the line of sight versus the actual path of the bullet. Line of sight is the unobstructed view of the target with the eyes held at the appropriate level to align the sights. A standard configuration rifle or carbine may have a differential of one inch or more between the front sight and the center of the barrel bore. But the AR15 or AK-47 platforms may have your eyes tracking as much as two and a half inches or more above the path of the bullet. This means when firing a long gun from cover or con-

cealment you may clearly see the target aligned perfectly in your sights but the muzzle is blocked. Until you realize the problem, all you're going to hit is the doorframe or some other impediment. This problem is much easier to avoid when firing a handgun because the bore line to sight line differential is typically only about one-half inch.

It may also be easier to become proficient shooting a handgun because practice ammunition is cheaper and generally more plentiful than rifle ammunition. Another factor that makes practice easier is that there are more available places in which to practice. Many shooting ranges, especially urban and suburban indoor ranges, do not have the space or distance to accommodate rifle fire. Nor do they have the necessary backstop to safely capture rifle ordnance. This reality should also be kept in mind when considering the structure of your home and the possibility of over-penetration.

When it comes to choosing your first or next firearm, it's a good idea to find a shooting range that rents guns so you can try out more than one. Here are some guidelines specifically tailored to helping choose which high-capacity handgun is best for you. Since the grip shape and circumference of a high-capacity semi-automatic handgun must be larger to accommodate wider magazines, the first concern should be choosing one that affords you a solid grip and a natural index. Here is an example of what is meant by natural index. If you had, say, five handguns lined up on a table and you picked them up one after another, the gun or guns with natural index would point at the target with the least amount of effort on your part. If, after a couple of tries, you still have to shift the gun in your hand to align the sights on a distant object, that gun should be disqualified.

The next check in your tests should be the trigger and sights. I prefer to blend the two characteristics because when it comes to accuracy, the only thing that matters is the alignment of the sights when the gun goes off. You must be able track the relation of the front sight to the rear sight the entire time you are pressing the trigger. Naturally, holding the gun firmly in the hand while keeping the trigger finger supple enough to move the trigger in a smooth, consistent motion does present a physical contradiction and takes practice.

Here is another simple test you can perform without even loading the gun that can help you choose one gun over another. Try aiming, or better yet steering, the sights while pressing the trigger. Whichever gun allows you to more easily coordinate sight alignment with trigger press may be the better choice for you.

Beyond isolating the trigger finger for fine motor action versus the gross motor action of holding the grip and tracking the sights, there are at least two other factors to consider—recoil and rate of fire. Again, I like to connect them because one has a direct effect on the other. Recoil is not just the opposite response to pushing the bullet forward but also the various inertial factors produced by the machinery of the gun as it cycles the ammunition. This includes a certain amount of twisting or torque as the stationary bullet is forced to rotate inside the barrel. Even a double-action revolver suffers torque-over as the cylinder starts and stops.

Choice of caliber, bullet weight, and velocity all make a difference in how much recoil is produced and how much work it takes for you to reacquire a usable sight picture. But choosing a grip that suits your hand and a style of trigger press that you can easily coordinate with alignment of the sights will ultimately be the key to speed and accuracy no matter how much recoil is produced.

There are many high-capacity handguns in production today. Government restriction, be it state, federal, or local, may affect maximum-capacity handguns now or in the future. Eventually, restrictive laws may be lifted. It has happened before. Either way, the most popular guns sold today are magazine-fed semi-automatic handguns with the rounds stored in a staggered or offset column to take maximum advantage of the interior space. Even if laws were passed to prohibit the mere possession of high-capacity magazines, the pistols would likely remain in production. Only the capacity of the magazines themselves would change. Therefore, mastering a high-capacity pistol is still the best choice.

Defending the Home with a Firearm

Home invasions and burglaries are rarely an accident. Whether the criminal plans for weeks to violate your home or over the course of just a few minutes, the decision is most often based on an equation of risk versus reward. Even if drugs that decrease inhibition and increase aggression are part of the mix, it still comes down to how much they want what you've got divided by how easy it is to take. The concept is universal. In conversation with professionals as diverse as a Texas Ranger and a personal security consultant from South Africa, we learned closely related concepts about crime prevention by preparation. Prevent the home from being targeted by keeping valuables discretely hidden and avoid attention-grabbing practices, such as taking home the day's receipts from the family business. Maintain a secure profile by hardening your home with solid fences, multiple doors, high-impact windows, and prominently posting notice of a monitored-alarm system.

Methods such as these are your first line of defense and could be referred to as external preparation because the purpose is to keep the threat from coming inside the home. But what preparations can be made for when the criminal has made it past the front door?

According to news sources such as CNSNews.com, the American public purchased 70,291,049 firearms between February 1, 2009 and March 31, 2013. This is based on data released by the FBI on the amount of background checks performed, and does not account for private sales or arms passed from generation to generation. It would be a stretch to assume that each one of these purchases was completed by a first-time gun buyer or to assume that there are now seventy million more armed citizens than there were before the current administration took office. But given the astounding computation indicating that as many as thirty-two legal purchases of a firearm took place every minute during this time, the possibility that a homeowner in the United States may be armed is now greater than it has been for several generations.

That means when someone breaks into a home, they are more likely to face someone holding a loaded firearm instead of a baseball bat or some other kind of improvised weapon. The question is—once the criminal has gotten past the double doors, the impact resistant glass, and the wailing security system—what else does the home occupant have on their side other than firepower? How about home-field advantage?

Home-field advantage in sports is not just when the majority of people in the stands actively root for the home team. It can also mean being familiar with certain characteristics of the field or court that offer a distinct advantage. Perhaps the most famous home-field advantage ever enjoyed in professional sports was the parquet floor at the old Boston Garden, on which the Boston Celtics basketball team won many championships. Celtic players knew the floor intimately, where there were soft spots and what slats were loose or settled at an angle. Not only did the home team know where not to dribble the ball, but also tried to steer their opponents toward these imperfections to make stealing the ball easier.

In terms of home defense, home-field advantage begins with no one being more familiar with the interior of your home than you and your family. Yet home occupants rarely envision the interior of their homes as a battleground. If they did, the first thing new tenants would do is determine which features of each room's layout and construction could potentially offer a tactical advantage.

What you would be looking for are natural points of concealment and cover. Plus hallways or doors that could limit visual access to make it easier for the home occupant to potentially ambush anyone who was moving around inside the house.

In terminology related to an armed confrontation, concealment is anything you can stand, crouch, kneel, or lie down behind that prevents the enemy from seeing you. Not sure where the best place for concealment is in your house? You can solve that quickly by inviting over some of the neighborhood kids for a game of hide-and- seek. It won't take long for them to find the best places to hide. Nor should it take them long to find the best place to take one another by surprise, yell out "Tag, you're it!" and run away.

A better version of concealment that can also prevent the enemy from seeing you is cover. A barrier referred to as cover is better than a barrier classified as concealment because cover will stop a bullet. A wooden interior door, such as those commonly used to divide rooms, is classified as concealment because it is not likely to stop a bullet. In comparison, a column of granite is impenetrable and therefore classified as cover. A doorframe or a corner constructed of wallboard and wood is concealment but could also function as cover if it is thick enough. The ability for walls not specifically built to be impenetrable may have the ability to change the path of a bullet, depending on its interior. Therefore, its cover value is unreliable.

Furniture is generally considered to be a barrier, not cover. But heavy wood furniture, especially those constructed in multiple layers, such as a chest of drawers, might be able to provide cover as well as concealment. So might a complex structure like a couch or retractable lounge chair that could have a metal frame, or contain gears, ratchets, or an electric motor to provide vibrating massage. But impact with any of these components is not guaranteed, so its value as cover is not reliable.

Two additional aspects of tactical planning are distance and surprise. Distance is important because it offers the opportunity to escape or move to a more advantageous position. Bear in mind that distance equals time. The greater the distance between you and an attacker, the longer it takes for him or her to get to you or, in tactical jargon, close the distance. Distance also slows down the shooting process. At close range, the outline of the gun superimposed over the body of an attacker may be all that is necessary to confirm that your shot will hit the target. But once sight alignment becomes necessary, the process of making an accurate shot becomes more complex and requires more time to deliver.

Even when distance is not that great, hitting a smaller target area is going to require more precision. That's why you will often see marksmen and -women practicing at short range with miniaturized targets. The reduction in size replicates greater distance by imitating how small the targets would appear if they were farther away.

Similarly to how increasing distance can force your attacker to shoot slower or waste more ammunition trying to hit you, cover can have the same effect. Cover makes you less vulnerable not only by shielding a portion of your body, but also by slowing down the rate of incoming fire as your attacker is forced to take more careful aim.

The element of surprise is unfortunately something that is more likely to be in favor of your attacker. The only way to reduce the advantage of surprise is to see trouble coming. The more barriers in the way of an attacker, the greater the possibility you will have an opportunity to notice when trouble is brewing. The first barrier is awareness: Recognizing that a strange car is stopping in front of your door or footsteps in the hall are approaching your apartment. Perhaps there are individuals moving about in the neighborhood who appear out of place.

Do you have any other barriers that might eliminate advantage by surprise? Is your alarm set to instant? Does your dog bark or does your parakeet sound off or move nervously inside his or her cage whenever someone approaches? Will the intruder have to first open an exterior door before breaking the lock or kicking down the door? Or have you witnessed all of this via a security camera while relaxing in a back bedroom?

Early warning systems are just one part of home-field advantage. They give you time to react. But most intruders will not be surprised that you have an alarm system and they will be determined to act quickly while it blares away. It could be said that criminals have more experience acting under chaotic conditions than the average person. In addition, they know a certain amount of time will pass before help arrives if you do have a monitored alarm system. But you can't just stand in front of an intruder with a gun and expect that to be enough to scare them off.

Merely being armed might not be enough of a surprise to take back the advantage. In a gunfight, firing from a position of cover is your most effective defense. But to mount such a defense, you must be able to take cover quickly. The only way to reach cover quickly is to know in advance which elements of the interior structure of a room, which furnishings, or both afford you the most effective cover.

To determine the best firing points in a given room, you will need to analyze the layout and its furnishings in relation to a series of straight lines drawn between two positions that would likely be taken by combatants. Each line represents the line of sight. If you can do this with a spouse or other housemate it's going to go a lot faster and yield more accurate results. One of you, taking the part of the intruder, should be facing inside the house or room, as if entering. The other player, taking the part of the occupant, should be facing the door from the interior of the house. Both participants should be armed with a camera. A cell phone with still or motion picture capability will be sufficient.

For this study to be of real value, the occupant should be pointing an unloaded firearm or a dummy that replicates the firearm that they would actually use. But, as a point of warning, before participating in this drill with an actual firearm, go to a different room than the one that will be studied. As always act on the assumption that the gun is loaded. Unload the firearm and use a safety device to deactivate it. This might necessitate installing a faux plastic barrel such as one of the 5.11 Blade-Tech Pistol Tactical Training barrels, which are bright yellow. Or insert a brightly colored wire or cable-tie into the chamber. The safety device should remain visible at all times. In addition, any ammunition removed from the weapon should remain in the other room, and loaded magazines should be emptied and remain in the other room, as well. If your pistol requires the magazine to be in place to complete its grip profile, remove the magazine spring and follower before reinserting it into the rehearsal weapon.

The purpose of using a dummy model or an actual weapon that has been deactivated is so that body and hand positioning from cover will be accurate. Keep in mind that the head must be in a certain position to properly aim any weapon, and a pistol must be extended to provide an adequate sight picture. Without a weapon in hand, you could end up approving a specific position that will not be usable in an actual confrontation. The result could be not only a faulty firing position but greater body exposure, especially the occupant's head or limbs.

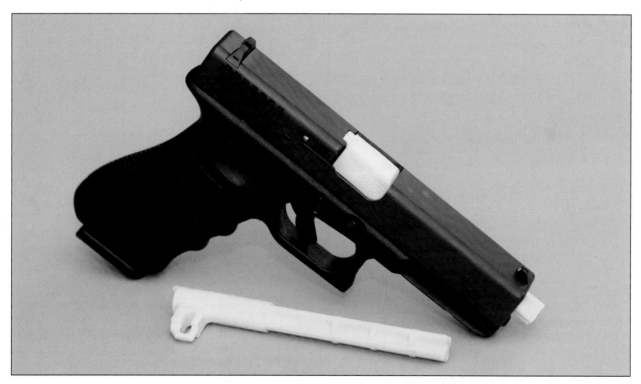

▲ To learn where inside the home you can take cover or at least benefit from a measure of concealment, you must actually take each position one by one with a partner standing opposite to check for physical exposure. Have your partner take a photograph so you can see what changes might be necessary to protect your body from incoming fire. This study is most effective when performed holding a firearm so the shooter's setup accurately reflects the posture necessary to acquire an adequate sight picture. The only problem with this method of study is how to ensure safety. After clearing the weapon of all ammunition from both the chamber and the magazine, additional steps must be taken. Insert a chamber flag or otherwise disable the firing mechanism. One product that does an excellent job of providing safety is the brightly colored 5.11 Training Barrel. Precisely made to fit most popular handguns, they offer instant recognition to ensure safety. By using your own firearm, you are fully exposed to the finer points of aiming and handling your firearm in limited conditions, such as cramped spaces. *Photo by R. Eckstine courtesy of Brownells, Inc.*

The next step in understanding what characteristics of your home's interior can help you in a gunfight is to classify each piece of furniture as either cover or concealment and file it in your memory. Take time to check what physical positions would be required to use each piece of furniture as a shooting station. But since the exact positioning of furniture can be easily changed through whim or during a scuffle, using furnishings for cover or concealment might better be left as something to improvise from rather than depending on it to always be there. Next, visualize the room as if it were empty of all furniture. Now, classify each component of the room's permanent physical structure as being cover or concealment. If the room is just one big box without any vertical stanchion or countertops, then positions of cover or concealment will most likely be limited to the doorframes leading from the room. You'll want to choose one door over the others or prioritize each one based on where the door leads to, or where you are likely to be standing at the time of engagement. Do you want to escape to a backyard, a room with more weapons, or a room that offers a position of cover and puts you in a much better tactical position from which to engage? An example of a better tactical position would be one that offers true cover or a great deal of concealment. Just transitioning to an adjoining room could force an intruder to come through the door blindly. The advantage you will have in this situation is that the intruder will need to look

▲ Even the heaviest pieces of furniture may not be reliable in terms of stopping a bullet. But, it is still a good idea to try setting behind each component of your home's interior to recognize all potential points of tactical advantage.

for you. Meanwhile, you merely have to focus on the doorway or at the point where he becomes visible as he rounds the corner.

In developing this chapter with the help of active law enforcement professionals who specialize in serving dangerous warrants, we continually referred to it as a study of angles. For example, line of sight or a straight line drawn between two combatants would represent a 180-degree angle. Which, in effect, is no angle. If neither combatant had any barrier between them to reduce physical exposure, they would both be equally vulnerable. This would amount to the proverbial Western showdown and one might as well say to the other, "Draw, pardner."

To get a better understanding of how to avoid being caught in a Western showdown, have your partner, the so-called intruder, stand outside the front door. Is there a room to the left or right that you would likely spend time in, such as an office or a sewing room? Let's say you have a study just off the foyer so the front door is a few feet away from its entrance. If the intruder rang the doorbell and you, the occupant, went to answer the door, how far from the door would you be standing when your body was in full view of the door, a 180-degree or no-angle confrontation? What could you do about it if the door was kicked in suddenly or jimmied open with the use of a crowbar?

The problem is that the distance between the front door and the entrance to the study cannot be increased. The only factor that can be changed is the angle or how much of your body is exposed as you look out to the front door. To minimize exposure, move toward the front door but stop so that the edge of your body is not visible beyond the outer edge of the study room door. Then, to get a line of sight, you should lean outward until the front door is visible. To backtrack a moment, if you heard someone at the front door, whether expected or not, the first move could be to look out the window. If the front door is not visible then check to see what car or truck is outside. A particularly cautious person would acquire their handgun first. The key component in this confrontation would be not going up to door fully exposed. It's better to be leaning out for a line of sight with the pistol held out of view by the inside hand. Held in this manner the pistol would be out of sight and there would be

▲ Leaving the key inside the interior lock means you might as well not have spent the extra money on a double key dead bolt lock. Never mind, this crook prefers to force the door open with a crowbar anyway (see the telltale diagonal line through the glass). What could you do about it once he is inside?

▲ Merely being alert when hearing an unexpected knock at the door is not enough. Can you name four things this homeowner is doing correctly? First of all, what he is not doing is approaching the door. What he has done is taken up arms. He is not exposing the firearm, but is keeping it in a relaxed ready. He has limited his physical exposure by placing his off hand on the doorjam, preventing him from unconsciously taking a step beyond a basic position of cover. (For the moment we'll assume the structure of the door frame has the potential to stop or at least redirect a bullet.) Instead, he is leaning outward to get a better look at what may be approaching.

no danger of alarming an innocent person or escalating a misunderstanding. However, it would be readily available if there were an intruder actively breaking through your door or an unwelcome solicitor that may be up to no good and testing to see if someone is at home.

In the case of an exchange of gunfire from the doorway, using the door frame to limit visual access and hopefully block or redirect incoming rounds becomes vital. To demonstrate how much target area the occupant presents to the intruder while standing at the edge of the doorway, have your partner, the intruder, take your picture. See how much of the occupant's body is exposed while still being able to acquire a sight pic-

ture. Take a series of pictures so the occupant can get a feel for how much body can be positioned behind the doorframe while still maintaining a usable sight picture. You might even be able to establish a specific go-to position based on, say, placing the outer foot in line with a border in the pattern of the rug, or a stain in the carpet. As the intruder enters the door, you will probably need to rotate into the room, but establishing a solid first position of defense can give you a big advantage.

A second position from this same room in relation to the front door would be, again, keeping as much of the occupant concealed by the doorframe—but this time standing farther back. Have the intruder take a second photograph. In comparing the two photographs, it will be evident how much less target area remains available to the intruder just by increasing the distance only two or three feet. The farther back from the edge of the doorframe the occupant moves, the more effective it becomes as a visual barrier. The amount of target area available to the intruder gets narrower and narrower. An added benefit for the occupant is the fact that by moving to the rear just a shuffle step or two more, space

▲ The homeowner is using the same corner break for cover/concealment. By standing further back, she not only becomes a smaller target, but also has more options for lateral movement that can adjust the amount of exposure and offer greater possibility for escape.

▲ In the event of engagement, the homeowner is using the corner break to limit her exposure to approximately half of his body.

becomes available for lateral movement. By moving sideways, the occupant can continually adjust how much of their body is exposed by keeping a section of the doorframe between himself and the intruder.

An added benefit to standing back from a point of cover or concealment is this makes the gun less vulnerable to a takeaway. You can feel safe behind cover, but if the gun is sticking out, for example, across the threshold of a door, you might not see an attacker approach from the side and reach in to trap the gun. Operating with a long gun can be even more inviting to a takeaway because much of its length is open and available. While a handgun is almost completely covered by the hands, holding a shotgun or rifle leaves plenty of surface area uncovered. This means there is plenty of leverage literally up for grabs.

Suppose we try another scenario with the start position away from the front door. It is not uncommon for the front door to lead into a small foyer, then directly into a large room. Perhaps this is the living room or a living room and kitchen combination with hallways and doors feeding off toward the bedrooms. The intruder is still coming in the front door, but this time the occupant becomes aware of it while in a distant room.

The benefit of the increased distance is additional time to prepare. You should already have planned for defense by knowing the strengths of each room in the house, including the one you are in. Move yourself and all others to the position of greatest cover and concealment. If there is more than one occupant but only one weapon, give the non-shooter the telephone and have them call 911. Keep the gun pointed at the door through which the intruder must pass and be ready to fire. If it is nighttime, be ready to illuminate the target. It is always best to identify all targets to avoid accidents. Plus, the lights will afford you better aim and might temporarily blind the intruder, making their attack all the more difficult.

If you must surveil the front door, do so from the farthest end of the room. Move sideways a little at a

▲ Shotguns (and carbines for that matter) offer more power per shot than handguns but require more space to be operated properly. When searching or setting up a shooting position, stand back from the edge of the doorway. Take a wide turn. Let your vision enter well before your muzzle. Unfortunately, the element of surprise may be enough to defeat the homeowner in the tug of war that has just begun. If the homeowner were holding a pistol in outstretched arms instead of a shotgun mounted high on his shoulder, the mechanics of this ambush may well have been the same.

Defending the Home with a Long Gun: Some Shortcomings

Much of the information in this chapter focuses on defending the home with a handgun, and for good reason. Handguns are the most widely owned firearms and, with the exception of the AR15, AK-47, and other carbines, handguns offer the highest-capacity magazines. Handguns are more versatile, being easier to stow, more portable, and requiring less overall space to aim properly. Indeed, you can fight with a handgun even with the body contorted behind tight cover. Long guns, even those with collapsible stocks, demand lots of space for a low ready scan and on sights target-firing positions. Bunching up behind cover with a carbine, such as the AR15 or AK-47, can create another problem. These weapons are typically aimed with sights that stand well above the barrel. The result is that the shooter can obtain a perfectly clear sight picture, but the barrel may not yet be clear of cover and shots that should have been on target will instead ricochet off line, or worse yet, deflect back toward the weapon and shooter.

One thing that long guns, including shotguns and carbines, offer is superior firepower on a per shot basis. While the length of shouldered weapons can be a problem within the confines of the home, their extra length can also offer added protection specifically from attack with an impact weapon, such as a baseball bat or crowbar.

▲ Handguns are more versatile than shotguns or rifles if only because you can still take aim effectively no matter how scrunched up you need to be to take advantage of concealment or cover.

▲ AK-47 and AR15 carbines operate with sighting systems that ride well above the center of the bore. At very close range, one could aim at a specific point but the bullet hole will print two to three inches lower than expected. When firing from behind cover or concealment, it is possible to have a perfectly unobstructed sight picture. But, the bullet may still be blocked as it leaves the barrel.

◄ Even with carbines like the AR15 that offer a collapsible stock to minimize length, a low, ready search position still takes up a lot of space front to back.

◄ Once on target, rifle-caliber carbines are devastating weapons. But movement can be limited due to overall length, the necessity for a strictly defined visual index, and the necessary position of support against the body. Also, the presence of a scope can interfere with peripheral vision.

Overhead block.

Side block.

Horizontal redirect.

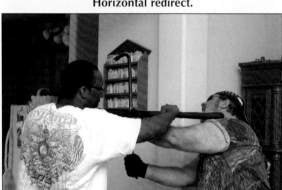

Diagonal redirect.

Strike, step back, and challenge.

Strike, step back, and challenge.

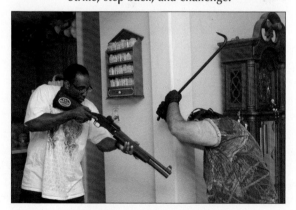

▲ Defending with a long gun offers the added advantage of providing the means to defend against attack with a blunt instrument such as a crowbar, which is often used to force entry into the home. But it's not enough to simply block the first strike because more will follow. You will need to go on offense. This means creating an opening to use the shotgun or carbine for its intended purpose rather than merely as a device for blocking. Whether the line of attack is from overhead or from the side you must stop the oncoming blow and redirect its force. In each sequence portrayed from top to bottom the crowbar is stopped at the center of the shotgun. The defender then pivots from the point of contact rotating the weapon so that the butt of the shotgun strikes the attacker in the head. Where the head goes the body follows so this is the most direct way to put your attacker off balance. Note that response to a vertical strike is a direct horizontal rotation accompanied by stepping forward with the strong side foot. Response to a blow from the side requires more aim on the part of the defender pushing the butt of the shotgun diagonally in order to strike the attacker in the head. Similar defensive actions with strikes coming from all angles may need to be repeated until there is an opportunity for the defender to step back and create enough distance so that the muzzle of the weapon can be moved to a position from which he can demand compliance or apply devastating force by firing a shot.

time until you get a line of sight with the door. Even if you are standing in open space, lean sideways as if there were a solid barrier directly in front of you that you needed to peer around the side of. Actually, there is a solid barrier to peer around. But in this case, it is positioned well in front of you. It may be the edge of the hallway leading to the front door or the front doorjamb itself. Be prepared to move quickly in retreat before you are caught in a face-to-face 180-degree Western showdown without any cover. In this case, safe retreat is an equation of distance versus time for both the occupant and the intruder: the time it takes the intruder to reach you physically or draw a weapon, acquire an adequate sight picture, and deliver an accurate shot versus the time it takes you to acquire a weapon and take cover.

Aside from having an impenetrable safe room, forcing an intruder to move toward you through a door while you aim from behind cover is perhaps the best option available to most homeowners. Even if the room to which you are retreating were nothing more than a square box with no cover or concealment available, you would still have the option of setting up at an acute angle from the door. A corner situated along the same wall as the doorway is the better choice. If the intruder must pass through a door that is hinged on its right side and therefore opens to his right, it will probably be easier for him to see you if you are to his left. There is no guarantee, but odds are that it will be safer to lay in wait at the corner to his right. If the door was located at the end of the hallway and was wide open, meeting the room at its center so that it formed a T-shape, it's a 50/50 chance that the intruder will first look to his right or left. Nevertheless, you will still see the intruder first unless he is skilled and slows down and checks all angles before entering. If you live in a two-story house, setting up behind cover at the top of the stairs can be a certain death trap for an intruder because there are too many angles for anyone coming up the stairs to defend at one time.

With so much written about clearing rooms and homes, keep the following information in mind. You are at a disadvantage whenever you seek to advance.

▲ The point of concealment or cover is as much as fifteen feet from the homeowner as she leans out to peer around the corner to avoid excessive physical exposure. There has no need to move closer to see if trouble is coming down the hall. Greater distance from the possible threat means that you are a smaller target. In addition, there are more options for retreat and more time to act, whether that means moving to a better position to cover and engage or to escape altogether.

Even being the good guy doesn't help. When asked about clearing a home, each of our entry experts agreed that it would take as many as three or four SWAT personnel to neutralize a single occupant if they were armed and properly positioned behind cover. That's why tear gas and flash bangs are so heavily relied upon by entry teams. If you are intent on defending your home with a firearm, never stop developing your ability to shoot quickly and accurately. But you must also learn every corner of your environment. Find the best positions from which to defend and never give up home-field advantage.

Range Sessions

The *Shooter's Bible Guide to Home Defense* is not necessarily a book about shooting. But with the historic proliferation of gun ownership that will likely continue for years to come, ignoring the subject of shooting instruction would be completely unrealistic. After all, if this were a guide to homebuilding that only covered styles and choice of materials but ignored skills like measuring, painting or sheet rocking, it would be far from complete.

The analogy drawn between construction skills and shooting was not chosen at random. Construction skills require visualization and the ability to transfer planning into a strictly measured result. Hand-eye coordination is required to operate both simple and power-driven tools to fabricate or modify a structure for the purpose of shelter, storage, or general security. For anyone wishing to master construction skills, it would be difficult to consider one's education complete without learning to handle a hammer and saw. Merely drawing up blueprints and hiring workers to do virtually everything else would be like going on safari and asking the guide to do all the shooting.

It's not going to be possible to reach out through the pages of a book and actively show someone how to deploy a firearm or press the trigger. Nor will it be possible to watch someone shoot and analyze form or technique. Instead, the goal of this chapter is to offer information about some of the finer points of gun handling and shooting that are often overlooked by instructors and instructional media. In addition, this chapter will cover how to make the most of your range sessions by understanding the nature of commonly available facilities, such as a public shooting range.

If the subject were trapshooting, instruction would focus on gun fitting, stance, where to focus the eye, and those sorts of things. If the subject were long-distance rifle shooting, then breathing, bipod loading, trajectory, and reading the wind would be part of the syllabus. This chapter will be tailored to developing practice sessions where gun-handling skills are closely related to home defense.

Developing home-defense skills with a firearm requires that the owner of the firearm, no matter which configuration—shotgun, carbine, or handgun—first acquire basic shooting skills. For this, it is recom-

mended that the owner take hands-on instruction with a qualified instructor. Ask around at your local shooting range or contact the NRA. A common question is "How many lessons should I take?" As many as necessary until you can pass a basic proficiency test where you can deliver on demand an appropriate level of accuracy as defined by the instructor and have no incidents of safety violations.

A safety violation would be pointing the muzzle of your weapon at something you are not willing to destroy, such as another living being. Another violation would be holding the gun in one hand and thoughtlessly pointing or sweeping the opposite hand or other part of the body. Think of the barrel of your gun not

▲ Whenever you handle a firearm in practice, competition, hunting, or in the midst of an actual crisis, never let the muzzle cover anything you are not willing to destroy. This includes parts of your own body. Be particularly careful when reaching out with the free hand.

▲ This is a perfect example of sweeping. The operator is so concerned with opening the door that she is unaware that the imaginary line extending from the gun's barrel is intersecting with her opposite hand.

ing the chain that operates the switch to turn it on, so never pick up a gun with your finger on the trigger or inside the trigger guard.

In regard to demonstrating proficient accuracy, it's easy to say that this means you should be able to match your point of aim to where your bullets hit (point of impact) at a given distance, depending on the weapon. Rule of thumb distances at which to test for proficient accuracy are fifteen yards, or forty-five feet, with a handgun and fifty yards, or one hundred fifty feet, with a carbine or short rifle. But some people like to measure the interior of their house and say that since the farthest shot they could possibly make from the back bedroom to the front door is fifty-five feet, all they need to do is be able to hit a bull's-eye about fifty to sixty feet downrange. Or, since my property stretches about two hundred yards until the tree line, I need to be able to set up and shoot accurately at a two-hundred-yard target. Without question, these are valid considerations. But true proficiency means that no matter what distance is to be overcome, the necessary level of accuracy should remain consistent. Five hits dead center and five shots completely missing from the target at any distance does not demonstrate proficiency.

Once the firearms owner has achieved a basic level of safe handling and accuracy, developing advanced skills is the next step. The term advanced could be seen as being somewhat misleading. In the shooting world, fundamentals such as grip, sight alignment, and trigger control are king. There is no situation where the fundamentals of shooting are irrelevant or have no effect. Advanced shooting skill in regard to home defense is the ability to apply fundamentals successfully under a variety of circumstances that are other than ideal. Another way of looking at an advanced level of skill is the ability to overcome all obstacles to performing the fundamentals without hesitation.

Before drawing up a list of drills designed to develop advanced skills, you will need to locate a suitable firing range. Not every public shooting range—indoor or outdoor—in the country allows targets to be shot in any manner other than stand-and-shoot or seated at a bench. This is understandable due to liability concerns. After all, a public range, by description, has little control over who comes through the door and whether a

as a tube that ends at the front of the gun. Think of it as a line or laser beam extending to infinity. The only way to prevent lasering someone else is to be constantly aware of the line permanently extending from the muzzle. This state of awareness is a habit you must develop and is referred to as maintaining a safety mindset.

Another component to the safety mindset is to never touch the trigger until you are ready to fire. One of the great misconceptions connected to handling a firearm is that the trigger is a part of the grip. It is not. The grip is a solid structure designed to enable the shooter to support and stabilize the gun. The trigger is a hinged movable lever designed to be unstable. Its sole purpose is to set into motion the firing sequence, an act that is irrevocable. You don't lift a table lamp by grasp-

customer will cause a dangerous situation is difficult to predict. But some ranges are willing to accommodate more in-depth practice sessions so long as you ask for permission first.

If you are affiliated with a shooting range either by membership or as a result of studying with one of its certified instructors, you will probably be able to secure a time or specific area of the range where you can practice advanced drills. Alternatives to using a public range are semiprivate membership-only ranges that basically offer turnkey access. Or visit with a shooting club that gathers at the range on a weekly or monthly basis for competitive shooting in a format that loosely replicates a shooting confrontation. Referred to as Practical Shooting, these types of matches can be an excellent opportunity to develop fast handling gun skills, which is but one key facet to defending your home with a firearm. To find these types of clubs, you can visit the websites of national organizations, such as the International Defensive Pistol Shooting Association (IDPA.com) and the United States Practical Shooting Association (USPSA.org). You may not be ready to join in the competition, but some of the participants will be able to tell you which shooting ranges in your area would be willing to accommodate the practice of advanced drills.

Other options for training in advanced drills include taking a course with one of the commercial tactical trainers that accept civilian students. These men and women are usually police or military veterans. Several of the firearms and target manufacturers have also set up shooting schools with courses tailored to shooters with a wide range of experience, including first-time students and professional operators. This would include Action Target, Smith & Wesson, and Sig Sauer. Training courses are often held at sites away from the main facility so, for example, you need not necessarily travel to Springfield, Massachusetts to attend a Smith & Wesson course. None of the schools run by firearms manufacturers demand that students use their products. So choosing which school to attend should be driven primarily by what classes are offered, rather than by the brand of firearm you now own.

But you don't have to be a member of a shooting club, have a fancy custom gun, or a lot of gear to advance your skills or improve your ability to apply fundamentals. You don't have to be interested in competition, either. Not everyone wants to get up in front of a group and shoot a course of fire any more than they want to get up in front of an audience and give a speech. But at some point, you may want to take a training course if for no other reason than to meet like-minded people. For now, let's take a look at what it takes to get the most out of your own personal range sessions.

Unless you are fortunate enough to have your own shooting range, there are limitations on how you can perform even the most basic drills at a public or privately shared range. Some of these limitations are based on whether the range is located outdoors or inside a building. One of the primary differences between outdoor- or indoor-range facilities is how and where the targets are fixed. An indoor range will typically be constructed so that no one is able to advance downrange between the shooting positions and the targets. Instead, the targets are retrieved via a mechanical system that brings the target board to you for change and inspection and allows you to position the target at the distance you prefer. Most indoor ranges offer a maximum distance of twenty to twenty-five yards.

Outdoor ranges offer target boards or what might simply amount to a fence upon which the targets are attached at distances typically beginning at seven yards from the firing line. Additional target positions are usually placed at a distance of ten, fifteen, and twenty-five yards for pistol fire, with rifle range targets beginning at the fifty-yard line. A narrow table or bench often divides the shooter from downrange at both indoor and outdoor ranges. Rifle ranges offer a table for seated rifle fire.

Since the targets at the outdoor ranges are fixed rather than retractable, the mounting of targets or target changes are performed during ceasefire periods called by the range officers. All shooters are called away from the firing line during a ceasefire. Sometimes the range officers will perform all target mounting, but at most outdoor ranges the shooters will go downrange while the range officers keep an eye on the firearms left behind at each bench or in a rifle rack. In addition, it is also the range officer's job to prevent anyone from handling a firearm during the ceasefire period. Before the shooters are allowed downrange, all firearms are cleared of ammunition.

▲ Indoor ranges offer the convenience of targets that can be individually illuminated and positioned at any distance from the shooter. The shooting action is continuous, without the interruption of regularly scheduled ceasefires to allow shooters downrange to check or post targets. Without the need to leave your shooting position, guns and gear are more secure and you're never rained out. The ambiance of indoor shooting ranges varies, but see through dividers help keep them shooters from feeling closed in. Note the three wide-angle cameras overhead and the computer control panels located at each station. This is the VIP range at Tactical Firearms in Katy, Texas, where we conducted our lights and lasers range session.

Now that we have established what facilities can be expected to be available for a practice session, let's isolate a couple factors that are part and parcel of facing an imminent threat. First, there is a limited yet undetermined amount of time available before an attacker puts his hands on you physically and either strikes you or cuts you. Or , he or she could bridge the gap by projecting a deadly weapon such as a bullet fired from a gun. So the ability to acquire the weapon, and put it on target quickly is a key concern.

The next challenge is accuracy. Accuracy is directly related to the available target area and distance. Certainly distance makes shots more difficult as one's vision plays a part. But so does the ability to hold the gun steady, so the sight picture is where you need it to be when the shot goes off. Target area is often a subject of much discussion with police and entry teams, where an armed criminal may be only partially exposed but willing to fire while holding a hostage. It is not unheard for an armed confrontation to take place with just a few feet between combatants and the criminal holding a hostage in front of them, covering all but a very small area. Both time and shot placement are two problems that can be addressed in a common range setting.

▲ American Shooting Centers, located inside West Houston's scenic George Bush Park, offers several different shooting facilities. The primary rifle and pistol range, shown here, offers benches and fixed target locations ranging in distances from seven to one hundred yards. The handgun benches are designed for standing off hand and the rifle positions may be shot prone or from a bench.

Volumes have been written about stance, grip, sight alignment, and trigger control, but rarely addressed is the process that comes well before any of this can take place. That is, getting the gun into your hand. Perhaps the most basic and most necessary skill for home defense is the ability to pick up the gun and shoot it accurately. Since most people do not think of wearing a holstered gun while inside the home, the skill of acquiring the gun safely from a drawer, tabletop, predetermined fixed position, or from inside a small personal safe must be practiced. Firing drills beginning with the aforementioned predetermined fixed position such as a bedside or wall mount holster is not going to be easily or safely executed at a range, let alone in your home. So would deployment beginning with the opening of a drawer. Each of these drills would have to be staged in dry-fire mode—meaning with an empty gun—exclusively. Practicing picking up your gun from

a flat surface can be easily staged on the line at a shooting range. But, don't attempt this drill unless you have first obtained permission from range management to do so.

Practicing picking up the gun and firing while at the shooting range should begin with checking the surface of the bench you will be working on. Indoors or out, many such benches that divide the shooter from the area downrange have a vertical piece in front to prevent loose rounds or anything else from rolling off the bench, onto the ground, and downrange. If so, place a sandbag, which should be readily available at the range, so the gun sits higher than the barrier in front of the gun. Otherwise, if an accident happens and a round is fired before the muzzle clears the barrier, it could cause a ricochet or other unfortunate result.

One last piece of advice is before shooting any type of drill to perform the first few repetitions in dry-fire

▲ If live-fire practice of the pickup drill is permissible at the range, it is best to make sure there is no form of obstruction in front of the barrel. In this case, placing sandbags beneath the gun was the most stable way to elevate the gun and clear the muzzle.

▲ Before starting any dry fire training session it is essential that all firearms be empty of ammunition. Revolver rounds are stored individually in separate chambers within the cylinder. This is the most efficient way to hold a revolver and work the ejector rod.

mode. The purpose of dry-fire rehearsal is to increase focus on the processes that take place before the gun goes off. Dry-fire not only gives you the time to visualize, but also helps to make visualization a habit. To those who see range time as being for live-fire only, dry-fire practice may seem like a waste of time. But it will pay off by saving ammunition and increasing focus, thanks to less total repetitions being necessary to solidify or improve a given technique.

Entering dry-fire mode begins with clearing the gun of all ammunition. To clear a revolver, release the cylinder and push the ejector rod repeatedly until all the ammunition is clear. Raise the cylinder to your eyes to make sure you can see all the way through each chamber. Stow loose rounds in your pocket or a separate compartment of your range bag. To clear a semi-automatic pistol, drop the magazine. Work the slide to pull the loaded round from the chamber. Do not try to catch the round as it leaves the chamber. Let it fall where it may. Next, lock back the slide and look into the breech to confirm that the chamber is empty. Or slip a pencil down the barrel until it is visible inside the breech. If you have difficulty pulling back the slide and pushing the slide latch upward into the notch, try this: Insert an empty magazine and pull the slide back. This should automatically lock the slide in the rearward position. Stow loose rounds in your pocket or a separate

compartment of your range bag. Now you are ready to rehearse your first drill.

Start position for the pickup drill is as follows: With the gun lying on its side, slide forward in ready position, with the muzzle pointing downrange. If your gun is equipped with a manual safety, it should be in the on position. If your gun has a decocker, use it to lower the hammer. If you are right-handed, the handgun should be lying on its left side. The object is to pick up the gun quickly off the bench, acquire front and rear sight alignment on a designated target, and press the trigger. If this sounds simple, the reality is that there are a number of pitfalls. The first and most common mistake would be breaking the shot before sights are on target. This could mean the shooter's finger was on the trigger prematurely and the discharge was unintentional. Or the shooter's initial grip was so faulty he or she was unable to acquire an acceptable sight picture and gave up, firing the shot out of desperation.

Getting a good grip on a handgun means the sights are easily aligned without having to shift the gun in your hand, the trigger comfortably within reach, and the grip surface of the gun in full contact with the inside of your hand. If there is a gap, the gun will shift in your hand during recoil and you will likely

▼ Clearing the chamber starts with dropping the magazine and pulling back the slide until the round is pulled from the chamber and drops to the ground. The A-Zoom aluminum snap cap is just about to eject, but this gun is not yet clear.

need to reset your grip after each shot. So the question becomes how you pick up a gun from a tabletop or inside a nightstand drawer and attain a good grip. Two methods are widely recognized. One method utilizes both the weak and strong hands, meaning for the right-handed shooter, the left and right hands respectively. The second method utilizes only the strong hand.

When picking up the gun using both hands, the strong hand hovers momentarily over the handgun with the palm down and index finger extended as if pointing, but neither tense nor locked straight out. The three remaining fingers are curled but open enough to accept the grip frame. The thumb is ready to be wrapped around the left side of the gun. At the moment of contact with the gun, the weak hand will be nearly palm-up, with middle finger reaching beneath the handgun at or just forward of the rear sight. The strong hand does not reach down for the gun. Rather, the middle finger of the weak hand lifts the gun upward so the strong hand can wrap around the grip as the weak hand takes its position in supporting the handgun.

When using the strong hand only to pick up the gun, the middle finger and thumb take a leading role. Start by touching the tip of your middle finger to the tip of

▼ With the slide locked back, a visual inspection of the chamber may not be enough. Slipping a pencil down the barrel provides unmistakable proof. Note the operator keeps her hand outside of the trigger guard at all times.

your thumb. Now separate the two, leaving enough space to wrap around the grip of the handgun with the middle finger placed just below where the trigger guard meets the grip frame. Unlike the two-handed method, which is a lift and catch, in the one-hand method the thumb and middle finger pass tightly around the grip and, with a slight squeeze or pinching motion, the gun pops up into the hand. Keep in mind that the trigger finger remains outside the trigger guard, extended but relaxed until the gun is raised and sights are on target.

The strong-hand method is very fast but more difficult to perform consistently. In addition, the middle finger could mistakenly be placed inside the trigger guard, especially in low-light conditions. To compare efficiency, try picking up the gun in dry-fire mode using both methods, say twenty or thirty times each. How many times did you have to make an adjustment to your grip to get a good sight picture using the one-handed method versus utilizing the two-handed method? If necessary, how much easier was it to adjust your grip with the gun held in both hands versus when it was held in only one?

Now that you have rehearsed one or both methods of picking up the gun, it is time to load it and make ready for live-fire practice. However, this does not mean it is time to speed up. The objective is to build muscle memory, and bear in mind that your body learns more quickly from a series of consistent, smoothly executed moves than it does from going too fast and produc-

▼ When picking the up the gun from a tabletop or inside a drawer, the goal is to acquire a usable shooting grip in the shortest time possible. The dangers of rushing to make the shot are unintentional discharge, dropping the gun, or simply raising the gun to your eye only to find that you must shift the gun in your hand before you are able to fire. The method shown tips the gun up off the table into the palm of the hand. Key points are middle finger lifting the gun from beneath the rear sight unit and keeping your receiving hand open and relaxed. A word about dropping a gun; let it fall. Modern guns, pistol or revolver, have internal mechanisms to prevent ignition upon impact with the ground. The greater danger is finding your finger inside the trigger guard and pressing the trigger as your grip closes to catch it. If the gun should fall, think of it as a ball of fire.

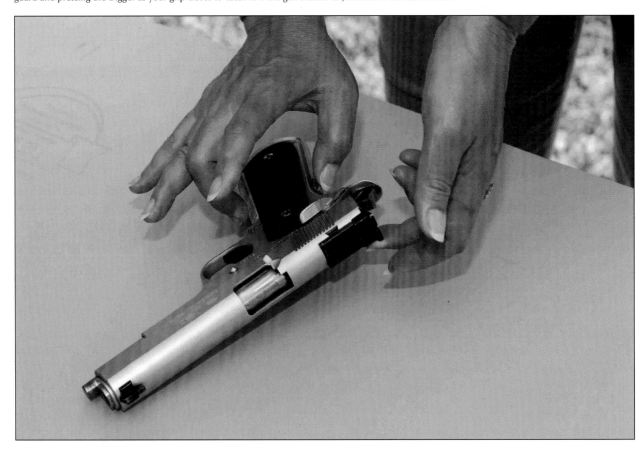

ing a chain of stuttering stops and starts. Begin with posting a near target. For this drill, a target mounted five to seven yards downrange is all that is required. Shooting at greater distance may be helpful for refining accuracy, but most professional speed shooters agree that practicing at closer targets is more effective in developing speed.

The configuration of the target chosen for this exercise is less important than how you aim at it. No matter what the target looks like or how big it is, the key is to aim for a specific point. Whether that means the eye socket of a paper bad guy or just a dot you've scribbled on a blank piece of paper, the objective is the same. Pick up the gun, find the sights on target, and deliver an accurate shot.

Shooting in the context of a confrontation is never going to be as easy as it is at the shooting range. The difference is stress, and once a defensive shot becomes necessary, the sooner you can get off an accurate shot the better. Probably the most helpful tool for building speed is the shot-recording timer. Shot-recording timers deliver an audible start signal and, by the use of an internal microphone, record elapsed time each time it hears a shot. This means you can keep a record of how fast it takes you to acquire the gun and take the first shot and all shots thereafter. It wasn't always so, but today's shot-recording timers enable you to review not only the elapsed time from start signal to last shot fired but the intervals or split times between each individual shot as well.

▼ Picking the gun up using only one hand is a skill that requires practice and an empty gun. Notice the small yellow chamber flag protruding from the ejection port. Its length continues into the chamber and down the barrel. The key point to the single-hand method is the pinching action applied by the thumb and middle finger to the frame just beneath the trigger guard and at the hollow located at the top of the back strap. Performed correctly, the gun should pop up into the hand. The danger here is for the middle finger to enter the trigger guard and press the trigger instead of grasping the frame.

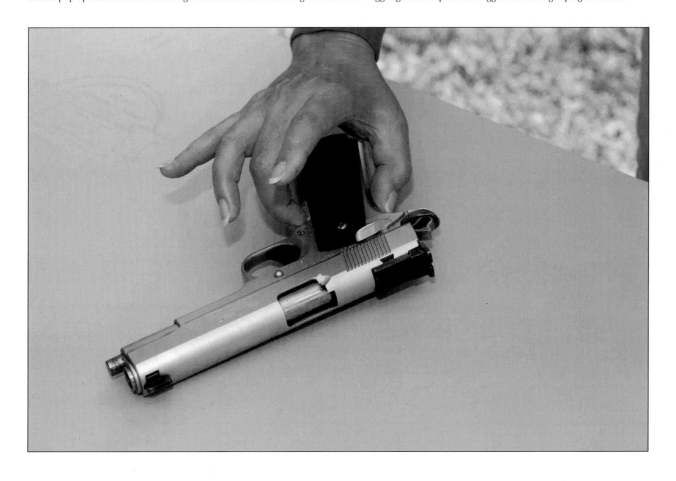

Timers can also be set with a fixed or par time. If, for example, your first attempt at the pickup drill registered an elapsed time of 2.0 seconds, you can set the timer to deliver a stop signal after 2.0 seconds have elapsed. This offers you a way to compete against yourself and register progress. For example, for your next range session you can set par time at 1.75 seconds and try to beat that time consistently. Using par time also helps you to build an inner clock. The net effect will be that time appears to slow down and you can learn to better manage the individual movements that make up how you acquire the gun and deliver your shots.

The shot-recording timer is a great tool, but you can substitute other means. Perhaps the most valuable feature of a shot-recording timer is its start signal. This can be replicated with a cooking timer or anything else that makes a noise because it need not be precise. Indeed, shot-recording timers are best used with the start signal set to chime at random intervals after pressing the start button. The objective is to develop the ability to listen hard and avoid reacting to mere anticipation. Short of having a mechanical device, have a companion tap you on the shoulder to serve as a start signal, the less predictably the better.

There are a lot of ways to make a simple shooting exercise such as the pickup drill more valuable to your defensive skills. You could begin the drill firing at an eight-and-a-half by eleven-inch piece of paper. After you can hit it consistently, try folding it in half, then in half again. Or change your start position. Begin with your hands in your pockets, stand off a

▲ The shot-recording timer is one of the most effective tools a shooter can use to increase their skills. It can provide a start signal at random or fixed intervals after pressing the start button. This teaches you to listen and react rather than anticipate or overreact. You can keep a record of how long it takes you to perform a drill the first time and then monitor your progress. Shot recording timers not only report elapsed time and interval between shots, but can be programmed to designate a specific window of time, called par time. Performing a specific set of tasks, such as pick up the gun, fire, reload, and fire again, within a fixed amount of time can increase your ability to manage time and better perceive actions taken under stress.

few feet so you have to step up to the gun, or begin the drill with your back turned, facing up range. The point of such variation is to force you to adjust and be able to acquire the gun smoothly and safely no matter what the situation. But, keep in mind that these are drills that should be cleared with range management before every session.

In rehearsing of the two-handed versus single-hand pickup, it should become obvious that being able to use a second hand to support the gun is a big advantage, if not a luxury. There is no question that it is easier to fire faster and more accurately with the gun held in both hands. Not only does a two-handed hold make sight alignment steadier to begin with, but it also makes getting the sights back on target after recoil faster and more efficient, as well. But in terms of armed combat, having both hands available to shoot with is not always possible. One hand may be injured, struggling to hold off an attacker, or needed to push or pull an innocent person out of the way. One hand may also be needed to operate a light so you can navigate in the dark or identify a possible target.

To prepare for shooting with the gun held in only one hand, begin your practice session without the distraction of having to pick up the gun as the first step. Just stand and shoot, taking your time for each shot. This should be practiced with both the right and left hands. However, here is where a lot of gun owners get into trouble. Naturally, shooting with one hand is going to be more accurate and efficient than shooting with the other. And with more gratifying results from the superior hand, it is common, if not human nature for the shooter to practice more with the gun held in the better shooting hand. But to advance your skills and feel secure, you must be willing to fail and learn from your mistakes.

If that sounds like your range sessions will never be fun again, try dividing your shooting time into two different activities, pleasure shooting and skill building.

Pleasure shooting is not necessarily devoid of the opportunity to learn. It's just that in pleasure shooting mode, you are not necessarily trying to learn something new or install muscle memory by engaging in a series of challenging repetitions. Pleasure shooting rarely takes the participant outside their comfort zone.

Pleasure shooting should not be confused with plinking. A popular interpretation of the word plinking is the practice of throwing shots down range with less than complete determination to hit a given target. If this is the true definition of plinking, then I, like many serious trainers, object to it. Here is why. Every fired shot hits something. The only acceptable outcome for any given shot is to connect with the desired target and not hit anything else. This is an extension of at least two safety rules for handling firearms, which tell us to never point a firearm at anything you do not wish to destroy, and be conscious of what lies behind your target. One key to effective defensive shooting is to develop the habit of firing to hit only the designated target.

When it comes to skill building, probably the least practiced drills are the ones where the handgun is fired while being held in one hand. The sport of bull's-eye shooting is a target sport wherein all shots are fired holding the gun with only one hand, and the annual matches at the famous Camp Perry draw hundreds of shooters. But this is not what I'm referring to. In a situation that involves an imminent threat, it may not be possible to focus all your effort, conscious and unconscious, on stabilizing, aiming, and firing a handgun.

Firing handguns requires both fine- and gross-motor skills. Gross-motor skills are used to physically support and aim the gun in general alignment with the target. Fine-motor skills are required to aim the sights to a specific point and press the trigger in a manner that presents as little movement as possible from the desired point of aim specifically at the moment of ignition. Dialing 911 on a cell phone, switching it to speaker, or just putting it to your ear also requires a series of gross- and fine-motor skills. Can you operate a cell phone with only one hand and maintain a safe direction of aim for your handgun in readiness to engage?

One of the biggest dangers to safely handling a firearm is unconscious and sympathetic movement within the hands, especially under stress. One example of unconscious movement is the closing of the hands during a slip and fall. In an earlier chapter we spoke of what many anthropologists feel is one of two fears innate to the human race, the fear of loud noise. The second fear considered to be innate or hard-wired into our psyche is the fear of falling. A common response to a slip and fall is to close the hands, which may be related to the desire to grasp on to something on the way down. How does this relate to firearm safety? If you are moving with a firearm and have your index finger inside the trigger guard, should you fall the reaction of closing the hand will likely result in pressing the trigger and releasing an unintentional shot.

A second phenomenon commonly related to unintentional discharge of a firearm is that of sympathetic movement. During the performance of certain tasks with one hand, the opposite hand tends to mimic the same movements without any clear necessity to do so. But when holding a firearm, you can't afford to have your grip tighten suddenly or flinch. Nor can you allow your trigger finger to move in consort with motions initiated by the opposite hand. This could mean turning a doorknob, activating a cell phone, or turning on a flashlight.

Drills designed to insulate the motion of one hand from the other can be performed in both dry-fire mode or live-fire at the range. But since there will be no report from the empty weapon and this is a drill that delves into the unconscious, dry-fire rehearsal requires not only an empty gun but also a partner to watch the action of the trigger finger. A good first drill could be as simple as holding the pistol in the strong hand while holding and squeezing a rubber ball in the other.

A good second exercise would be holding a retractable pen in the weak hand with the thumb pressing and releasing the action. This relates directly to the use of a tactical style flashlight, which in today's configuration are typically controlled by an on/off switch located on the tail cap opposite the bezel or source of the beam. The ability to use a flashlight to search or identify is key to the ability to make decisions, another factor in defending your home with a firearm. As such, live-fire practice while operating a flashlight provides an excellent opportunity to advance your shooting skills.

Taking the above drills to the range for live-fire shooting is the next step. Indoor ranges that can offer reduced lighting upon request are ideal. But with the strength of today's flashlights, the beam should be visible in all but the very brightest of room conditions. The first challenge to manipulating a flashlight in your opposite hand should be as simple as keeping the beam on the target while delivering an accurate shot. This means setting the switch to the on position and firing two or three shots at a time, concentrating on

accuracy rather than speed. The next drill would begin with the light off and the handgun held at a low-ready position, which means the gun is aligned with the target in terms of centering to the left and right. But the gun has been lowered from dead center just enough so that the shooter can see over the gun and has a clear view of the periphery. The low-ready position can be found by aiming the gun at the desired point of impact then lowering it into the bottom area of your peripheral vision. This way, you'll be able to track the sights into position when you raise the gun.

Having an audible start signal or just having a partner say "ready, standby, go," will help you develop visualization and avoid overreaction due to anticipation. On the start signal, switch on the light, illuminate the target, raise the gun to align the sights to the desired point of impact, and deliver a shot. The first variation should be to deliver more than one shot to learn how to recover from recoil and control both the pistol and the beam of light. If your flashlight offers a momentary illumination mode that requires constant pressure to the tail cap or other type of switch, this same drill should be repeated using this feature.

Subsequent variations on this drill have to do with the complexities of the on/off switch in your particular flashlight and the way you hold it. In this regard, today's tactical flashlights may offer several options. The tailcap switch might provide illumination as long as it is depressed but constant illumination requires turning down the end piece until contact with the batteries is achieved. Or the tailcap of your flashlight may be set up to provide momentary illumination as long as the switch is held down, as well as constant illumination by delivering a quick, deep stab to the tailcap, locking the switch into position. Still other variations include pressing sharply on the tailcap switch to adjust the width of the beam, the intensity of illumination, or both. Some flashlights even provide a strobe in an operational protocol as complicated as pressing the tailcap once for increased intensity and twice in rapid succession for strobe. Whether any of these features beyond constant or momentary illumination will help you in a defensive situation depends mainly on your ability to use them without being distracted by the operational protocol they require.

There are several different ways to hold the flashlight in coordination with pointing the gun. In one method, commonly referred to as the FBI hold, the flashlight is held away from the body at arm's length at approximately 10 o'clock. This is an ideal first position for the exercises above because stabilizing the gun with the arm extended can be challenging and requires the most effort. The FBI hold also serves as a very good search position. Once a target is found the light can then be pulled in to a position against the body or joined with the gun. One of the intentions behind development of the FBI method was to provide a margin of safety to the operator. This is based on the theory that by holding the light away from the body the natural response of an adversary will be to shoot toward the source of the light and away from the operator of the flashlight. Indeed, many professionals swear by this method.

A second hold indexes the flashlight below the operator's jaw line to offer illumination in line with the operator's eyes. It also presents a compact profile and brings in your center of gravity to provide better overall stability of your shooting platform. Another hold crosses the wrists with the flashlight in the weak hand held below and to the outside of the pistol. This is often referred to as the Harries technique. Yet another puts the hands side by side so that the barrel of the gun is parallel and at nearly the same height as the flashlight. Developed by Ray Chapman, this is ideal for using traditional design flashlights where the on/off switch is located along the barrel of the unit rather than at the end. In this method, the hand holding the light offers additional support to steady the pistol. Another method that offers more integration between holding the gun and the flashlight places the barrel of the light between

▲ Practicing while operating a flashlight challenges the shooter to isolate the fine-motor skills needed to fire a handgun from the movements necessary to turn on the flashlight and aim the beam. While this method may not provide a solid base to shoot from, the theory is that return fire will be directed at the beam of light and away from the operator.

Indexing the beam along the jaw-line offers nearly automatic coordination with the line of sight. It also can be used to assist in sight alignment by vaguely illuminating the sights if that should become necessary. Keep in mind that one thing you never want to do is catch the beam on an opposing surface so the light is reflected back at you, revealing your profile. But one other advantage of this method is with the arm in tight, you become a smaller target and can move more easily within cramped spaces, such as a hallway. Finally, keeping the arm in tight helps avoid suffering any type of pendulum effect that might amplify recoil and disturb your aim.

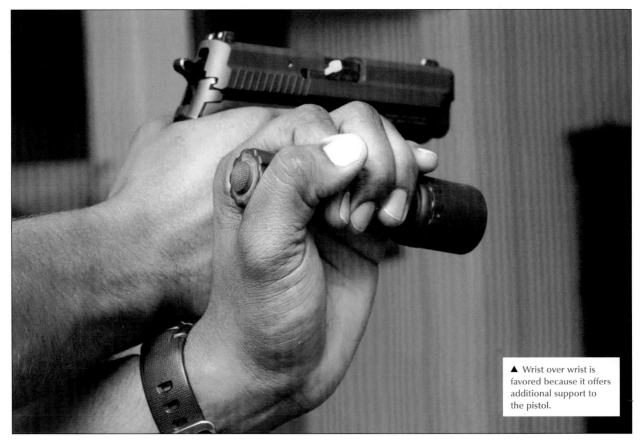

▲ Wrist over wrist is favored because it offers additional support to the pistol.

◀ Gun and light held side by side with the thumb over the top is a good choice when using larger flashlights with the on/off switch in its traditional position along the casing.

▼ Holding the flashlight side by side with the handgun but with the thumb behind the tail cap achieves two purposes. First, this accommodates flashlights that operate from a tail cap switch, and second, it enables the flashlight to be used in striking directly forward. This is not to say that the thumb over side by side technique cannot be used as a platform from which to deliver a strike. But striking from a thumb over grip favors an overhead strike that requires first raising the unit and telegraphing the strike. Held with thumb behind the tail of the flashlight, the flashlight is braced by the thumb for a quick jab that offers no telltale warning.

▲ Smaller flashlights can be integrated into a grip that holds the gun with both hands by splitting the fingers. The original Bill Rogers grip puts the flashlight in the support hand with the tail cap switch sustaining pressure against inside of the palm. Shown here in variation, the tail cap is being compressed against the front strap of the grip frame for momentary illumination.

the middle and ring fingers with pressure applied to the tailcap switch against the inside of the palm. This method was developed and popularized by firearms training innovator Bill Rogers. A variation of this method, places the tailcap against the front strap of the handgun frame itself. This variation on the Rogers grip is more applicable to smaller flashlights. Probably the biggest challenge is activating the momentary on feature in these two positions without affecting accuracy.

The question becomes which method should you learn? The answer: all of them. You can prioritize based on preference, but it's always valuable to have plans C and D ready to go if plans A or B are not possible. Choosing which methods will be your favorites should become obvious during your first dry-fire practice session. It should also be emphasized that initial applications of each method should be rehearsed without a loaded gun. Even when you take your practice session to the range, you should rehearse in dry-fire mode before engaging targets with live fire. For most operators, the type of hold that can be achieved the fastest and maintained with the most consistency of both illumination and accuracy with the handgun ultimately becomes the preferred method.

Weapon-Mounted Lights and Lasers

*I*n the previous chapter, Range Sessions, the objective was to introduce simple training methods to help the reader develop advanced skills and overcome some of the rudimentary problems that crop up in the real world away from the shooting range. The chapter finishes with the very real challenge of having to shoot with one hand and manipulate a flashlight with the other. An alternative to splitting tasks between the two hands is to have the source of illumination mounted on the weapon itself. There are several advantages to utilizing a weapon-mounted light. In terms of handguns, you can not only hold and control the weapon with both hands, but when you reach for the gun, the light comes along with it. In terms of lights mounted on shotguns or carbines, effectively using a flashlight is much more difficult if your forehand grip is responsible not only for supporting the weapon but holding and aiming the flashlight. A solid mount also prevents the flashlight from falling away during recoil or in the midst of reloading or any other task that might become necessary.

Another weapons-mounted system that can be helpful is a laser-aiming unit. Key advantages to using a laser-aiming device include not having to align the gun perfectly in front of the shooter's eyes, nor bring the eyes back to the sights, leaving the target in the periphery.

Weapon-mounted lights and lasers have been around for quite a while. Nevertheless, I have not always been a fan of using lasers or weapon-mounted lights for home defense. Some of the reasons include battery life and the sheer bulk of the units. Plus, not only do you have to see the dot on the target for the first shot, but you have to be able to find the dot after recoil and replace it onto a target that has probably moved. But there has been a lot of improvement, especially since the beginning of the war in Iraq, where demand spurred innovation and design. The only way to address these concerns and learn more about the possible advantages of the latest lights and lasers was to shop around for some products that would hopefully address each of these concerns and take them to the range for tests.

In choosing a weapon light, my preference is that the unit be quick and easy to apply and to remove. But of primary importance is that the unit stay attached to the gun and be able to withstand abuse not only during recoil but when, not if, the gun was dropped. Long battery life is another concern. Powerful illumination in a moderately wide beam should, in my opinion, be a given, but without reliability, no amount of lumens or for that matter candlepower is going to be of any importance.

The handgun weapon light chosen for the tests was an old reliable from my personal collection. The SureFire X200 has since been supplanted in production by very similar models, such as the X300 and X400 handgun weapons lights. The Surefire X200 was chosen over a number of other handgun weapons lights because it proved to be not only the easiest to get on and off the guns, but in fact was the only one that didn't loosen up or leave the gun altogether during some hard shooting in practice for the test session. Choosing a laser projection system was more complicated.

Part of my reluctance in the past to utilize a laser-projection unit was based on my color blindness. For a long time, laser beams for small arms only came in red. Frankly, I found the color too dark to pick up quickly, and the size of the dot was typically too small. But with the introduction of green laser beams, my interest was renewed. Am I actually able to see green? No, not really, but to my eyes the green laser is much brighter and far more capable of capturing the eye.

▲ For our range tests we tried out a number of different handgun weapons lights. But, in the end we chose to use a SureFire X200. This unit was an old warrior that proved to be the best suited and, indeed, the most reliable unit we had at our disposal. The SureFire X300, shown here, is the latest version of this pocket-sized flame thrower. *Photo courtesy of SureFire*

The next step up in laser innovation was the introduction of a pulsating beam or strobe effect. With the addition of the strobe comes a splashing effect that makes the dot appear to be larger and bolder. A second advantage to the strobe relates to persistence of vision, the same phenomenon that makes flashing a series of still photographs before the human eye result in the illusion of motion. In this case, the strobe light, or stroboscope, produces the opposite effect as per its definition found online at Webster-dictionary. org: "Strobe: a scientific instrument that provides a flashing light *synchronized with the periodic movement of an object; can make moving object appear* stationary." This plays into the reinforcement of shooting skills perfectly. Here is why. One of the most desirable shooting skills is the ability to call your shots, or knowing where the shot will land based on sight alignment at the moment the shot went off. How does one know this? Calling a shot requires a flash sight picture, meaning mentally realizing a snapshot of what the sights looked like when the gun went off. Combined with the brightness of a green laser, the strobe laser offers the shooter faster recognition, making recovery of aim after recoil much easier in reduced light or in a brightly lit room.

The issue of added bulk was addressed with the choice of two different products from Lasermax, each one producing a green strobe laser beam. A Lasermax LMS-2281 guide rod that contained the laser unit was installed on a Sig Sauer P229 pistol, chambered for .357Sig ammunition. This was an older pistol, produced before the option of an accessory rail dustcover was available. As such, area illumination would have to be provided by a hand held flashlight. A .45 ACP Glock model 30SF was also fit with a Lasermax laser guide rod, part number LMS-1191. Since the G30SF comes with an accessory rail, we were able to use it with the SureFire light attached.

The second laser unit chosen was designed to be attached to the pistol at the dustcover accessory rail. It was, nevertheless, compact. The Lasermax (LMS-UNI-G) added barely more than one half-inch to the depth of the dustcover of the dustcover and supplied a second rail for piggyback style application of the SureFire light. The on/off switches on the Lasermax units could be activated from either side of the pis-

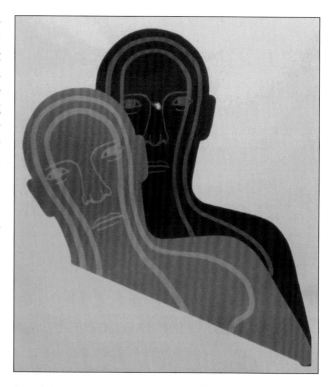

▲ Daylight recognition is not always fast or even possible with many laser units, especially if you are colorblind. To simulate a bright, sunny day, we had the Range Master at Tactical Firearms in Katy, Texas fully illuminate the range, including the work lights and fire emergency beams. The splash of the strobe from the LaserMax LMS-UNI-G proved unmistakable on this Coast Guard CG-2 target mounted some twenty-five yards downrange.

tol. In each case, the laser units were activated using the weak hand thumb. After firing had ceased, we removed the finger from the trigger and used it to turn off the laser. Adding a visual scan left, right, and to the rear before turning off the laser is one way our test procedure could be turned into a valuable defensive drill.

One might ask why a combined light and laser system was not chosen. The answer is none of the combined laser light systems I was able to find offered a bright enough laser for my somewhat compromised vision. Nor were any of the lights truly sufficient in terms of intensity. It was as if one unit sharing both tasks had compromised the full value of either the light or the laser. Furthermore, most of the combination units were just as bulky or more so than stacking two units together. I prefer the added flexibility, too. For example, if it's daylight and I am only going to need the laser I wouldn't be stuck with the extra mass of an attached light.

▲ The LaserMaxLMS units take the place of the factory guide rods. This is an ideal solution for pistols that do not offer an accessory rail. Zeroing the laser beam was automatic upon installation with point of aim set to match point of impact at a distance of twenty yards. Separate guide rod units were mounted in a .45 ACP Glock 30SF and an older Sig Sauer P229 chambered for .357Sig. Reliability proved 100 percent in both pistols. In fact, the P229, which had been recently refreshed at the Sig Sauer factory, appeared to cycle more smoothly with the addition of the LaserMax guide rod than with the stock recoil unit in place. Operation of the guide rod units was ambidextrous, with a cross-bolt on/off switch integrated with the slide stop.

Armed with an imminently visible laser system and a rugged weapons light, we sought to evaluate the efficiency of each unit and how they might offer an advantage to the homeowner in a defensive scenario. The first step was to take part in timed fire tests to establish a base line for comparing speed and accuracy when firing from four different combinations of illumination and aiming devices. The combinations were handheld light utilizing the standard pistol sights, attached weapon light with standard pistol sights, attached weapon light with rail-mounted laser, and guide-rod-mounted laser with attached weapon light.

For tests, we visited Tactical Firearms a state-of-the-art indoor shooting range in Katy, Texas, where we were able to easily control not only the distance to each target but more importantly the amount of available light. In fact, the bulk of our tests were conducted in near darkness.

For accurate, reliable ammunition, we relied upon both new manufacture and remanufactured rounds from Black Hills Ammunition, produced in Rapid City, South Dakota. Choice of test ammunition included 180-grain .40 S&W full metal jacket, 230-grain .45 ACP jacketed hollow-point and 100-grain .357Sig Frangible ammunition.

Targets used were the CG-2 Coast Guard training targets, available from Law Enforcement Targets, Inc. The CG-2 shows a gray silhouette of a hostage, head and torso, canted at about a forty-five-degree angle in front of a dark silhouette figure representing a predator

▼ The Lasermax LMS-UNI-G contributes little to the profile of the pistol and supplied a secondary rail for attachment of other accessories.

attempting to shield themselves behind the hostage. This is not a character photograph but facial features such as eyes, nose, and ears are depicted. The CG-2 target was chosen to add tension, with only about 70 percent of the hostage taker's head and neck exposed.

Targets were set up at a distance of precisely ten yards by computer control from the firing line. Start position for all tests was with the light on and the gun in hand (or hands) resting on the shelf that divided the shooting booth from the downrange area. In tests where the laser was used, the respective laser unit was switched on as the shooter moved the gun into the ready position. A random start signal and a record of elapsed times for each shot were recorded using a Competitive Edge Dynamics CED 8000 shot-recording timer. Test procedure was to deliver three shots on target after an audible start signal. This procedure was repeated four times for a total of five separate strings of fire. By checking the size of the group delivered to the hostage taker and the elapsed times, we would be able to ascertain

the efficiency of our shooting. This would provide the insight necessary to determine which devices or combination of devices we would prefer to rely upon.

Our first test was firing a .40 S&W Springfield Armory XDM 3.8 Compact pistol with the SureFire X200 handgun weapon light attached to the rail. The XDM 3.8 Compact was chosen because it can serve as either a carry gun with short grip or as a high-capacity weapon for home defense by simply loading one of the supplied sixteen-round magazines with grip extension. The supplied pistol sights, which were of the standard low-mount notch-and-post configuration without any source of illumination, such as tritium, were used for aiming. How fast the shooter was able to acquire an acceptable sight picture was indicated by first shot times ranging from 1.29 seconds to 1.69 seconds after the start signal. Four out of five second shots were recorded at approximately the 2.30-second mark. But, the fastest second shot was reported after 1.95 seconds had elapsed. The fastest overall time for the three shots was 2.68 seconds, but the other four strings of fire took a little more than 3.01 seconds to complete. The target showed a nine-inch-wide group with seven of fifteen hits not impacting the hostage taker.

Next, we removed the SureFire light from the XDM pistol. For this test, the gun was held in the strong hand only with the shooter again utilizing just the supplied pistol sights. But this time, illumination was provided by a flashlight held in the shooter's weak hand. On average, the first, second, and third shots took more time to deliver, by as much as .72 seconds, 1.06 seconds, and 1.42 seconds, respectively. Regarding the hits, target first shots were the most accurate with about a five-inch-wide five-shot group forming on the lower right side of the hostage taker's face. But shots that were fired after recovering from recoil were more likely to be off. Overall, only seven shots hit the hostage taker.

Firing strong hand only, the biggest disadvantage was the amount of work it took to steady the gun and put the sights on target after each shot. Illuminating the target and getting enough light on the sights was also challenging. With the light mounted on the gun, there was enough light splashing back from the target to offer a sight picture. Using the FBI hold with the weak side arm extended, pointing the light at the target, proved to be an extra task in itself. Plus, the sights were difficult to decipher. Moving the flashlight to along the side of the jawline helped aim the light at the target and offered a solid index that the shooter could move to and lock into place quickly. But, the handheld flashlight had two settings on its beam. The first setting we tried put out an extra-wide beam, which caused a glare on the rear sight unit that made sight acquisition nearly impossible. Using the narrow beam solved this problem, but intensity in this mode was less than desirable. Changing to a single-beam flashlight was the better choice because there was less to think about, making turning on the light and positioning the beam almost automatic.

The five strings of fire in near total darkness was repeated this time with both the SureFire X200 handgun weapon light and the Lasermax LMS-UNI-G laser attached to the accessory rail on the Springfield Armory XDM 3.8 Compact pistol. This combination produced the fastest and most consistent shots of the range session. Three separate runs began with a first shot at the 1.30-second mark. Two others began with a first shot computing to an average of 1.165 seconds after the start signal. On average, second shots were recorded at the 2.08 mark. Third shots ended the string with an average elapsed time of 2.78 seconds. The target showed a twelve-shot nine-inch-wide group on the hostage taker.

The next test would feature a different combination of light and laser. Switching to the Glock 30SF, the Lasermax guide rod unit was installed and the SureFire handgun weapon light was attached. One advantage we noticed right away when comparing the guide-rod laser unit to the rail-mount system was how much simpler it was to zero the laser beam so it matched the point of impact dictated by the sights. The laser beam produced by the rail-mount unit was adjusted by turning separate windage and elevation screws with the supplied tool. And zeroing the beam was as easy as steering the laser beam until it was hidden directly behind or just above the front sight blade. But, zeroing the guide-rod laser unit was far less complicated. Our range session showed all that was required to place the beam at an accurate point of aim was to install the guide rod properly. We noticed that the unit was dead-on in our tests, especially when shooting at distances of fifteen to twenty-five yards. In fact, Lasermax reports that the guide-rod systems are zeroed for precisely twenty yards. Variation at longer distances would depend on the trajectory of individual loads and calibers. For example, flat shooting calibers, such as a 125-grain .357Sig round, would probably maintain proper elevation longer in flight than a 230-grain round of .45 ACP ammunition that tends to rise and fall over a longer distance.

One of my biggest concerns with installing the guide-rod laser unit was depending on the Lasermax guide rod to deliver reliable performance. But my concerns proved unfounded. Reliability in both the Glock 30SF and the Sig Sauer P229 remained 100 percent. In the case of the older Sig Sauer P229, controllability seemed to be improved over the original equipment, despite having been recently tuned and updated at the Sig Sauer factory. Taking a break from timed fire and from shooting in the dark, we asked for the range to be fully illuminated. Our range officer responded by turning on all of the work lights so the room was nearly

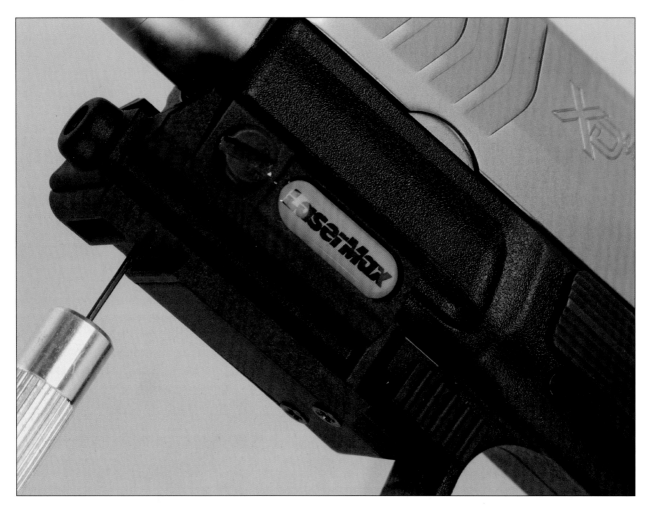

▲ Changing the point of impact of theLMS-UNI-G laser beam was accomplished with the supplied tool. The bottom access is for adjusting elevation, and the small hole located on the side directly beneath the set screw is for changing point of impact to the left or right. Once set, our adjustments stayed true.

as brightly lit as a sunny day. Using the Sig Sauer P229 with guide-rod laser in place the green strobe laser was clearly visible. Aiming at the bridge of the nose of the hostage taker on the ten-yard CG-2 target, the shooter delivered ten shots of continuous fire resulting in the best single group of the session to point of aim measuring 2.4 inches across.

In my opinion, changing guns, let alone from what is ostensibly a forty-caliber service pistol to a .45 ACP subcompact with a different trigger system, should have resulted in an unfair if not uneven comparison. But, the elapsed times achieved firing the Glock 30SF with laser guide rod and SureFire handgun weapons were actually quite close to the numbers recorded

firing the Springfield Armory pistol. While first and second shots trailed on average by about .37 seconds and .29 seconds, respectively, total elapsed times for all three shots were less than 0.40 seconds apart. Accuracy was impressive, with 75 percent of the shots shredding the target in about an eight-inch group squarely upon the face of the hostage taker.

It was no surprise to find out that aiming and firing in a dark room with a weapon-mounted light was more efficient than shooting with a flashlight in one hand and the gun in the other. The ability to steady both the weapon and the light for initial aim and in response to recoil was the obvious difference. Also, with the laser in place there was no need to move the gun very far

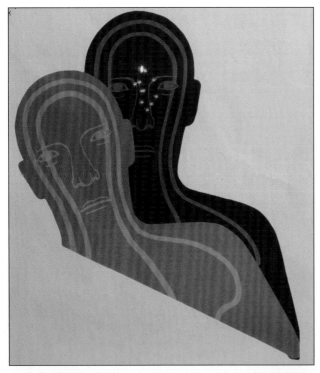

◀ Our best group in our lights and lasers test session was achieved using the Sig Sauer P229 with the LaserMaxLMS-2281 guide rod installed. With the range brightly lit, all ten shots were landed in rapid fire with the gun held below eye level, elbows bent gently hugging the rib cage in a variation of a compressed-ready stance. This showed that laser-equipped pistols can be shot accurately without the necessity of raising the gun from a commonly used search position.

from the start position. Throughout our timed drills, with both the light and the laser units illuminated, all of the shots were taken with the arms pulled into a lock position, elbows almost hugging the rib cage, and the eyes looking over the gun at the target. This replicated near-ready, or as some call it, the compressed ready position that in daylight could be considered the basis of a search-and-scan position.

One last test was performed firing the Glock 30SF with Lasermax guide rod and weapon-mounted light. In this test, the shooter simulated firing from an awkward position of cover for the sake of presenting as little target as possible to incoming fire. Reaching around the right side of a barricade with only one hand holding the pis-

▶ By mounting a light and laser, we were able to shoot more effectively from awkward positions, even when one hand was disabled. Here, the shooter is shown clutching his off hand to his chest to prevent the arm from introducing a pendulum effect that can interfere with the aiming process, especially in recovery from recoil.

▶ Firing from an awkward position with a handheld light is difficult. But in combination with a laser-equipped pistol, you needn't be concerned with several key factors. The amount of light splashed on to the sights becomes irrelevant and so does sight alignment altogether. In fact, the gun may be fired accurately from any position you can manage. This adds up to faster, more accurate shooting in conditions that would make normal procedures difficult or impossible to perform. *Photo by R. Eckstine*

tol and no more of the shooter's dominant eye than was necessary to aim the laser, three-shot strings of fire were delivered to a target placed seven yards down range. The left hand was brought tightly into the chest for the purpose of avoiding any sort of pendulum effect from rocking the body upon recoil. Total elapsed times averaged 3.09 seconds and more than half the shots landed on the hostage taker's silhouette.

Every system of fire has advantages, yet every system has shortcomings, too. First and foremost to electronic devices is maintaining power. Today's batteries, lights, and laser units do offer much greater staying power, and the units themselves typically draw less energy than earlier models. But if you are the type of person who never cleans their gun or services their magazines, then maybe you are not likely to replace batteries on schedule, either.

Using a handheld flashlight is also considered to be safer in reducing accidental shootings. During our dark range session, it was difficult to avoid the temptation of using the light mounted on the handgun to check handwritten notes or get a better look at the timer. If you should ever need to perform a search or

hold a position because you heard something go bump in the night, the beam of your weapon-mounted light might only find the family pet or a child who couldn't sleep. But so would the muzzle of your gun. And that would be a bad time to be startled.

Another aspect that should not be overlooked is how the laser or the light is turned on and off. In so many words, simple is better. You don't want to start confusing digits when one of them is responsible for releasing a shot.

But the greatest strength of weapon-mounted lights and lasers for defending the home should not be taken lightly. Very few shooting positions from cover are going to be ideal. Inside the home, you may be setting up from behind a doorframe or forced to shoot from an awkward prone position lying sideways behind a bed. Getting the eyes behind the gun for an accurate shot and then continuing to support the gun for repeat fire can be almost impossible and cause overexposure beyond the point of reliable cover. Of all the positives and negatives related to weapon-mounted lights and lasers, the ability to acquire an effective sight picture from awkward positions of cover is their greatest asset.

BEST BETS FOR HOME DEFENSE 2013–2014

Introduction to Best Bets for Home Defense

Whenever I am asked what gun I like best the answer is likely to be whichever gun I happen to have with me. Asked what a good gun looks like I prefer to see only the target and a clear view of the front sight. But, when asked what gun is best for home defense I believe the category is then narrowed considerably. Out go my preferences for what I might bring to a pistol match, to the Trap range or on a prairie dog hunt. When choosing a gun for home defense all I am concerned with is reliability, high capacity and mobility.

Reliability means never having to think about whether or not the gun will fire each time I press the trigger. Reliability means the sights will stay locked into the desired position and the magazine will not fall out due to wear, breakage or as a result of the release lever being too prominent and making it prone to being activated by incidental contact. Reliability means that with reasonable maintenance the gun should function continuously. Reasonable maintenance means cleaning and lubrication plus proper attention paid to the condition of the magazines. You should always have more than enough magazines, (three per gun would be the minimum). One to remain loaded inside the gun and another one loaded for when the first magazine is empty. Or, to replace the first magazine should it fall out of place or otherwise malfunction. The third magazine should be stored empty so that the magazine spring has the opportunity to relax and regain any strength it may have lost from being compressed. Although it only takes a couple of days for the spring to regain its resilience magazines should be rotated monthly, in my view.

But, the key to running any semi-automatic weapon is the ammunition you choose. Understandably, it is less expensive to practice with full metal jacket ammunition but your home or personal defense gun should be tested regularly for its ability to fire hollow point rounds or what ever round you intend to rely on. If you do in fact practice primarily with ammunition other than your defense rounds then 50 to 100 rounds of your defensive ammunition shot twice a year should provide an adequate test to determine its reliability. If you find a specific type of defensive round that performs well in your gun it would be worth your money to stock up on it so you do not have to retest the gun every time you replace ammunition.

In terms of (high) capacity I prefer that a home defense gun hold approximately 15 rounds of ammunition or more. A friend of mine relates a story where his personal security detail needed to move from behind their vehicles to inside a small cottage in Zimbabwe before being shot by pursuers who were trying to stop them. The answer was to leap frog or, take turns delivering suppressive fire to cover one another as they moved from one position of cover to another on the way to safety. My friend was armed with a very high capacity 9mm pistol and his partner had an 8+1 shot 45. The 9mm pistol could be heard firing continuously but the report from the 45 repeatedly cut short well before my friend was able to make it to his next point of cover. When they finally reached safety my friend asked, "Why does your gun keep breaking?" "It's not broken. I had to reload," was his answer.

In some states it is illegal to purchase or even possess magazines with a capacity greater than 10 or in some cases as little as 7 rounds. The ability to enforce such laws retroactively has yet to be tested but let's address this problem in its worst-case scenario. Be ready to

▲ The most common scenario is to have only one firearm at your immediate disposal and be limited to the amount of ammunition that is already loaded into the weapon. But, if you have an audible alarm system, be it canine, electronic or simply enough fences or doors to make forced entry a noisy affair you may have time to access spare ammunition. Especially if it organized on a rigid belt that can be quickly buckled around your waist. The rig in this picture is set up with spare ammunition for 12 gauge shotgun as well as for pistol. The shotgun shell holders are by California Competition Works.

▲ Extra magazines are best carried in a belt-mounted pouch on the side of your body opposite to your primary shooting hand. But it's a good idea to practice shooting while holding a spare magazine in your support hand for when an emergency forces you to access the weapon and retain a spare magazine without the benefit of tactical gear. Remarkably powerful the .357Sig Sig Sauer P239 semi-automatic pistol is compact, easy to handle and its 7 round magazine makes it New York legal.

▲ If the defender in this picture needs more than the 7 rounds of .357 Magnum he can perform a New York reload by dropping the empty gun and drawing his other Smith & Wesson 686 Plus. Albeit not concealed this is but one example of how to legally carry 14 rounds of ammunition in the Empire state.

reload or transition to a second gun. Keep a loaded magazine next to your defense gun and practice picking up the gun with one hand and the spare magazine with the other. Place the magazine in a pocket right away and devote both hands to the gun. No pockets available? Keep a belt with quick buckle and magazine pouches close by.

Hopefully you have an early warning system such as an audible alarm or a barking dog that will give you enough time to put the belt on. Or, practice shooting your pistol with the spare magazine integrated with your support hand grip.

One other way to get around low capacity laws is to simply have two guns. Instead of having spare magazines on your belt how about a pair of matching holsters.

Dropping an empty gun and picking up a loaded one has for some time been referred to as a "New York reload". It is ironic that New York is the very state that has actually adopted laws that dictate how many rounds a tax paying citizen is allowed to use per gun or per magazine creating a situation that may indeed force home defenders to transition to a second or even third gun.

If I were limited to only one revolver then the 8-shot Taurus and Smith and Wesson revolvers would be my

only choice. In terms of semi-automatic pistols there are some high capacity 45s I would choose but there are far more choices in calibers 9mm and 40 S&W. Whichever handgun I thought I could shoot more accurately, (specifically with only one hand by the way) would be my choice. If you want to know why I specify the ability to perform under compromise then just think worst-case scenario.

When I say that a firearm for home defense should provide mobility this is not the same feature or characteristic offered by a "carry" gun. There is no need to conceal a home defense handgun. You are not in public nor should you need to carry it specifically on your person. Home defense handguns are generally bigger so they can carry more rounds. Even 9mm polymer handguns that are remarkably light in weight when they are empty become heavy shooting irons when filled to capacity. But, increased weight can also go a long way to tame recoil so shooting multiple shots with a bigger, heavier gun is actually easier and more comfortable for the operator.

Whereas home defense handguns tend to be larger I prefer that long guns or shoulder mounted weapons be smaller. Rifles or rather carbines are shorter end to end making them easier to negotiate in tight spaces. Many carbines offer an adjustable length buttstock and 16 inches is the minimum legal barrel length for rifles. But it is possible in most states to obtain a carbine with a barrel that is shorter still. However, the barrel must then be extended to legal length with the attachment of a sound suppressor, for example. The minimum legal length for a shotgun barrel is 18 inches. Given the magazine tube rides underneath the barrel maximum capacity for the shotgun with minimum barrel length is typically 7 or 8 rounds of 2 ¾ inch long cartridges. Shotguns are intimidating weapons and loaded with buckshot or slugs the 12 gauge shotgun is a devastating weapon. But, it can also be heavy and cumbersome to use in close quarters. Shotguns chambered for 20 gauge ammunition are less effective than 12 gauge models but still offer more than adequate power. Less recoil and lighter weight makes them attractive to smaller operators. But due to the long thin shape of the 20 gauge rounds they can be more difficult to cycle and the guns themselves more difficult to reload.

The following selection of handguns, shotguns and carbines was culled from the Shooter's Bible 104th Edition which is as close to being a complete listing of currently available firearms as anyone has been able to compile. My choices were based on nothing more than each weapon's ability to deliver what I would expect to have at my disposal for the task of home defense.

Overview—Author's Picks

Handguns

Browning Hi Power 9mm Standard

The Browning Hi Power is an older design that a lot of people have forgotten about or may be totally unaware of. But long before the Glock polymer pistol fostered a revolution in design, the Hi Power successfully blended high-capacity firepower with a single-action trigger and thumb-operated safeties, both of which are huge advantages in my view. One makes the gun easier to shoot, and the other safer to handle. The Hi Power pistol is renowned for its accuracy. When the sport of practical shooting was in its infancy, the Hi Power was dominant. This is remarkable because the 9mm Hi Power competed at a disadvantage. That's because in IPSC (International Practical Shooting Conference) pistol competitions, larger caliber handguns that are more difficult to control are awarded an extra point for each shot on target that lands outside of the A-zone, which is IPSC's preferred scoring area—the bull's-eye, if you will. So, any gun chambered for a minor caliber, such as the Hi Power, had to make up the difference by being more accurate.

The Hi Power is a steel-framed pistol feeding from a double-column magazine. Also available chambered for .40 S&W ammunition, the Browning Hi Power was once the gold standard for law enforcement, as well as competition. There was a period that the Belgium-made models were superior, but today's modern manufacturing methods have greatly improved the quality of current production Browning Hi Powers. It seems ironic to refer to a pistol that has been in production for decades as a best kept secret, but this might be the case. While many of today's polymer pistols resort to offering alternate grip panels to make their guns more comfortable in the hand, the Hi Power has always been famous for its remarkably ergonomic grip.

CZ SP-01, CZ SP-O1 Shadow Target, and CZ TS Czechmate

The CZ SP and TS series pistols are based on the model 75, which is an all-steel pistol made in—where else—the Czech Republic. (But this design goes back to when that country was referred to as Czechoslovakia.) One thing that has remained consistent is the quality of Czech steel, which is absolutely robust. The CZ

75 is an original design that is currently being copied by several manufacturers, so you will find CZ clones. Unique features include frame rails that reach up and over enveloping the slide rails. CZ feels this design makes the action less impervious to dirt and debris. The trigger on the CZ pistols operates in both single and double action. Load the chamber by retracting the slide and the hammer stays back. Thumb-operated safeties found on both sides of the frame can then be raised to lock the hammer back and make the gun safe to carry or store. Or the hammer can be lowered manually or by a decocker, depending upon the individual model. Manual lowering of the hammer requires the operator to hold on to the hammer and press the trigger until it clicks. Actually, the trigger press is an abbreviated movement and in this case it could be thought of as an on/off switch. While this is safer than it might sound, CZ pistols with a mechanical decocker offer a good compromise. The decocker levers take the place of the thumb safeties and are pushed downward to drop the hammer to a safe position. Once the hammer is down, the first shot will be performed double action. This means the trigger will not only release the hammer to strike the firing pin, but will also push the hammer rearward until it is released mechanically. The enhanced models, such as the SP series, are desirable because more attention has been paid to making the trigger action—specifically during double action fire—smoother and lighter. This results in greater accuracy because it makes it easier for the shooter to keep the sights in alignment throughout the duration of the trigger press.

One of the variations to choose from in the CZ lineup is barrel length, which also affects sight radius or the distance between the front and rear sight. Shorter sight radii is faster, but a longer sight radii is easier to read, especially for older eyes as near vision becomes more of a problem. Also, notice the difference in rear sight structure. Adjustable rear sights that feature a taller, more prominent vertical blade are more prone to damage or moving out of adjustment. Another aspect of the different models is the grip panels. This is a wide gun with an ergonomic profile, but the competition models ship with a set of flat-sided grip panels. They make it easier to command the gun, especially during the first shot double action, and they can be easily installed on other models, too. Whichever model you choose, I have found that a smooth double-action trigger and the flat grip panels are the most helpful upgrades to perfecting your CZ pistol.

Glock G34Gen4 and G21Gen4

Glock pistols just plain work, especially if you do not try to modify them. Yes, there are a lot of aftermarket enhancements now available, but those are best left to the arena of competitive shooting where, just like in auto racing, the mechanics are always looking for an edge and are willing to accept failure once in a while if they can succeed in the long run. But for home or personal defense, you will not have that margin of error. If you didn't win the match this week, well, there is always the next match. Have a gun go down during an engagement with an assailant and, like the name of the book by Bill Jordan, there is *No Second Place Winner*.

You will note that my picks from the Glock lineup are each Gen4 models. Gen is short for Generation. This is a designation used to identify the institution of specific changes to the original design. To date, many of the changes from the original Glock addressed the shape and texture of the grip. But it is a subtle change to the trigger unique to the Gen4 pistols that I like best. For me, what sets the Gen4 models apart is the increased trigger feel. Serving as a test professional for almost twenty years, there have been many range sessions where more than one type of pistol was being tested on the same day. When firing for the collection accuracy data, becoming accustomed to each different trigger system was the key to success. The challenge of moving from one trigger system to another was learning to read where you were in your controlled press in relation to when the shot would break. For my part, the Glock system has not always been readable, offering less feedback than other designs. And it didn't help that there was more than one trigger assembly being shipped for Glock. The Glock New York trigger, for example, was an attempt to make the trigger safer merely by being heavier and more difficult to operate. Never mind trigger feel or feedback. When it was time to shoot, some shooters likened it to punching a wall as hard as you could. This was not very good for accuracy, which is a safety factor too, because every shot hits something even if it is not your intended target. It's

better for the gun to communicate with the shooter, and the Gen4 trigger, which is moderate in trigger pull weight, has trigger feel in droves. I have chosen the models G34 9mm and G21 .45 ACP for their sight radius, power, and high capacity.

Heckler & Koch P30 LEM

Heckler & Koch (pronounced like "Coke") offers a slightly more expensive gun but one that is unique and well thought-out. The designation LEM stands for Law Enforcement Module and refers to the trigger mechanism. However, this is not necessarily available to law enforcement personnel only. HK pistols are extremely modular and offer variations in trigger protocol to suit, ranging from full-time double action only to a DA/SA decocking system with thumb-operated safeties. The HKs are hammer-driven guns, which I like, because with the hammer down I can handle the guns administratively in or out of a holster with my thumb on the back of the hammer. This provides me with an early warning system. If anything should press on the trigger, the hammer will begin to move and tell me to stop and inspect the pistol.

The HK design offers a unique magazine release system. The lower rear portion of the trigger guard includes a set of paddles on each side that release the magazine when pressed. This makes it almost impossible to accidentally release the magazine. The trigger guard itself is oversized, making the trigger more accessible even when gloves are worn. In addition, the base of the grip panels are indented, so if a magazine becomes stuck in place, it is easier to grab it and rip it from the frame. HK pistols were designed for military use, and they have proven to be reliable and accurate. The P30 series is not only one of the best looking polymer pistols you can buy, but it also comes with three sets of grip panels and back straps so you can customize the grip to fit your hands.

Para USA Black Ops 14.45

Para Ordnance was the first manufacturer to be successful offering high-capacity pistols that operate with the Browning 1911 design. Para Ordnance pistols took the practical shooting world by storm by offering more rounds per magazine so competitors could post faster times simply by not having to reload as many times during the match. Originally based in Canada, they have since moved to North Carolina and, after a recent restructure, they offer both single-stack and high-capacity 1911 style pistols. Now known as Para USA, the model 14.45 can be loaded with a total of fifteen rounds of .45 ACP. The .40 S&W models of this pistol will hold a maximum of seventeen rounds and when chambered for 9mm ammunition, maximum capacity is listed at nineteen rounds.

The trade off to obtain higher capacity by way of feeding from a double stack, or staggered column mag (one round on top of another, slightly offset), is additional width at the grip. This was more of an issue in Para's first offerings. Thanks to today's metals and machining techniques, the frames that surround the double column magazines are minimal in width. Certainly no more than the polymer pistols that have become so much more common since Para Ordnance arrived on the scene.

The big advantage to the 1911 style pistol is its precise trigger and safety features, such as a grip safety that must be depressed by the palm in order for the gun to fire. Also, ambidextrous thumb operated safeties that do not require the shooter to shift the gun away from the shooting grip, providing a veritable on/off switch.

Ruger SR9C and SR40

The Ruger SR series pistols work from double-column magazines, so maximum capacity is greatly enhanced. Use of fiberglass-filled nylon to construct the frame has allowed Ruger to create a pistol as thin as the original 1911, which can only store seven or eight rounds in a single vertical column magazine. The SR series pistols also offer ambidextrous thumb safeties and an indicator that pops up when the chamber is loaded. The indicator allows the operator to check the condition of the pistol by running a finger across the top of the slide. This could be useful in reduced light or in a situation where you can't afford to take your sights off line from an area of threat.

The SR9 and SR40 pistols (chambered for 9mm and .40 S&W respectively), are full-sized service pistols. The SR9C and SR40C have shorter barrels, but also shorter grips, too. Yet, the SR compacts are one of the few such pistols I would consider as a first choice for home defense. That's because the compact models will accept longer, higher capacity magazines reliably when fit with the proper adapter to extend the surface of the grip. This means you could carry the compact model concealed in a holster or purse and then replace the shorter magazine with the full size component for around the house and at night.

Sig Sauer P226

The P226 is the flagship full-size pistol from Sig Sauer. The Texas Department of Public Safety has chosen the P226 for their state troopers, and some of the more recently commissioned Texas Rangers have adopted this pistol, as well. The P226 pistols of the Texas DPS are chambered for .357Sig ammunition. This caliber was designed to replicate the stopping power of the .357 Magnum service revolver in a higher capacity semi-automatic pistol. Driving a 125-grain bullet about 1400 fps, this combination nearly achieves this goal, and its stopping power is far better than its commercial popularity would indicate. Detractors say that it's too loud in report, but I like it because it packs tremendous shock on impact and thirteen rounds of .357Sig weighs about as much as nine rounds of 230 grain 45 ACP and about the same as thirteen rounds of less powerful 9mm ammunition.

There are several different models of P226, but most of them differ only in color, finish, or grips. The model P229 is a more compact version and offers the same maximum capacity as the P226. But in my experience, the P226 is easier to shoot due to its increased sight radius and less muzzle flip.

Besides choice in caliber and finish, the P226 is available with four different trigger systems. They are traditional double action (DA/SA), double action Kellerman (DAK), single action only (SAO), or enhanced short return trigger (SRT). Standard and least expensive is the DA/SA. This means the first shot is fired after a longer and heavier trigger pull than the shots that follow. That's because the first pull has to move the trigger rearward as well as release it. Subsequent shots are made with the trigger beginning further to the rear inside the trigger guard and the hammer remains cocked having been set by rearward movement of the slide. The advantage of this system is that after the first shot is fired, the trigger is extremely easy to manipulate and accuracy and cycling speed are greatly increased.

A decocker lever on the left side of the pistol is used to return the hammer to a safe down position. DAK was developed to provide the same double-action trigger pull for every shot and avoid the complication of a transition. The trigger stroke is, however, shorter in length than the double action that begins the firing sequence on the DA/SA model. The SAO system means the hammer stays to the rear when the chamber is loaded and a thumb safety is used to lock it into place. The trigger stroke is short and light, serving only to drop the hammer. The SRT system improves the double-action pull in the DA/SA sequence and makes the transition to single action much easier to discern. It also reduces the distance and time it takes for the trigger to travel to the point where is reset to fire. No matter which system you choose, the Sig Sauer pistols are durable, accurate, and reliable.

It was not long ago that Sig Sauer pistols were priced higher than many other handguns. Sig Sauer pricing has not really changed, but it is remarkable how much the cost of other pistols has risen, putting many more pistols in its price range. But Sig Sauer is still a cut above many other choices.

Smith & Wesson Revolvers
M327 Night Guard, M327 TRR8,
and M627/M&P R8 Pistols
M&P9JG and M&P357

When the Smith & Wesson M&P pistols entered the market, they distinguished themselves primarily by offering superior ergonomics as well as high capacity. Prior to this, most polymer pistols were renowned for having take it or leave it accommodations for the hand that forced shooters to look past their strange grips to benefit from their high capacity. The M&P was also among the first to introduce alternate grip panels so that the size and shape of the frame exterior could be changed to suit different sized hands. Since their introduction Smith & Wesson has improved the overall performance of the M&P series. But, from the very beginning the M&P pistols were easy guns to learn how to shoot. First-time shooters will take to this design very quickly.

Thanks to Smith & Wesson's participation in the shooting sports, most notably ICORE (the International Conference of Revolver Enthusiasts), the modern 8-shot revolver was developed for the practical shooting competitor. The M327 Night Guard is a short-barreled revolver in the snubbed-nosed tradition. Thanks to its scandium alloy frame it weighs less than steel framed models making it a good candidate for concealed carry as well as home defense. The downside to this is however that its ultra-light weight allows the gun to recoil quite a bit. One answer is to have the barrel ported by experts in the field such as MagNaPort. Magnaporting produces an instant transformation to a flat shooting gun but can also make the gun exponentially louder and unattractive for indoor use. Another answer is to keep the gun loaded with 38Special rather than comparatively volcanic .357Magnum rounds. My favorite 38Special loads are frangible rounds from MagSafe. MagSafe loads a hollow-point bullet with small BBs affixed in epoxy. Even the standard pressure 38 Special Defender rounds from MagSafe deliver devastating blows without over-penetration that can push a missed shot from one room to another.

The 327 TRR8 is another eight-shooter that is built on a scandium frame, but its five-inch barrel puts the weight right where you need it to make the gun more controllable and comfortable to shoot. The M&P R8 takes this gun further into the tactical world by offering a Picatinny accessory rail to the underlug. (The underlug is the mass below the barrel.) The model 627 is Smith & Wesson's original stainless steel framed eight-shooter. The 627 weighs the most of all the eight-shot revolvers and shoots the softest. All of the eight-shot revolvers can be loaded using a full moon clip, a circular bracket that holds all eight rounds in place aligned with the individual chambers. This makes ejecting and reloading much quicker. One additional advantage to using a revolver for home defense is that the gun will fire any round that can be fit into the chamber and reliability will not be affected by leaving the gun loaded indefinitely.

Springfield Armory XDM and XDM Compact

The XDM polymer pistols are Americanized versions of the Springfield Armory XD pistol, which came to the Geneseo, Illinois, manufacturer's attention after years of service as the pistol used by the Croatian police. This is a striker fired pistol that offers good ergonomics and has an added safety feature. The grip safety is a lever that must be depressed by the web of the shooter's hand for the gun to fire. This feature remains unique to striker fired pistols and is especially helpful during reholstering. With the operator's thumb pushing down on the rear of the slide as the gun enters the holster, the grip safety remains untouched so that any incidental contact with the trigger, such as snagging on a shirttail, will not result in the gun firing accidentally.

I refer to the XDM series as being Americanized because its reshaped grip mimics the ergonomics of the Browning 1911, a pistol that is unique and decidedly American. But, the biggest advantage the XDM pistol has over the original XD is that during field stripping the trigger need not be pressed to remove the slide from the frame. The XDM also comes with three full sets of grip panels to adapt the pistol to a variety of different size hands.

The Compact XDM pistols are nothing more than the full size pistol with a shorter grip. But all of the XDM Compact pistols ship with a full-length magazine and grip extension that restores not only full capacity but completes the grip frame, as well. One characteristic to pay attention to, especially when operating with the compact magazine, is that the grip safety must be compressed in order to operate the slide manually, such as during the process of loading the chamber. But, thanks to perhaps the best trigger of all striker fired handguns, the XD/XDM series pistols are among the easiest and fastest guns to learn to shoot accurately.

Steyr Arms C9-A1 and M40-A1

If this were a music awards column, the Steyr Arms pistols would win the prize for talent deserving wider recognition. The Steyr pistols will fit most everyone's hands like a glove. And their accuracy is well above average. Grip angle and the undercut at the web of the hand enhance control and make follow up shots quick and easy. The triggers on these pistols are just the right weight. Takeup and reset after each shot is likewise very predictable. Imported from Germany to the facility in Trussville, Alabama, Steyr products are respected worldwide, but until recently were popular only among aficionados of fine weaponry.

STI Edge, Eagle, and VIP

After Para Ordnance took over the practical shooting sports with high-capacity frames married to the superior SAO Browning 1911 action, Sandy Strayer developed a modular design to achieve the same end, integrating a polymer grip frame to a metallic receiver. It has been said the polymer grip offers a degree of flex that helps soak up recoil. The result has been nearly complete dominance of a sport that scores its competitors in an equation of accuracy and speed. But, today the STI modular 2011 pistols offer race car, or rather race gun, performance for self-defense, as well as competitive shooting. Capacity remains high in the full-size models, as well as the VIP. The Edge, thanks to a full-length dust cover, is the heaviest and should make for a superb pistol for home protection. The Eagle is somewhat lighter and could serve as a duty weapon, as well as for home defense. The VIP utilizes a shorter barrel and could be considered a high-capacity version of Colt's famous Commander sized 1911. But when chambered for 9mm or .40 S&W, its maximum capacity is considerably more.

Taurus 608, Pistol 24/7 G2, and 809

The Taurus 608 revolvers are big, steel-framed guns. Only the Taurus Raging Bull series is larger overall. But this makes the 608 comfortable to shoot with even the most ferocious .357 Magnum ammunition. The barrel is ported, but the Taurus system adds less to the noise of each shot than other porting configurations, so indoor use is not much louder than other non-ported revolvers. The cylinder is not machined to accept moon clips, but a number of gunsmithing houses will provide this service.

The Taurus 24/7 G2 series is reasonably priced and offers comfortable ergonomics, an accessory rail for light or laser, and thumb-operated safeties. Maximum capacity for the 9mm pistol is eighteen rounds, despite the gun being relatively compact. The .40-caliber model holds sixteen rounds. The trigger on the 24/7 G2 pistols operates in the DA/SA pattern similar to the Sig Sauer. The trigger of the model 809 series pistol is more straightforward. Designed to compete for a military contract, it features one pattern of short double-action trigger pull making the 809 easy to master. One added benefit is the ambidextrous thumb-operated safeties and low-mount sights that provide an excellent sight picture.

Shotguns

Pump

Benelli Nova Pump Tactical

In stock form, the Nova Pump shotgun carries only 4+1 rounds but that can be easily increased with an aftermarket magazine extension. In the mean-time, the Nova can chamber 3- and 3½-inch shells, as well as the more common 2¾-inch variety. The Tactical model actually differs little from the hunting or field version, save for the addition of ghost ring or notch and post rifle sights. While tritium ghost ring sights are also an option, ghost ring sights put the line of sight well above the bore. The standard rifle sights sit much lower and help prevent the problem of shooting from behind cover and clearing all obstructions. Frankly, some tacticians swear by rifle sights and others say having to align sights slows them down. Traditional methodology tells us if the shotgun is properly fit, no sights are indeed necessary to put shot where you point the gun. So the question becomes should you spend extra for the Tactical model. Here is one good reason to buy it. Given, the stock is synthetic and difficult to remodel to specific length or cast, the rifle sights may be the best choice overall. By relying on the sights, precise fit to the individual shooter as would be necessary when firing the field model, becomes less critical. Overall, the Nova pump is a smooth operating versatile shotgun.

Ithaca Model 37 Defense Synthetic

In the book *Point Man*, the biography of a founding member of the U.S. Navy SEALS by James Watson and the brilliant modern military historian Kevin Dockery, Chief James "Patches" Watson recounts his time in the Vietnam War. Watson's favorite weapon was an Ithaca Model 37 with a sawed off wooden stock. Watson's account of one particular confrontation, wherein he reloaded and fired single shots repeatedly at close range, is absolutely breathtaking. Having spent time with the Ithaca model 37, albeit in trap gun configuration, the design of Ithaca bottom eject system should take some credit in assisting Chief Watson. Indeed, on a flight where he was supposed to fly unarmed, he refused to give up his Ithaca and the crew ulti-

mately had to bow to his wishes. Today, the bottom eject remains unique and the light-weight, bare bones model 37 Defense Synthetic remains a formidable weapon that one might consider as a piece of history.

Mossberg 500 Tri Rail Tactical and 590A1 Adjustable Tactical Tri-Rail 9-Shot

Both the 500 and 590 series shotguns from Mossberg offer two very helpful features. First, the safety is located on the tang, the area atop the stock directly within reach of the shooter's thumb on the primary hand. This makes it possible to operate the safety quickly and not interfere with the shooting grip. Many feel this is better than a cross-bolt safety operated by the trigger finger, but others say that this tempts the lazy shooter to leave his or her trigger finger inside the trigger guard when there is no need for it to be there. Personally, I agree with the former rather than latter. Another positive aspect is that the trigger finger is relieved from the chore of unlocking the slide. The slide release is located directly behind the trigger guard so that the inside edge of the middle finger has immediate access to unlock the slide whether you are right handed or left handed.

The 590A1 was developed specifically for military trials and the result of such military testing was that the 590A1 was the only shotgun that stood up the abuse heaped upon it and kept on running. The 590A1 was used extensively by the military in Middle Eastern urban warfare as a breeching tool well before other shotguns were designed specifically for this purpose. Having become known as the skeleton key, the 590A1 differs from the model 500 series in terms of construction. Whereas the Moss 500 was designed as a general purpose field shotgun for civilian use, the 590A1 is much sturdier and heavier built. Having put thousands of rounds through the 590A1 I can attest that it is a tank of a machine that is amazingly reliable requiring almost no maintenance.

Remington 870 Express and 870 Express Tactical

The beauty of the Remington 870 is that you can purchase the fanciest tactical model or the least expensive base model and, thanks to a wealth of aftermarket parts, build whatever you want. The wood stock can be easily cut and modified. Both the wood and synthetic stocks are simple to mount with bias left, right, up, or down. Magazine tube extension kits and spare parts are easy to find. If you want to leave it beneath the bed in case of emergency, mount the short barrel. If you decide to go bird hunting, deer hunting, or trap shooting, just mount the proper barrel or change the choke. Whereas most pump action shotguns are just as versatile, the range of key components readily available for the 870 is astounding. Not long ago the 870 was a competitive trap shooting gun. I know first-hand that first rate used trap and skeet barrels can be purchased on the internet that you can slap on to your home defense gun in less than a minute, go to the range, and shoot a perfect score. Sights and scope mounts are also available, making the 870 possibly the most versatile all-around weapon available today.

Winchester Super X Pump Defender

The Winchester Super X Pump or SXP shotguns distinguish themselves by offering fast pump action. The slide is light short and heavily ribbed. The actual distance necessary to work the slide is somewhat shorter than other pump-action shotguns. This can certainly make a big difference in a confrontation. In addition, Winchester has contoured the stock and pistol grip to offer maximum control, adding to shooter confidence.

The SXP Extreme Defender adds an AR15 style adjustable-length butt stock and ghost ring sights. In addition, the receiver is topped with a Picatinny rail for mounting a scope. Like the Remington and Mossberg pump-action shotguns, a corrosion-resistant finished marine model is available. In this case, the coating is hard chrome. This can be an asset aboard ship but highly reflective surfaces can be a liability, especially during a confrontation in low-light conditions where concealment and deception are key tools for survival.

Semi-automatic

Benelli M4 Tactical

The Benelli M4 may be as close to the gold standard for tactical shotguns as you can get. The M4 series is a gas-operated shotgun, unlike the M2 series, which is recoil-operated. The M4, like the legendary Super 90 that came before it, offers an extremely fast cycling speed with greatly reduced recoil, making quick target to target transitions possible.

CZ 712 Utility

The CZ 712 utility is just that. A bare bones gas-operated 12-gauge shotgun selling for a reasonable price. Having spent time with the 712, I was impressed with how fast and smoothly it would cycle. And, despite the most minimal of recoil pads, the 712 transferred surprisingly little impact to the shooter. In tests with a shot-recording timer, the 712 was found to deliver multiple shots faster and with less felt recoil than the other shotguns I was testing that week, despite the lack of specialized equipment or a fancy name. All I would add to the CZ 712 would be a magazine tube extension kit. In subsequent tests, the 20-gauge version of this shotgun, the CZ 720, proved to be reliable and accurate, as well. If there's a best buy in the shotgun category, the CZ 712 and CZ 720 are strong contenders.

Mossberg SPX Pistol Grip/SPX 8-Shot

Mossberg has always had an image of providing a good product of consistent reliability at a fair price, but in recent years they have jumped into the competitive shooting market. Not in trap or skeet, mind you, but into the speed shooting or pseudo-tactical world of competitive shooting. Just before they jumped in with both feet by hiring the Legendary Three-Gun shooter Jerry Miculek (and family), they released an eight-shot semi-automatic with ghost ring sights for the tactical market (the 930 Tactical). The 930 was actually quite good and proved fully reliable. But the latest special purpose shotguns in the SPX category are an improvement over the 930. Mossberg reliability has always been solid, but thanks to input from professional speed shooters, attributes like cycling speed and handling continue to improve.

Weatherby SA-459 TR

A lot of good shotguns are coming out of factories in Turkey, and the Weatherby shotguns are no exception. Gas-operated with an oversized bolt the SA-459 is an easy shotgun to operate. Its length of pull is more than I typically like, but with the ghost ring sights in place or a red dot scope mounted on the provided Picatinny rail eye relief and natural alignment are not critical. The eighteen-inch barrel is extended about two inches by attachment of a removable ported choke. A lot of tactical shotguns are fit with barrels that are not threaded but simply contoured for cylinder bore or improved cylinder constriction. I like to make my own choices and, provided you are not satisfied with the stock component, top-quality aftermarket chokes can make a big difference. Integrating the sling swivel with the magazine cap is another small feature that is a big plus in my view.

Carbines

Armalite AR-10T Carbine and SPR Model 1 LE Carbine

If you have ever wondered what the letters AR mean, they stand for Armalite Rifle. In civilian form, the .223 Remington (or 5.56mm) Armalite Rifles are referred to as AR15s. The same design on a slightly larger scale built to chamber .308 Winchester (or 7.62X51mm NATO) ammunition is designated the AR10. When it comes to carbines, I like to stay with a sixteen-inch barrel or shorter to enhance maneuverability. The option of firing the larger ordnance in a small package is what makes the AR10 attractive. If I had property to defend aside from just a suburban plot or home interior, the AR10 would offer more power at an extended range. It also would be more effective against a vehicle that might be coming up the road to my house. But, the Model 1 LE is an excellent handling rifle because its minimal weight and well thought-out rail system leaves plenty of room for mounting iron sights, optics, lasers, and lights.

Arsenal MTK90 Jubiliee AK-47

The AK-47 is an imported weapon known the world over for power and reliability. Originally a select-fire weapon, civilian versions are limited to semi-automatic fire. The long trigger pull is, in my opinion, better suited to full-auto fire than one press, one shot, semi-automatic fire. Nevertheless these stamped steel guns can be as robust as they are crude. Quality can vary but Arsenal imports some of the best AKs and companies like Timbersmith can provide enhanced wood stocks or furniture, as is the popular terminology. AK-47s typically run well on surplus 7.62X39mm ammunition and, in some cases, more reliably than when loaded with the latest commercial ammunition. Since these guns are imported, their availability may be in jeopardy due to the passing of prohibitive gun laws.

Benelli MR1

The MR1 was designed for military trials seeking to replace the M16, which is the military version of the AR15 rifle. As such, it feeds from the same magazines you may already own for your AR15. The gas-operated recoil system is the same one used on the M4 shotgun. This is the A.R.G.O or Auto Regulating Gas Operated system with rotating bolt. The MR1 has a synthetic stock and pistol grip that offer the same profile of the M4. It has both a ghost ring or military-style aperture sight system and a Picatinny rail for optics. The MR1 may not have been able to replace the M16 but it's a really fun gun to shoot.

Bushmaster .308 ORC, ACR Basic Folder, MOE Gas Piston Carbine, and Quad Rail Patrolman's Carbine A3

The Bushmaster ORC, Optics Ready Carbines, chambered for either .308 or .223 offers a trim basic platform ready to add your choice of optic. I like 1-4X variable power scopes because they do not rely on battery power and a 1X magnification reticle is very fast and accurate from a few feet to fifty or one hundred yards, depending on the size of the target. Such variable power scopes are sometimes marketed as shotgun scopes meant to be fit on to slug-shooting shotguns, for the purpose of hunting deer. This guarantees that they are rugged, because if they can handle a shotgun blast, they can stand up to rifle fire. Prices for this type of scope range from in prices from about eighty to four hundred dollars.

The MOE gas piston carbines are said to run longer without cleaning and also shoot with less heat and back draft towards the shooter. This is true to some degree but what I really like about the Bushmaster MOE carbines is the exterior components by MagPul. These include the sure-locking adjustable buttstock, the ergonomic pistol grip and the comfortable fore end that offers several options for adding Picatinny rails for the attachment of lights and lasers.

The Quad rail Patrolman's carbine is a hard use working man's carbine. There is no play in the fore end and, as much as I like carry handles for picking up the weapon quickly or protecting the integrity of the rear sight, I also like having the option of removing it to mount a long distance scope.

The ACR Adaptive Combat Rifle basic folder was built to compete for a military contract that valued modular versatility. This model has a folding stock. To date, the ACR lineup remains underappreciated by the buying public. Do most people need modularity extending to quick replacement of the barrel for caliber change? Well, I may not be an operator arriving in an urban combat zone in the Middle East carrying a carbine that makes me look like any other Marine, but I have a longer .308 barrel tucked away for more specialized countersniper work. Then again, I wouldn't want to waste. 30 caliber ammo on prairie dogs at Hoffman's Rifle Ranch in South Dakota, either. But I might want to switch out from .223 to hunt bigger game on the same hunting trip. If you're bored with your AR15 and can't think of another way to customize it, the ACR will get you noticed.

Colt LE901-16S and Match Target

Match rifles usually operate from a barrel measuring twenty inches or more in length. And indeed the Colt Match Target is available with a twenty inch barrel, but I would like to take advantage of what this construction has to offer with the optional sixteen inch barrel in place. I like the collapsible iron sights and full A4 flat top design. Also, for indoor work a non-threaded barrel can be a little less disconcerting as it pushes all the bullet debris and gas forward. I realize that most people say a flash hider is necessary to reduce the blinding flash of each shot, but this is not always the case as per choice of ammunition.

The LE901-16S is another example of a .308 carbine offering extra punch at extended range without being cumbersome. In addition this carbine offers ambidextrous controls so the safety, magazine release, and bolt catch can be operated from either side.

DPMS Panther Lite 16 and Compact Hunter

The Panther Lite 16 is another high-quality standard design AR15 that will get the job done. Think of it as a Leatherman tool. Its light weight makes it highly maneuverable and it's not as tiring to shoot standing unsupported. Especially if you spend all day at the range training in shoot and move scenarios.

The Compact Hunter with SOPMOD (B5 Systems Special Operations Peculiar Modification) is a very good example of a compact AR10 style carbine. I find it most desirable for a number of features and characteristics. I like the carbon fiber hand guard fore end because it is smooth and won't catch on anything I brace the gun on. Also, the carbon fiber will not transmit heat like the aluminum hand guards. The handguard is hard mounted and won't shift as they surround the free-floated barrel. The rail on the top strap is all I'll need for attaching an optic and the barrel is just hefty enough to help fight recoil without attaching a compensator. I prefer the Hogue grip over other such products, and it comes standard. I might opt for a railed gas block, however, so I can attach folding iron sights front and rear. In fact, I might prefer a set of low mount sights instead of a scope after all. DPMS has a good reputation for installing variations and upgrades to existing models for a fair price so this shouldn't be a problem at all.

FNH FNAR Standard and SCAR 16S & 17S

FNH offers two very distinctive carbines. The FNAR Standard is likely so named because its layout is based on a standard straight rifle stock but with a couple of appealing variations. The FNAR features a synthetic stock with raised Monte Carlo style comb and vertical pistol grip. The comb itself can be offset to accommodate left and right handed shooters or make room for gear, such as ballistic MOLLE vests worn by operators in the field. The technology used to adjust the comb was borrowed from the competition shotguns produced by FN's stateside affiliate Browning of Morgan, Utah. The fore end of the stock is fitted with picatinny rails on the underside, at 3 o'clock and at 9 o'clock, as well as offering sling studs front and rear. The receiver has a scope mount that stretches a long way so there is plenty of room for plenty of options. Operation is semi-automatic and chamberings include .308 Winchester and 7.62X51mm NATO. In my tests, this was a rewarding weapon to shoot when fit with either the twenty inch fluted or twenty inch heavy barrel. That this weapon is now available with a sixteen-inch long heavy barrel is very exciting.

The SCAR is another one of the full-bodied modular weapons designed for military use. It has several interesting features including adjustable length stock and even an adjustable height comb. Both these features disappear into the bodywork when not in use and the sling attachment points are cleverly unobtrusive as well. Having shot both the 17S .308 and the 16S .223 caliber SCAR weapons extensively, I can say that most people will prefer the lighter caliber. Although efficient in terms of reliability, I have always felt that when loaded with .30 caliber ammunition, the system was performing dutifully but was not in any way enjoyable to shoot. Barreled for .223, the SCAR platform really comes alive. If both the Armalite Rifle and the SCAR system had been made available at the same time way back when, we might all be shooting the SCAR 16S instead of the AR15.

HK MR556A1

Long before the shortage of AR15 magazines or .223 ammunition the steel-bodied magazines produced by Heckler & Koch were in demand and hoarded at every opportunity. Many of the policeman I was acquainted with owned more than one brand of magazine, but only the HK magazines were trusted to stay loaded at the ready in the magazine wells of their carbines for an extended period of time. Such is the quality of HK products, which are, for the most part, actual military weapons made available for the commercial market. While not an exact definition, the term MilSpec can be described as meaning within specifications delineated by the United States Military to meet rigorous technical and physical demands. And yet the term MilSpec is at times thrown around carelessly. The 556A1 may not offer extraordinary features but the execution of the design is in my view far above average.

LWRC International M6A2 SPR IC and M6 IC

LWRC International is another manufacturer of AR15 style weapons that sets the bar high and delivers. They specialize in carbines and rifles that operate with a short stroke piston rather than gas impingement designs. A two position gas valve offers enough adjustment so that the weapon will cycle with any choice of ammunition and continue to operate in the most extreme conditions, clean or fouled. The SPR (the acronym associated with the term special purpose rifle) is nonetheless a carbine as defined by its 16.1-inch barrel. The M6 IC, (individual carbine) has a slightly shorter barrel but is augmented with an extended flash hider. Both models are built to reflect the requirements of the United States Military Individual Carbine

program and provide ambidextrous operation of all controls, including bolt catch and release, safeties, and magazine release.

Rock River Arms LAR-PDS and LAR 6.8 Coyote Carbine

Rock River Arms is a quality manufacturer. The LAR-PDS is appealing because the fore end or rather the hand guard surface favors the human hand over attachment of accessories. Although a tri-rail hand guard (with skeletonized Picatinny spec rails at 3 o'clock, 6 o'clock, and 9 o'clock) is available there is also enough room on the top rail to attach components that can ride side saddle, putting them directly in front of your support hand without obscuring the sights. Whereas most of today's AR15s feature an adjustable length stock the LAR-PDS goes one step further with a hinge that allows the buttstock to be folded completely out of the way, making the carbine much easier to transport. PDS stands for Piston Driven System.

The Rock River Coyote Carbine offers a sleek profile barrel with a Smith Vortex flash hider that adds a measure of recoil control, and the flat-top design with railed gas block that I favor. Chambered to launch a slightly bigger bullet, (6.8 SPC II) this is essentially a varmint hunting rifle with the added mobility of a carbine length barrel. Note the oversized trigger guard that can speed acquisition especially when wearing cold weather or work type gloves.

Ruger Mini Thirty

As much as I like the .223 Remington Mini 14, especially in its original straight-stock configuration, I think this platform really comes alive when chambered for 7.62X39mm .30-caliber ammunition. Somehow, from laden weight to recoil impulse, it seems to me that this was the result that the designer had in mind from the very beginning. Maybe that's because its roots are in the .30-caliber M1A battle rifle. Ruger also makes a good piston drive AR15 series, but the Mini Thirty makes for a really good ranch or truck rifle that is affordable and a natural for home defense.

Sig Sauer 516 Patrol

When Sig Sauer, (then Sigarms) first offered an AR15 style carbine in the United States, it included an ambidextrous safety and gas-piston design. I felt the gas-piston system made the gun top heavy and it seemed like I was dealing first with recoil from ignition and then more distraction from movement of the piston. Also, the right side safety dug into my knuckles, not necessarily interfering with my trigger press but it was uncomfortable and distracting. My reaction was hey, just make an AR15 at Sig's usual high level of quality and I'll be happy. The 516 series does just that. It still has the gas-piston system but now there's a four position gas regulator to temper and balance movement from the piston according to how much gas it needs to operate. There are other choices in the Sig Sauer lineup but the 516 Patrol is my favorite.

Smith & Wesson M&P 15T and M&P 15-22

Since jumping in to the AR15 market, Smith & Wesson has come a long way in terms of features and quality. Little things, such as numbers on the railed hand guard, help you find and retain the proper eye relief for optics and the best placement for a light or laser system. In addition, I prefer its single-stage trigger to slower two-stage designs. The 15T also has a folding stock by Magpul, one of several quality suppliers that Smith & Wesson has teamed up with to produce good weaponry.

The Smith & Wesson M&P 15-22 is not recommended for home defense. But, when it comes to a training weapon to improve you skills operating an AR15 the M&P 15-22 is too good to pass up. It is the only rimfire replica of the AR15 that operates and field strips almost exactly like a centerfire AR15. In a time when .223 ammunition has become scarce and expensive, many professional trainers are allowing students to take training courses with rimfire replicas. But, such training is only valuable if the 22 version truly offers the same operational protocol as the full-size weapon. And that is what the M&P 15-22 delivers in spades.

Springfield Armory SOCOM II

It's hard to think of a more powerful battle-proven weapon than the 7.62X51mm (.308 Winchester) M1A design. In the SOCOM II Springfield Armory has reduced barrel length to 16.25 inches and attached a rugged accessory rail system by Vltor. Two versions are available, one with the breech left open with clip guide, and the other with the top rail extending all the way back to

the rear sight with Enlarged Military Aperture, which is a fancy way of saying ghost ring. The front sight is a highly visible .125-inch post by XS Sights treated to a lively Tritium insert. The top rail has a trough in its center to make sure you can see the line of sight that is actually quite low in relation to the center of the bore. Feeding from ten or twenty round steel bodied magazines but much easier to handle than its ten pounds of weight would suggest this is one of the most reliable and very likely the most overpowering carbine you can buy.

Steyr AUG and A3 SA USA

Not everyone can become accustomed to spent brass being ejected in the vicinity of their right shoulder, but the AUG design shrinks overall length so that the entire weapon reaches little further than your support hand. As you can tell, this weapon is best for right-handed shooters. Its forte is cycling speed and its ability to make you and your AUG a small package able to hide behind cover and move quickly. When moving about, there is much less danger of a gun takeaway because even when passing through a doorway with the gun mounted at the shoulder there just isn't that much of gun exposed beyond your grip. Despite being limited to semi-automatic fire, the sensation experienced by the AUG shooter is in my view a lot closer to the old Tommy Gun than to a more typical rifle or carbine. This is a fun gun to shoot and the Steyr AUG is probably the best production of this design currently available to the general public.

Wilson Combat Recon Tactical

The Wilson Combat Recon Tactical might not look extraordinary but the reputation for products that leave Bill Wilson's shop in Berryville, Arkansas is such that the owner is assured of a lifetime of reliable service from a high quality weapon. It might be easier to get into Fort Knox than it is for a flawed weapon to make past Wilson's quality control. Parts, such as sears and pins, may look the same but if you order a custom firearm from other shops chances are the internal parts are from Wilson's catalog of "Bullet Proof" parts. Accuracy from the Recon is at or near the top of any list. The Recon is available chambered for 6.8 SPC, 300 Blackout, and 7.62X40mmWT as well as 5.56mm ammunition.

Rifles

ARMALITE, INC. AR-10T CARBINE

Action: Semi-automatic
Stock: Synthetic
Barrel: 16 in.
Sights: Open
Weight: 8 lb. 10 oz.
Caliber: .308
Magazine: Detachable box, 10 & 20 round mags
Features: Free float handguard in black; two-stage NM trigger; flash suppressor; black case; black stock
MSRP $1914

ARMALITE, INC. AR-10T CARBINE

ARMALITE, INC. SPR MOD 1 LE CARBINE

Action: Semi-automatic, short gas system
Stock: Synthetic
Barrel: 16 in.
Sights: 3 detachable rails
Weight: 6 lb. 8 oz.
Caliber: .223, 6.8mm SPC, 7.62x39mm
Magazine: Detachable box, 30 rounds
Features: Muzzle flash suppressor; black synthetic tactical stock; aluminum handguard; tactical two-stage trigger, sling; black case
MSRP $1554

ARMALITE, INC. SPR MOD 1 LE CARBINE

ARSENAL, INC. MTK90 JUBILEE SERIES AK-74

Action: gas-operated autoloader
Stock: U.S.-made black polymer
Barrel: 16.3 in.
Sights: 1000m rear leaf sight and scope rail
Weight: 7 lb. 5 oz.
Caliber: 5.45x39.5mm
Magazine: 10-shot Russian and 30-shot Bulgarian boxes included
Features: Created to celebrate the 35th anniversary of AK-74 and the 90th anniversary of M.T. Kalashnikov; limited edition; Russian-made receiver; includes matching rifle case, gloves, and certificate
Silver Edition: $3500

ARSENAL, INC. MTK90 JUBILEE SERIES AK-74

BENELLI USA MR1

Action: A.R.G.O (Auto-Regulating-Gas-Operated)
Stock: Synthetic tactical pistol grip (ComforTech optional)
Barrel: 16 in.
Sights: Military-style aperture sights with Picatinny rail
Weight: 7 lb. 14 oz.
Caliber: .223 Rem.
Magazine: Detachable box, five shot
Features: Self-cleaning stainless piston system with gas port forward of chamber; accepts high-capacity M16 magazines; hard chrome lined barrel
MSRP . . . . $1299–$1429

BUSHMASTER FIREARMS .308 ORC

Action: Semi-automatic
Stock: Synthetic
Barrel: 16 in. (carbine), 20 in., (rifle)

Sights: None
Weight: 7 lb. 12 oz.
Caliber: .308 WIN, 7.62 NATO
Magazine: Detachable box, 20 rounds
Features: Milled gas block; heavy, chrome lined barrel; A2 Birdcage flash hider; receiver length Picatinny optics rail with two .5 in. optic raisers; heavy oval hand guards; six position telescoping stock; shipped in lockable hard case with yellow safety block; black web sling included
MSRP $1476.99

BUSHMASTER FIREARMS ACR BASIC FOLDER COMBINATION

Action: Semi-automatic
Stock: Synthetic
Barrel: 1.5 in., 14.5 in., 16.5 in.
Sights: None
Weight: N/A

Caliber: .223/5.56mm NATO to 6.8mm Rem. SPC
Magazine: 30 round PMAG
Features: Cold hammer forged barrel with melonite coating; A2 birdcage-type hider; tool-less quick-change barrel system; quick and easy multi-caliber bolt carrier assembly; free floating MIL-STD 1913 monolithic top rail for optic mounting; high-impact composite hand guard with heat shield; ambidextrous controls; composite stock comes in black or coyote.
MSRP $2490

BUSHMASTER FIREARMS MOE A-TACS M4 TYPE CARBINE

Action: Semi-automatic, pistol grip
Stock: Synthetic
Barrel: 16 in.
Sights: Magpul MSBUS rear flip sight
Weight: 6 lb. 7 oz.
Caliber: 5.56mm, .223 Rem.
Magazine: 30 round PMAG
Features: M4 profile barrel with gas piston system; receiver length Picatinny optics rail; Magpul MBUS rear flip sight; Magpul MOE adjustable buttstock with strong A-frame design; rubber buttplate; Magpul MOE vertical grip; stock available in A-TACS camo, black, Flat Dark Earth, or OD green furniture
MSRP . . . . $1181.59–$1391.48

BUSHMASTER FIREARMS QUAD RAIL A3

Action: Semi-automatic
Stock: Synthetic
Barrel: 16 in.
Sights: None
Weight: 8 lb. 5 oz.
Caliber: 5.56mm, .223 Rem.
Magazine: Detachable box, 30 rounds
Features: Chrome-lined barrel; A2 birdcage-type suppressor; free-float quad rail forend; six-position telestock for light weight and quick handling; ships with lockable hard case and yellow safety block
MSRP $1391.48

BENELLI USA MR1

BUSHMASTER FIREARMS .308 ORC

BUSHMASTER FIREARMS ACR BASIC FOLDER COMBINATION

BUSHMASTER FIREARMS MOE A-TACS M4 TYPE CARBINE

BUSHMASTER FIREARMS QUAD RAIL A3

Rifles

COLT'S MFG. LE901-16S

COLT'S MFG.
LE901-16S

Action: Semi-automatic
Stock: Combat-style, synthetic
Barrel: 16.1 in.
Sights: Flip-up front, adjustable post, flip-up rear
Weight: 9 lb. 6 oz.
Caliber: .308 Win.
Magazine: Detachable box, 20 rounds
Features: Matte black, monolithic upper receiver; .308 Winchester upper receiver group can be swapped out for Mil-Spec Colt upper in 5.56x45 NATO; ambidextrous controls on magazine release, bolt catch and safety selector; back up iron sights; full floated barrel; bayonet lug and flash hider
MSRP **$2423**

COLT'S MFG. MATCH TARGET RIFLE

COLT'S MFG.
MATCH TARGET RIFLE

Action: Semi-automatic
Stock: Combat-style, synthetic
Barrel: 16.1 in., 20 in.
Sights: None
Weight: 7 lb. 5 oz.–9 lb. 4 oz.
Caliber: 5.56 NATO x .223
Magazine: Detachable box, 9 rounds
Features: Flat top with optional carry handle and scope mount; two position safety; available with free floating monolithic handguard; available with flip up sights; available with match trigger; black stock with matte finish
MSRP . . . . $1230–$1835

DPMS PANTHER ARMS A3 LITE 16

DPMS PANTHER ARMS A3 LITE 16

Action: Semi-automatic
Stock: Synthetic
Barrel: 16 in.
Sights: Open
Weight: 6 lb.
Caliber: 5.56 NATO
Magazine: Detachable box, 30 rounds
Features: Chrome-moly steel barrel with A2 Flash hider; A3 aircraft aluminum alloy receiver with detachable carrying handle; A1 front and rear sights; DPMS Pardus carbine black stock; oval, carbine length GlacierGuards
MSRP **$769**

DPMS PANTHER ARMS COMPACT HUNTER

DPMS PANTHER ARMS COMPACT HUNTER

Action: Semi-automatic
Stock: Synthetic
Barrel: 16 in.
Sights: None
Weight: 7 lb. 12 oz.
Caliber: .308 Win.
Magazine: 4, 10, 20 rounds
Features: Designed for smaller statures and suitable for youth, female, and hunters who prefer a compact firearm; Teflon-coated stainless steel barrel; carbon fiber free-float tube; Hogue pistol grip; B5 Systems-Special Operations Peculiar Modification (SOPMOD) stock
MSRP **$1499**

Rifles

FNH USA
FNAR STANDARD

Action: Gas-operated autoloader
Stock: Synthetic
Barrel: 16 in., 20 in. standard fluted, 20 in. heavy fluted
Sights: Receiver mounted rail
Weight: 8 lb. 13 oz.–10 lb.
Caliber: .308 Win. (7.62x51mm NATO)
Magazine: 10, 20 round
Features: Extended bolt handle, hammer forged barrel with crown; comes with one magazine, three interchangeable recoil pads, three comb inserts and shims for adjusting for cast-on, cast-off, and drop at comb; stock is matte black synthetic with pistol grip and adjustable comb
MSRP. **$1699**

FNH USA
SCAR 17S CARBINE

Action: Gas-operated autoloader
Stock: Polymer
Barrel: 16.25 in.
Sights: Adjustable, folding, removable
Weight: 8 lb.
Caliber: .308 Win. (7.62x51mm NATO)
Magazine: 10, 20 round
Features: Fully adjustable stock; MIL-STD 1913 optical rail plus three accessory rails for attaching a variety of sights and lasers; free-floating, cold hammer-forged barrel; available in black or Flat Dark Earth tactical, telescoping, side-folding polymer stock
MSRP. **$3349**

FNH USA FNAR STANDARD

FNH USA SCAR 17S CARBINE

HECKLER & KOCH MR556A1

Action: Autoloading
Stock: Synthetic
Barrel: 16.50 in.
Sights: Open
Weight: 8 lb. 15 oz.
Caliber: 5.56x44mm
Magazine: Detachable box, 10 rounds
Features: Free-floating four-quadrant rail system; four Mil-Spec 1913 Picatinny rails; two-stage trigger; retractable buttstock
MSRP **$3295**

HECKLER & KOCH MR556A1

LWRC INTERNATIONAL M6 IC (INDIVIDUAL CARBINE)

Action: Short-stroke gas piston operation
Stock: Magpul MOE
Barrel: 14.7 in.
Sights: LWRCI folding BUIS
Weight: 6 lb. 14 oz.
Caliber: 5.56mm NATO, 6.8mm SPC
Magazine: 30 rounds
Features: New fully ambidextrous lower receiver with dual controls for bolt catch/release, magazine release, and fire control; 2-position gas block; user configurable rail system; features non-IR reflective Cerakote Stealth that makes the rifle "disappear" to image intensifying night vision (US Military applications only); initial production run will be flat dark earth only
MSRP . . . . **N/A**

LWRC INTERNATIONAL M6 IC
(INDIVIDUAL CARBINE)

LWRC INTERNATIONAL M6A2 SPR

Action: Short-stroke gas piston operation
Stock: Magpul ACS
Barrel: 16.1 in.
Sights: LWRC Skirmish BUIS
Weight: 7 lb. 6 oz.
Caliber: 5.56mm
Magazine: 30 rounds
Features: Rifles uses a lightweight sculpted rail derived from the LWRC REPR platform; SPR-MOD rail is lighter and longer than Mark-II-B rail; cold-hammer-forged barrel; spiral fluting; enhanced fire control group; Magpul MIAD pistol grip; Magpul ACS stock; available in black, flat dark Earth, OD green, and patriot brown
MSRP. **$2425**

LWRC INTERNATIONAL M6A2 SPR

Rifles

ROCK RIVER RIFLES LAR-6.8 COYOTE CARBINE

Action: Semi-automatic
Stock: Synthetic
Barrel: 16 in.
Sights: None
Weight: 7 lb.
Caliber: 6.8mm SPC II
Magazine: 1 round
Features: Smith Vortex flash hider; chrome moly barrel; RRA two-stage match trigger
MSRP **$1270**

ROCK RIVER RIFLES LAR-PDS CARBINE

Action: Semi-automatic
Stock: Synthetic
Barrel: 16 in.
Sights: None
Weight: 7 lb. 6 oz.
Caliber: .223 Rem.
Magazine: Detachable box
Features: Ambidextrous non-reciprocating charging handle; A2 flash hider; RRA two-stage trigger; Hogue rubber grip; tri-rail handguard available
MSRP . . . . **$1595–$1750**

RUGER MINI THIRTY RIFLE

Action: Autoloading
Stock: Synthetic
Barrel: 16.12 in., 18.5 in.
Sights: Blade front sight, adjustable rear
Weight: 6 lb. 12 oz.
Caliber: 7.62 x39mm
Magazine: 5 rounds, or detachable box, 20 rounds
Features: Garand style action, hammer-forged barrel; sighting system; integral scope mounts; black synthetic stock; sling swivels; stainless steel or alloy steel barrel in matte or blued finish
MSRP . . . . **$979–$1039**

ROCK RIVER RIFLES LAR-6.8 COYOTE CARBINE

ROCK RIVER RIFLES LAR-PDS CARBINE

RUGER MINI THIRTY RIFLE

SIG SAUER RIFLES SIG516 PATROL

SIG SAUER RIFLES SIG516 PATROL

Action: Semi-automatic
Stock: Tactical synthetic
Barrel: 16 in.
Sights: None
Weight: 7 lb. 5 oz.
Caliber: 5.56mm NATO
Magazine: Detachable box, 30 rounds
Features: Gas piston operating system; three-position gas regulator; free-floating military grade chrome lined barrel; M1913 Picatinny flat top upper; aircraft grade aluminum upper and lower receiver with hard coat anodize finish
MSRP **$1666**

SMITH & WESSON M&P15-22 RIFLE

SMITH & WESSON M&P15-22 RIFLE

Action: Semi-automatic
Stock: Synthetic
Barrel: 18 in.
Sights: Adjustable A2 front post, adjustable dual aperture
Weight: 5 lb. 6 oz.
Caliber: .22LR
Magazine: Detachable box, 25 rounds
Features: Six-position collapsible stock; functioning charging handle; two-position receiver mounted safety selector; cartridge case deflector; bolt catch; recessed magazine release button; match grade precision, threaded barrel
MSRP. **$499**

SMITH & WESSON M&P15T

Action: Semi-automatic
Stock: Synthetic
Barrel: 16 in.
Sights: Folding Magpul
Weight: 6lb. 14 oz.
Caliber: 5.56mm NATO
Magazine: Detachable box, 30 rounds
Features: 10 in. patent pending, anti-twist, free-floating quad rail; melonite barrel; chromed bolt carrier and gas key; gas operated; single-stage trigger
MSRP. **$1159**

SMITH & WESSON M&P15T

Rifles

SPRINGFIELD ARMORY M1A SOCOM II

Action: Autoloading
Stock: Composite
Barrel: 16.25 in.
Sights: Tritium front, ghost ring rear
Weight: 10 lb.
Caliber: 7.62x51mm NATO, .308 Win
Magazine: Detachable box, 10 rounds
Features: High-efficiency muzzle brake; cluster rail system mounts anything designed for standard Picatinny rail; composite black stock
MSRP. **$2176**

STEYR ARMS AUG/A3 SA USA

Action: Semi-automatic
Stock: Synthetic
Barrel: 16 in.
Sights: None
Weight: 8 lb. 2 oz.
Caliber: .223 Rem.
Magazine: Detachable transparent box, 30 rounds
Features: Synthetic black stock; lateral push-through type, locks trigger; 1913 Picatinny rail; changeable barrel; includes factory AUG sling and cleaning kit that fits inside butt stock
MSRP. **$2099**

WILSON COMBAT RECON TACTICAL

Action: Semi-automatic
Stock: Synthetic tactical
Barrel: 16 in.
Sights: Optional rail
Weight: 7 lb.
Caliber: 5.56mm, 6.8 SPC, .300 Blackout, 7.62x40WT
Magazine: Detachable box, 30 rounds
Features: Match grade medium weight stainnless steel barrel; forged 7075 upper (flat top) and lower receiver; mid length gas system with low-profile gas block; Wilson Combat T.R.I.M. rail; ergo pistol grip
MSRP . . . . **$2250–$2600**

SPRINGFIELD ARMORY M1A SOCOM II

STEYR ARMS AUG/A3 SA USA

WILSON COMBAT RECON TACTICAL

BENELLI USA M4 TACTICAL

BENELLI USA M4 TACTICAL

Action: Inertia operated semi-automatic
Stock: Synthetic
Barrel: 18.5 in.
Chokes: Standard choke (M)
Weight: 7 lb. 13 oz.
Bore/Gauge: 12
Magazine: 5+1

Features: The same Benelli M4 used by the U.S. Marine Corps for personal ownership; Picatinny rail; adjustable ghost-ring rear sight and fixed-blade front sight; black synthetic pistol-grip style stock
MSRP **$1899**

BENELLI USA NOVA PUMP TACTICAL

BENELLI USA NOVA PUMP TACTICAL

Action: Pump
Stock: Synthetic
Barrel: 18.5 in.
Chokes: Fixed cylinder choke
Weight: 7 lb. 3 oz.
Bore/Gauge: 12

Magazine: 4+1
Features: Available with ghost-ring or open rifle sights; push-button shell stop; grooved grip surface stocks in black synthetic stock
MSRP **$669**

CZ-USA (CESKA ZBROJOVKA) 712 UTILITY

CZ-USA (CESKA ZBROJOVKA) 712 UTILITY

Action: Semi-automatic
Stock: Synthetic
Barrel: 20 in.
Chokes: Screw-in chokes-F, IM, M, IC, C
Weight: 6 lb. 10 oz.

Bore/Gauge: 12
Magazine: 4+1 rounds
Features: 3 in. chamber cross bolt safety; black synthetic stock; matte chrome black barrel
MSRP **$488**

Shotguns

ITHACA GUN COMPANY MODEL 37 DEFENSE

Action: Pump
Stock: Synthetic, walnut
Barrel: 18.5 in., 20 in.
Chokes: None
Weight: 6 lb. 8 oz.–7 lb. 2 oz.
Bore/Gauge: 12, 20
Magazine: 4+1, 7+1
Features: Choice of walnut or black synthetic stock; three-inch chamber; matte blued finish barrel; Pachmayr decelerator recoil pad
Walnut: **$769;**
Synthetic: **$685**

MOSSBERG SHOTGUNS 500 TRI-RAIL TACTICAL

Action: Pump
Stock: Synthetic
Barrel: 18.5 in.
Chokes: Cylinder-choked barrel

Weight: 6 lb. 12 oz.
Bore/Gauge: 12
Magazine: 6, 8, or 9 rounds
Features: Bead front sight; matte black synthetic, adjustable stock; tri-rail forend
MSRP **$593**

MOSSBERG SHOTGUNS 590A1 ADJUSTABLE TACTICAL TRI-RAIL 9 SHOT

Action: Pump
Stock: Synthetic
Barrel: 18.5 in.
Chokes: Cylinder bore
Weight: 7 lb. 4 oz.
Bore/Gauge: 12
Magazine: 9 rounds
Features: Six-position adjustable stock with a tri-rail forend; ghost ring sights; parkerized finish; speedfeed, black

stock; heavy barrel wall; Blackwater logo
MSRP **$839**

MOSSBERG SHOTGUNS SPX PISTOL GRIP/SPX 8-SHOT

Action: Semi-automatic
Stock: Synthetic
Barrel: 18.5 in.
Chokes: Cylinder bore
Weight: 7 lb. 12 oz.
Bore/Gauge: 12
Magazine: 4+1, 7+1 rounds
Features: Smooth cycling, dual-gas vent system; Picatinny rail; magazine extension; ghost ring rear sight; M16-style front sight; pistol grip full-length black synthetic stock available
Standard: **$787;**
Pistol Grip: **$883**

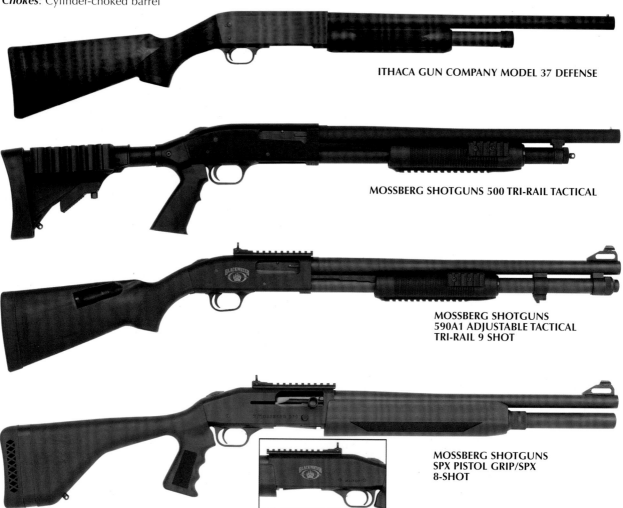

ITHACA GUN COMPANY MODEL 37 DEFENSE

MOSSBERG SHOTGUNS 500 TRI-RAIL TACTICAL

MOSSBERG SHOTGUNS 590A1 ADJUSTABLE TACTICAL TRI-RAIL 9 SHOT

MOSSBERG SHOTGUNS SPX PISTOL GRIP/SPX 8-SHOT

REMINGTON SHOTGUNS
MODEL 870 EXPRESS

Action: Pump
Stock: Hardwood, synthetic, laminate or camo
Barrel: 18-28 in.
Chokes: Modified Remington choke, Extra full Rem.
Weight: 6 lb.–7 lb. 4 oz.
Bore/Gauge: 12, 20
Magazine: 2-7 rounds depending on model
Features: Single bead sight; standard express finish on barrel and receiver; rubber recoil pad; twin action bars ensure smooth, reliable non-binding action; solid steel receiver; optional thumbhole stock in some models
Express: **$411;**
Syn. 7-round: **$428;**
Syn. Deer: **$457;**
Turkey Camo: **$485**

REMINGTON SHOTGUNS MODEL 870 EXPRESS

REMINGTON SHOTGUNS
MODEL 870 EXPRESS TACTICAL

Action: Pump
Stock: Synthetic
Barrel: 18.5 in.
Chokes: Screw-in tube
Weight: 7 lb. 8 oz.
Bore/Gauge: 12
Magazine: None
Features: Synthetic stock available in A-tacs digitized camo; Tactical Rem choke SpeedFeed IV; pistol grip stock; SuperCell recoil pad; adjustable XS ghost ring sight rail with removable with bead front sight; Picatinny-style rail
A-Tacs Camo: **$685;**
Express Tactical: **$572**

REMINGTON SHOTGUNS MODEL 870 EXPRESS TACTICAL

Shotguns

WEATHERBY
SA-459 TR

Action: Semi-automatic
Stock: Synthetic
Barrel: 18.5 in.
Chokes: Ported cylinder choke tube
Weight: 7 lb.
Bore/Gauge: 12, 20
Magazine: 5+1 rounds
Features: Pistol grip stock with a rubber textured area; chrome lined barrel; Picatinny rail for mounting scopes and optics; ghost ring style rear sight, front bead sight; black synthetic injection-molded stock is matched by black matte metal finishing
MSRP **$699**

WEATHERBY SA-459 TR

WINCHESTER REPEATING ARMS
SUPER X PUMP DEFENDER

Action: Autoloader
Stock: Composite
Barrel: 18 in.
Chokes: Fixed cylinder choked barrel
Weight: 6 lb. 4 oz.
Bore/Gauge: 12
Magazine: 5+1 rounds
Features: Uses Foster-type slugs; non-glare metal surfaces with a tough black composite stock; deeply grooved forearm for control and stability
MSRP **$400**

WINCHESTER REPEATING ARMS SUPER X PUMP DEFENDER

BROWNING HI-POWER STANDARD

Action: Autoloader
Grips: Select walnut, cut checkering
Barrel: 4.6 in.
Sights: Low profile fixed or adjustable with ramped front post
Weight: 32 oz.
Caliber: 9mm
Capacity: 10+1 rounds
Features: Locked breech action; single-action trigger; ambidextrous thumb safety; extra magazine; steel, polished blue finish barrel
MSRP . . . . **$1069.99–$1149.99**

CZ-USA (CESKA ZBROJOVKA) 75 SP-01

Action: Autoloader
Grips: Rubber
Barrel: 4.7 in.
Sights: 3-Dot tritium night
Weight: 38.4 oz.
Caliber: 9mm Luger
Capacity: 18 rounds
Features: Based upon the Shadow Target; decocking lever; safety stop on hammer; firing pin safety; steel frame
MSRP **$660**

CZ-USA (CESKA ZBROJOVKA) 75 SP-01 SHADOW TARGET

Action: Autoloader
Grips: Cocobolo
Barrel: 4.7 in.
Sights: Competition style, fiber optic
Weight: 38.4 oz.
Caliber: 9mm
Capacity: 18 rounds
Features: Single or double action; manual safety; steel frame; TRT rear sight; competition springs; CZ custom stainless guide rod
MSRP **$1321**

CZ-USA (CESKA ZBROJOVKA) 75 TS CZECHMATE

Action: Autoloader
Grips: Aluminum
Barrel: 5.4 in.
Sights: Fixed, C-more red dot
Weight: 48 oz.

Caliber: 9mm
Capacity: 20 or 26 rounds
Features: Built upon a modified version of the CZ 75 TS frame; interchangeable parts allow the user to quickly configure the gun for both roles; features a single-action trigger mechanism; red-dot sight; includes spare barrel; includes three 20-round magazines and one 26-round magazine; all-steel pistol is finished in black matte
MSRP **$3220**

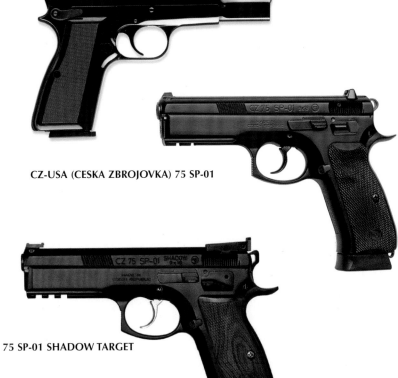

BROWNING HI-POWER STANDARD

CZ-USA (CESKA ZBROJOVKA) 75 SP-01

75 SP-01 SHADOW TARGET

CZ-USA (CESKA ZBROJOVKA) 75 TS CZECHMATE

GLOCK G21 GEN4

GLOCK G34 GEN4

Action: DAO autoloader
Grips: Synthetic
Barrel: 5.31 in.
Sights: Fixed
Weight: 23.1 oz.
Caliber: 9x19
Capacity: 10, 17, 19 rounds
Features: This "Tactical/Practical" GLOCK 9x19 is the G17 extended to the overall length of the Government Model 1911 pistols.
MSRP **$729**

GLOCK G21 GEN4

Action: DAO autoloader
Grips: Synthetic
Barrel: 4.61 in.
Sights: Fixed
Weight: 26.46 oz.
Caliber: .45 Auto
Capacity: 10, 13 rounds
Features: The GLOCK Pistol that validates the .45 cartridge and its 100 year history by providing all the necessities for superb accuracy and functionality. The dual recoil spring assembly and adjustable backstraps offer increased shooting comfort and control. Sleek, powerful and affordable are the hallmarks of this remarkable handgun.
MSRP **$687**

GLOCK G34 GEN4

HECKLER & KOCH P30 LEM

Action: Autoloader
Grips: Polymer
Barrel: 3.86 in.
Sights: Fixed
Weight: 25.6 oz.
Caliber: 9mm, .40 S&W
Capacity: 10, 13, or 15 rounds
Features: Interchangeable backstraps and side panel grips in small, medium, and large sizes; ambidextrous slide and magazine releases levers; integral Picatinny rail; modular design allows DA trigger or DA/SA system, with a decocking button
MSRP **$1054**

HECKLER & KOCH P30 LEM

PARA
BLACK OPS 14•45

Action: Autoloader
Grips: Beavertail
Barrel: 5 in.
Sights: Trijicon 3-dot night sights
Weight: 41 oz.
Caliber: .45 ACP
Capacity: 14+1 rounds
Features: Stainless steel frame;
oversized flared ejection port; ramped
barrel; adjustable skeletonized trigger;
black IonBond finish
MSRP $1299

PARA BLACK OPS 14•45

RUGER SR9C

RUGER
SR9C

Action: DA autoloader
Grips: Black, glass-filled, nylon
Barrel: 3.5 in.
Sights: Adjustable 3-dot
Weight: 23.4 oz.
Caliber: 9mm Luger
Capacity: 10 or 17 rounds
Features: Compact version of SR9;
black alloy or brushed stainless
six-groove rifling; high visibility sights;
accessory mounting rail
MSRP $529

RUGER SR40

RUGER SR40

Action: Autoloader
Grips: Black, high performance, glass-
filled nylon
Barrel: 4.1 in.
Sights: Adjustable 3-dot
Weight: 27.25 oz.
Caliber: .40 S&W
Capacity: 10 or 15 rounds
Features: Glass-filled nylon frame;
ambidextrous operating controls;
trigger system and reversible; fully
adjustable three-dot sights; integral
accessory rail; backstraps are identical
to SR9; Nitridox pro black or brushed
stainless finish
MSRP $529

Handguns

SIG SAUER
P226

Action: DA autoloader
Grips: One-piece ergo grip, extreme model features Hogue custom G10 grips
Barrel: 4.4 in.
Sights: Contrast, Siglite night optional
Weight: 34 oz.
Caliber: 9mm, .357 Sig, .40 S&W
Capacity: 9mm; 10 or 15 rounds; .357 Sig: 10 or 12 rounds, .40 S&W: 10 or 12 rounds
Features: Black hard anodized frame finish; nitron slide finish; accessory rail; extreme model features SRT trigger and front cocking serrations

Standard: **$993;**
Night Sights: **$1068;**
Extreme: **$1213;**
Elite SAO: **$1218;**
Engraved:. **$1289;**
Engraved Stainless: **$1402**

SIG SAUER P226

SMITH & WESSON
M327 TRR8

Action: SA/DA revolver
Grips: Synthetic
Barrel: 5 in.
Sights: Interchangeable front; adjustable V-notch rear
Weight: 35.3 oz.
Caliber: .357 Mag., .38 S&W Special +P
Capacity: 8 rounds
Features: Scandium alloy frame; stainless steel cylinder; matte black; large size frame; exposed hammer; equipment rails

MSRP **$1289**

SMITH & WESSON M327

SMITH & WESSON
M627

Action: SA/DA revolver
Grips: Synthetic
Barrel: 4 in.
Sights: Interchangeable front; adjustable rear
Weight: 41.2 oz.
Caliber: .357 Mag., .38 S&W Special +P
Capacity: 8 rounds
Features: Stainless steel frame and cylinder; matte stainless; large size frame; exposed hammer

MSRP **$1249**

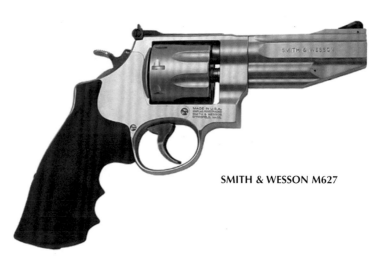

SMITH & WESSON M627

SMITH & WESSON
M&P357

Action: Autoloader
Grips: Polymer
Barrel: 4.25 in.
Sights: White dot dovetail front; steel low profile carry rear
Weight: 25.5 oz.
Caliber: .357 Auto
Capacity: 15 rounds
Features: Three interchangeable palm swell grip sizes; black melonite; thumb safety; polymer frame/stainless steel barrel and slide
MSRP **$727**

SMITH & WESSON
M&P R8

Action: SA/DA revolver
Grips: Polymer
Barrel: 5 in.
Sights: Interchangeable front, adjustable v-notch
Weight: 36.3 oz.
Caliber: .357 Mag., .38 S&W Special +P
Capacity: 8 rounds
Features: Single or double action; scandium alloy frame; stainless steel cylinder; integral accessory Picatinny style rail; precision barrel forcing cone
MSRP **$1289**

SPRINGFIELD ARMORY
XD(M)

Action: DA autoloader
Grips: Polymer
Barrel: 3.8 in., 4.5 in. match-grade
Sights: 3-dot
Weight: 28 oz. (29-30 oz. 4.5 in.)
Caliber: 9mm, .40 S&W
Capacity: 19 (9mm), 16 (.40 S&W)
Features: "M" features include carrying case, two magazines, paddle holster, magi loader, double magi pouch and 3 interchangeable backstraps and two magazines; "all-terrain" texture and deep slide serrations are standard
9mm: . . . . **$697–$815;**
.40 S&W: . . . . **$697–$876;**
.45 ACP: . . . . **$709–$896**

SMITH & WESSON M&P357

SMITH & WESSON M&P R8

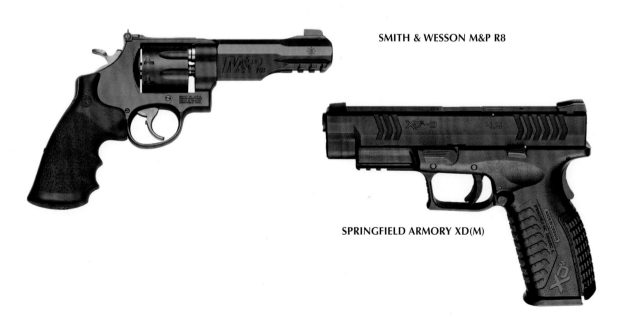

SPRINGFIELD ARMORY XD(M)

Handguns

SPRINGFIELD ARMORY XD(M) COMPACT

Action: Autoloader
Grips: Synthetic
Barrel: 3.8 in., 5.25 in.
Sights: Fiber optic front, adjustable rear
Weight: N/A
Caliber: 9mm, .45 ACP, .40 S&W
Capacity: 13, 19 rounds
Features: A handgun with improved accuracy, lessened recoil, faster shot recovery and greater sight radius of its newly enhanced performance. The Lightening cut in the slide reduces reciprocating mass which allows for faster cycling and allows a larger variety of loads to be used.
MSRP . . . . $705–$797

STEYR ARMS C9-A1

Action: Autoloader, striker-fired
Grips: Textured polymer
Barrel: 3.6 in.
Sights: Fixed triangular/trapezoid
Weight: 25.6 oz.
Caliber: 9mm
Capacity: 17+1
Features: Polymer frame; trigger, internal striker, internal gun-lock safeties; polygonal rifling; black matte Mannox finish; Picatinny rail
MSRP $560

STEYR ARMS C9-A1

STEYR ARMS M40-A1

STEYR ARMS M40-A1

Action: Autoloader
Grips: Synthetic
Barrel: 4 in.
Sights: Fixed triangular/trapezoid
Weight: 27 oz.
Caliber: 9mm, .40 S&W
Capacity: 12 or 15 rounds
Features: Triangular or trapezoid shaped sights; synthetic black grips; Picatinny rail; ergonomic handle
MSRP $560

STI INTERNATIONAL EAGLE 5.0

Action: Autoloader
Grips: STI patented modular polymer
Barrel: 5 in.
Sights: STI front, STI adjustable rear
Weight: 33.5 oz.
Caliber: 9mm, .357 Sig, .38 Super, .40 S&W, .45 ACP
Capacity: 10+1 rounds
Features: Stainless STI grip, ambi thumb, ramped bull barrel; STI patented modular steel frame; STI rear serrations; blue finish
MSRP $1985

STI INTERNATIONAL EAGLE 5.0

STI INTERNATIONAL EDGE

STI INTERNATIONAL EDGE

Action: Autoloader
Grips: STI patented modular polymer with aluminum mag well
Barrel: 5 in.
Sights: STI front, STI adjustable rear
Weight: 38.5 oz.
Caliber: 9mm, .38 Super, .40 S&W, .45 ACP
Capacity: 6+1 rounds
Features: STI fully supported, ramped bull barrel; stainless STI grip and ambi slided thumb; STI recoil master guide rod; blue finish
MSRP $2040

STI INTERNATIONAL VIP

Action: Autoloader
Grips: STI patented modular polymer
Barrel: 3.9 in.
Sights: STI front, STI adjustable rear
Weight: 30 oz.
Caliber: 9mm, .40 S&W, .45 ACP
Capacity: 10+1 rounds
Features: STI rear slide serrations; STI long curved trigger; STI stainless grip and single sided thumb; matte blue slide with blue steel frame
MSRP $1690

STI INTERNATIONAL VIP

Handguns

TAURUS 24/7 G2

Action: DA/SA autoloader
Grips: Checkered polymer with metallic inserts
Barrel: 4.2 in.
Sights: Low-profile, adjustable rear
Weight: 28 oz.
Caliber: 9mm, .40, .45 ACP
Capacity: 18 (9mm), 13 (.40), 11 (.45 ACP)
Features: Blued or stainless steel; DA/SA trigger system; SA or DA only; contoured thumb rests; Picatinny accessory rail; compact model available at same price
Blue: **$539;**
Stainless: **$555**

TAURUS 608

Action: Revolver
Grips: Rubber
Barrel: 4 in., 6.5 in., 8.4 in.
Sights: Fixed front, adjustable rear
Weight: 44-51 oz.
Caliber: .357 Mag
Capacity: 8 rounds
Features: Matte stainless steel finish; transfer bar; large frame; steel frame; Taurus security system; porting
4 in.: **$702;**
6.5 in.: **$724**

TAURUS 809

Action: Autoloader
Grips: Checkered polymer
Barrel: 4 in.
Sights: Fixed
Weight: 3.2 oz.
Caliber: 9mm
Capacity: 17+1 rounds
Features: Black Tennifer finish; smooth trigger type; strike two capability.
MSRP **$497**

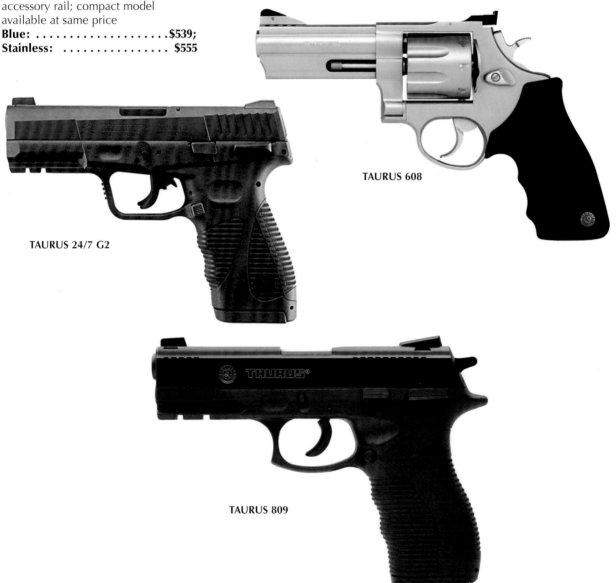

TAURUS 608

TAURUS 24/7 G2

TAURUS 809

AMERICAN SECURITY AM HOME SECURITY AM3020

Gun Capacity & Configuration: N/A

Ext. Dimensions: 30 in. x 20 in. x 20 in.

Features: All-velour interior; deep blue textured finish; spy-proof dial; 12-gauge steel body; three-wheel combination lock; five active locking bolts; four pre-cut anchor holes; fire insulation; AM4020 and AM2020 models also available

MSRP **$1130**

AMERICAN SECURITY AM HOME SECURITY AM3020

AMERICAN SECURITY BF SERIES BF6636

Gun Capacity & Configuration: 31+2 total

Ext. Dimensions: 65.25 in. x 36 in. x 26 in.

Features: U.L. Residential Security Container Burglary Classification; 11 bolts; DryLight insulation; Mercury Class III fire protection; Two Stage Dual fire seals; U.L. Listed Group II Lock; cam driven locking mechanism; available left or right swing door; mirrored back wall; Premium Door Organizer; E-Z Slant-Out Interior; also available in varying capacities

High Gloss: **$6380;**
Textured: **$5360;**
Two-Tone: **$5850**

AMERICAN SECURITY BF SERIES BF6636

AMERICAN SECURITY BARRETT BFB TACTICAL BFB7240

Gun Capacity & Configuration: 17+2 total

Ext. Dimensions: 71.25 in. x 40 in. x 26 in.

Features: Designed to store large caliber rifles, assault rifles, and tactical weapons; DryLight insulation; U.L. Residential Security Container Burglary Classification; eleven bolts; Mercury Class III fire protection; U.L. Listed Group II Lock; mirrored back wall; Premium Door Organizer; four pre-cut anchor holes; E-Z Slant-Out Interior; also available in SFB models

High Gloss: **$7515;**
Textured: **$6495;**
Two-Tone: **$7035**

AMERICAN SECURITY BARRETT BFB TACTICAL BFB7240

Gun Safes

AMERICAN SECURITY FV 45 MINUTE FIRE FV6036E5

Gun Capacity & Configuration: 38+2 total

Ext. Dimensions: 59 in. x 36 in. x 26 in.

Features: Mercury fire protection; 3/16 in. Steel Plate door; Two Stage Dual fire seals; 12-gauge steel body; AMSEC's ESL5 Electronic Lock with illuminated keypad; cam driven locking mechanism; three-point chrome tri-spoke handle; 14 bolts; Premium Door Organizer; four pre-cut anchor holes; FV7240E5, FV6030E5, and FV6032E5 models also available

MSRP **$2300**

AMERICAN SECURITY
FV 45 MINUTE FIRE
FV6036E5

AMERICAN SECURITY
HIGH SECURITY RF6528

AMERICAN SECURITY HIGH SECURITY RF6528

Gun Capacity & Configuration: 30 total

Ext. Dimensions: 72 in. x 35 in. x 29.5 in.

Features: Only U.L. Listed TL-30 burglary and fire-resistant gun safe on the market; ten bolts; 2¾ in. thick door with ARMOR steel plate; Mercury Class IV fire protection; Group 2M lock

High Gloss: **$9910;**
Textured: **$8480**

BROWNING
CLASSIC MODEL 24

Gun Capacity & Configuration: 9/18 + 7 DPX; 25 total
Ext. Dimensions: 60 in. x 30 in. x 22 in.
Features: DPX Storage System with a Quick Access barrel Rack; MAX Locking Bolts; 12-gauge steel; S & G Mechanical lock; fire insulation; also available in a 35 square foot model
Gloss: **$1699;**
Textured: **$1599**

**BROWNING
CLASSIC MODEL 24**

**BROWNING
COMPACT 9**

BROWNING COMPACT 9

Gun Capacity & Configuration: N/A
Ext. Dimensions: 30 in. x 24 in. x 20 in.
Features: Force Deflector Locking System; 12-gauge steel; two inches of fire insulation; door-mounted DPX panel; 180 degree external hinge for easy access
MSRP **$1099**

BROWNING DELUXE MODEL 45

Gun Capacity & Configuration: 22/33 + 10 DPX; 43 total
Ext. Dimensions: 72 in. x 43 in. x 25 in.
Features: MAX Locking Bolts with Reinforced Door Frame; Pry-Stop End Bolts; 11-gauge steel; Force Deflector Locking System; S & G Mechanical lock; fire insulation; also available in 26 and 37 square foot models
Gloss: **$3299;**
Textured: **$2999;**
Two-Tone: **$4199**

**BROWNING HUNTER
MODEL 37**

**BROWNING DELUXE
MODEL 45**

BROWNING HUNTER MODEL 37

Gun Capacity & Configuration: 22/33 + 10 DPX; 43 total
Ext. Dimensions: 60 in. x 43 in. x 25 in.
Features: Axis interior and DPX Storage System with Scope Saver; Pry-Stop End Bolts; 11-gauge steel; also available in a 26 square foot model
Gloss: **$2879;**
Textured: **$2559**

Gun Safes

BROWNING MEDALLION MODEL 39

Gun Capacity & Configuration: 22/33 + 10 DPX; 43 total

Ext. Dimensions: 60 in. x 44 in. x 26 in.

Features: OmniBarrier and Uni-Force Systems locking mechanism; 10-gauge steel; Pry-Stop Corner bolts; fire insulation; reinforced integrated door frame; Axis Adjustable Shelving; also available in 28, 47, and 60 square foot models

Gloss: $3999;
Textured: 3699

BROWNING PINNACLE MODEL 49

Gun Capacity & Configuration: 22/33 + 10 DPX; 43 total

Ext. Dimensions: 72 in. x 45 in. x 26 in.

Features: Gear Drive Locking System; 3/16 in. steel body; four Pry-Stop MAX Corner Bolts; fire insulation; cedar and simulated leather interior; available in seven colors; also available in 41 and 63 square foot models

Gloss: $6199;
Two-Tone: $7499

BROWNING PLATINUM PLUS MODEL 41

Gun Capacity & Configuration: 22/33 + 10 DPX; 43 total

Ext. Dimensions: 60 in. x 45 in. x 26 in.

Features: Grade VI Interior package; 3/16 in. steel body; Pry-Stop Corner Bolts; Uni-Force Locking System with Anti-Pry Tabs; OmniBarrier Lock Protection System; fire insulation; Interior LED light package; S & G Group II lock; cedar and simulated leather interior; also available in 49 and 63 square foot models

MSRP $5899

BROWNING PRESTIGE MODEL 39

Gun Capacity & Configuration: 22/33 + 10 DPX; 43 total

Ext. Dimensions: 60 in. x 44 in. x 26 in.

Features: MAX Locking Bolts; Gear Drive Locking System; Axis Adjustable Interior with DPX Storage System and Scope Saver; 10-gauge steel; S & G Mechanical lock; two inch fire insulation; simulated leather interior; also available in 28, 47, and 60 square foot models

Gloss: $3899;
Textured: $3599;
Two-Tone: $4899

BROWNING MEDALLION MODEL 39

BROWNING PINNACLE MODEL 49

BROWNING PLATINUM PLUS MODEL 41

BROWNING PRESTIGE MODEL 39

CANNON SAFES
ARMORY SERIES 64

Gun Capacity & Configuration: 80 total

Ext. Dimensions: 72 in. x 48 in. x 30 in.

Features: EMP keypad; five-spoke handle; seven bolt; split shelf; power supply and media outlet; door organizer kit; triple fin intumescent seal; 12-gauge steel; triple hard plate and interior light; also available in a Series 54

MSRP **$2799**

CANNON SAFES
ARMORY SERIES 64

CANNON SAFES
CANNON SERIES
CA33

CANNON SAFES
CANNON SERIES CA33

Gun Capacity & Configuration: 36 total

Ext. Dimensions: 60 in. x 40 in. x 22 in.

Features: EMP keypad; five-spoke handle; 60 minute fire protection; six bolts; split shelf; power supply and media outlet; door organizer kit; triple fin intumescent seal; anti-pry tab; 12-gauge steel; CA23 model also available

MSRP **$1699**

CANNON SAFES
COMMANDER SERIES 43

Gun Capacity & Configuration: 36 total

Ext. Dimensions: 72 in. x 40 in. x 26 in.

Features: EMP keypad; 90 minute fire protection; 12 bolts; split shelf; 5-spoke handle; power supply and media outlet; door organizer kit; dual relockers; 10-gauge steel; interior light; anti-pry tab; also available in Series 54 model

MSRP **$3699**

CANNON SAFES
COMMANDER
SERIES 43

Gun Safes

CANNON SAFES HOME GUARD H4

Gun Capacity & Configuration: N/A

Ext. Dimensions: 20 in. x 24 in. x 18 in.

Features: Toplite keypad; Drop one handle; Type one lock; 75 minute fire protection; three bolts; split shelf; power supply and media outlet; door organizer kit; Cannon's patented TruLock internal hinges; interior light; H1, H2, and H8 models also available

MSRP **$699**

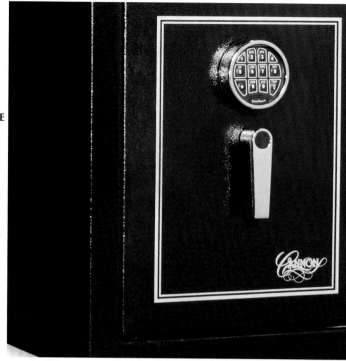

CANNON SAFES HOME GUARD H4

CANNON SAFES PATRIOT SERIES P14

CANNON SAFES PATRIOT SERIES P14

Gun Capacity & Configuration: 12 total

Ext. Dimensions: 59 in. x 22 in. x 18 in.

Features: Toplite keypad; three-spoke handle; 60 minute fire protection; five bolts; split shelf; power supply and media outlet; door organizer kit; anti-pry tab; TruLock internal hinges; 12-gauge steel; Triple Fin Intumescent Seal; P22 and P40 models also available

MSRP **$1199**

CANNON SAFES SCOUT SERIES 19

Gun Capacity & Configuration: 28 total

Ext. Dimensions: 59 in. x 28 in. x 20 in.

Features: Toplite keypad; three- spoke handle; 30 minute fire protection; four bolts; Type one lock; split shelf; power supply and media outlet; 12-gauge steel; anti-pry tab; Door Organizer Kit; also available in Series 14, 33, 40, and 45

MSRP **$1099**

CANNON SAFES SCOUT SERIES 19

CHAMPION SAFE CO. BIG YELLOW SAFE

Gun Capacity & Configuration: N/A
Ext. Dimensions: N/A
Features: Up to 2 layers of fire insulation; 240 cubic feet; 4-Way Active Door Bolts; 24- 2½ in. door bolts; 10-gauge steel; forklift cutouts at base for moving
Available upon request

CHAMPION SAFE CO. CROWN C-60

Gun Capacity & Configuration: 60 total
Ext. Dimensions: 72.25 in. x 44 in. x 27 in.
Features: Three interior configuration options; velour interior with LED light; Glass-Guard Relock system; Phoenix Class V fire protection; Double-Step door; S & G Group II Dial; four-way active boltworks; nine available finish options; C-30, C-40, and C-50 models also available
Available upon request

CHAMPION SAFE CO. BIG YELLOW SAFE

CHAMPION SAFE CO. MEDALIST M-31

Gun Capacity & Configuration: 28 total
Ext. Dimensions: 60.5 in. x 36 in. x 27 in.
Features: Three interior configuration options; All-Pro interior; 12-gauge steel body; Double-Steel Door Casement; four-way active boltworks; twelve bolts; Champion's Auto-Relock system; Phoenix Class II fire protection; S & G Group II dial lock; seven finish options; M-19, M-22, M-41, and M-45 models also available
Available upon request

CHAMPION SAFE CO. MODEL-T MT-21

Gun Capacity & Configuration: 24 total
Ext. Dimensions: 60.5 in. x 28 in. x 20 in.
Features: Phoenix Class I fire protection; S & G dial lock; four-way active boltworks; eight bolts; Roughneck bolt guides; three interior configurations; All-Pro interior; 12-gauge steel body; 4.25 in. composite door
Available upon request

CHAMPION SAFE CO. MEDALIST M-31

CHAMPION SAFE CO. MODEL-T MT-21

CHAMPION SAFE CO. CROWN C-60

Gun Safes

CHAMPION SAFE CO. SUPER SHORT SS-12

Gun Capacity & Configuration: N/A
Ext. Dimensions: 40 in. x 26 in. x 20 in.
Features: Internal locking detent; four-way active boltworks; eight bolts; up to two layers of fire insulation; 12-gauge steel; three interior shelves; SS-9 model also available
Available upon request

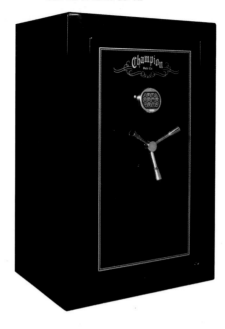

CHAMPION SAFE CO.
SUPER SHORT SS-12

CHAMPION SAFE CO. TRIUMPH T-75

Gun Capacity & Configuration: 84 total
Ext. Dimensions: 72.25 in. x 56 in. x 32 in.
Features: Phoenix Class IV fire protection; three interior configurations; Double-Step door; S & G Group II dial lock; Champion's Auto-Relock System; Cam-Lock; four-way active boltworks; velour interior with LED light; deluxe door organizer; 10-gauge steel body; five-spoke handle with slip clutch; Double-Steel Door Casement
Available upon request

CHAMPION SAFE CO.
TRIUMPH T-75

CHAMPION SAFE CO.
TROPHY TY-42

CHAMPION SAFE CO. TROPHY TY-42

Gun Capacity & Configuration: 52 total
Ext. Dimensions: 60.25 in. x 43 in. x 28 in.
Features: Three interior configurations; velour interior with door organizer; four-way active boltworks with 14 bolts; Phoenix Class III fire protection; 11-gauge steel; Champion's Auto-Relock System; S & G Group II dial lock; seven finish options; TY-19, TY-25, TY-35, TY-50, and TY-60 models also available
Available upon request

FORT KNOX DEFENDER

Gun Capacity & Configuration: N/A
Ext. Dimensions: N/A
Features: Quadrafold door frame; 10-gauge steel, Uni-body construction; up to 13 active door locking bolts; patented rack & pinion gear drive locking mechanism; bolt detent; drill stop hard plate; S & G Group II manipulation resistant lock; remote relocker; carpeted interior; customizable
Available upon request

FORT KNOX GUARDIAN

Gun Capacity & Configuration: N/A
Ext. Dimensions: N/A
Features: Reinforced fire door; Quadrafold door frame; 10-gauge steel, Uni-body construction; up to 20 active door locking bolts; Star Corner Bolts; drill deflector bolt guard; 5 to 1 reduction rack & pinion multi-gear drive locking mechanism; 5 spoke handle; S & G Group II manipulation resistant lock; carpeted interior; remote relocker; customizable
Available upon request

FORT KNOX DEFENDER

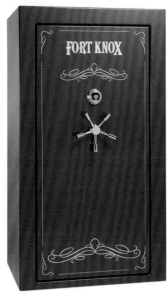

FORT KNOX
GUARDIAN

FORT KNOX LEGEND

Gun Capacity & Configuration: N/A
Ext. Dimensions: N/A
Features: Quadrafold door frame; 1.75 in. Reinforced Fire Door; 10-gauge stainless steel reinforced liner; up to 28 active door locking bolts; Star Corner Bolts; drill deflector bolt guard; 5 to 1 reduction rack & pinion locking mechanism with up to 55 machined gears; nickle plated gears and glass door panel; dehumidifier; remote relocker; electronic lock; carpeted interior; customizable
Available upon request

FORT KNOX MAVERICK

Gun Capacity & Configuration: N/A
Ext. Dimensions: N/A
Features: New Folded Door design; 5.5 in. thick door; 11-gauge steel

FORT KNOX
LEGEND

body; four active door locking bolts and locking dead bars; rack & pinion gear drive locking mechanism; up to eleven bolts; carpeted door panel; three way bolt work; drill stop hard plate; customizable
Available upon request

Gun Safes

FORT KNOX PROTECTOR

Gun Capacity & Configuration: N/A
Ext. Dimensions: N/A
Features: Quadrafold door frame; 10-gauge steel, Uni-body construction; up to 13 active door locking bolts; reinforced fire door; bolt detent; S & G Group II manipulation resistant lock; remote relocker; rack & pinion gear drive locking mechanism; drill deflector bolt guard; carpeted interior; customizable
Available upon request

FORT KNOX TITAN

Gun Capacity & Configuration: N/A
Ext. Dimensions: N/A
Features: Reinforced fire door; Quadrafold door frame; 10-gauge steel reinforced liner; up to 20 active door locking bolts; Star Corner Bolts; Drill Deflector Bolt Guard; bolt detent; 5 to 1 reduction rack & pinion multi-gear drive locking mechanism; gold plated S & G Group II manipulation resistant lock; dehumidifier; remote relocker; door organizer; carpeted interior; customizable
Available upon request

FORT KNOX TITAN

FORT KNOX ORIGINAL PISTOL SAFE

Gun Capacity & Configuration: N/A
Ext. Dimensions: 4.25 in. x 12.5 in. x 3.75 in.
Features: Gas strut to assist opening; Simplex lock; 10-gauge steel; wrap around door; exceeds the California Firearms Safety Device Requirements; Lifetime Warranty
MSRP **$249**

FORT KNOX ORIGINAL PISTOL SAFE

GUN VAULT
DRAWERVAULT GV 3000

Gun Capacity & Configuration: N/A

Ext. Dimensions: 4.25 in. x 10 in. x 12 in.

Features: Over 12 million user-selectable access codes; mountable; protective foam liner; spring loaded door; computer block access after repeated invalid entries; backup override key; uses 9v battery; also available in biometric model

MSRP **$229.99**

GUN VAULT
MICROVAULT MV 500

Gun Capacity & Configuration: N/A

Ext. Dimensions: 2.25 in. x 8.5 in. x 11 in.

Features: Over 12 million user-selectable access codes; mountable; protective foam liner; LED low battery warning; tamper indicator; computer block access after repeated invalid entries; backup override key; security cable included; uses 9v battery

MSRP **$159.99**

GUN VAULT
MICROVAULT MVB 1000

Gun Capacity & Configuration: N/A

Ext. Dimensions: 3.5 in. x 10.25 in. x 12 in.

Features: Biometric fingerprint scanning system; holds up to 120 unique fingerprints; mountable; protective foam liner; LED low battery warning; backup override key; uses a 9v battery

MSRP **$329.99**

GUN VAULT
MINIVAULT GV 1000D

Gun Capacity & Configuration: N/A

Ext. Dimensions: 5.25 in. x 8.25 in. x 12 in.

Features: Over 12 milllion user-selectable access codes; 16-gauge steel; mountable; protective foam liner; spring loaded door; audio and LED low battery warning; interior light; motion detector with audio alarm; tamper indicator; computer block access after repeated invalid entries; backup override key; external AC power supply; uses 9v battery; also available in a Standard and Biometric model

MSRP **$179.99**

GUN VAULT
DRAWERVAULT
GV 3000

GUN VAULT
MICROVAULT
MV 500

GUN VAULT
MICROVAULT
MVB 1000

GUN VAULT
MINIVAULT GV
1000D

Gun Safes

GUN VAULT MULTIVAULT STANDARD GV 2000S

Gun Capacity & Configuration: N/A
Ext. Dimensions: 8 in. x 10.25 in. x 14 in.
Features: Over 12 million user-selectable access codes; mountable; protective foam liner; spring loaded door; audio and LED low battery warning; tamper indicator; computer block access after repeated invalid entries; backup override key; uses 9v battery; available in Deluxe and Biometric models
MSRP **$189.99**

GUN VAULT NANOVAULT NV 300

Gun Capacity & Configuration: N/A
Ext. Dimensions: 1.75 in. x 6.5 in. x 9.5 in.

Features: Key Lock system; 18-gauge steel; memory foam interior; mountable; security cable included; NV 100 and NV 200 models also available
MSRP **$44.99**

GUN VAULT SPEEDVAULT SV 500

Gun Capacity & Configuration: 1
Ext. Dimensions: 6.5 in. x 3.5 in. x 13 in.
Features: Digital keypad; over 12 million user-selectable access codes; multiple mounting options; 18-gauge steel; protective foam liner; audio and LED low battery warning; tamper indicator; computer block access after repeated invalid entries; backup override key; uses 9v battery; also available in a biometric model
MSRP **$209.99**

GUN VAULT TACVAULT TVB 4810

Gun Capacity & Configuration: Fits AR style rifle with 30-round magazine or Tactical Shotgun
Ext. Dimensions: 48 in. x 10 in. x 19 in.
Features: Biometric fingerprint scanning; holds ten unique fingerprints; shelf for spare items; pre-drilled to secure to the floor; High Strength Lock mechanism; also available in a keypad model
MSRP **$549.99**

GUN VAULT SPEEDVAULT SV 500

GUN VAULT MULTIVAULT STANDARD GV 2000S

GUN VAULT NANOVAULT NV 300

GUN VAULT TACVAULT TVB 4810

LIBERTY SAFES
COLONIAL 23

Gun Capacity & Configuration: 25 Long Guns
Ext. Dimensions: 60.5 in. x 30 in. x 25 in.
Features: Certified 45 minute fire protection; 80,000 BTU fire rating; Palusol Heat Activated door seal; U.L. Residential Security Container burglary classification; triple case harded steel plates; up to 14 bolts; cam-drive bolt locking mechanism with slip clutch SURETIGHT; S & G group II lock; 3-in-1 Flex fabric interior; available in 23, 30, and 50 size models
From: **$1429**

**LIBERTY SAFES
COLONIAL 23**

LIBERTY SAFES FATBOY

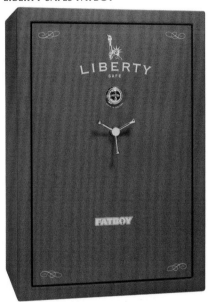

LIBERTY SAFES
FATBOY

Gun Capacity & Configuration: 64 Long Guns
Ext. Dimensions: 60.5 in. x 42 in. x 32 in.
Features: Palusol Heat Activated door; 83,000 BTU fire rating; U.L. Residential Security Container burglary classification; DX-90 Monster Mech over-center cam mechanism; 1.25 in. bolts with anti-pry tabs; fourteen bolts; S & G Group II lock; 3-spoke SURETIGHT handle with Slip-Clutch; velour interior with Double Sportsman Rack
From: **$2529**

**LIBERTY SAFES HOME
SAFES LH12**

LIBERTY SAFES
HOME SAFES LH12

Gun Capacity & Configuration: N/A
Ext. Dimensions: 42 in. x 26 in. x 22 in.
Features: Palusol 7X Heat Activated door seal; 83,000 BTU fire rating; 60 minute fire protection; S & G Electronic Lock; triple case hardened steel plates; 14-gauge steel door; clutch-driven mechanism; chrome hardware; velour interior with adjustable shelving; LH05, LH08, and LH12 models available
From: **$829**

Gun Safes

LIBERTY SAFES HOME SAFES LH12 LINCOLN 25

Gun Capacity & Configuration: 24 Long Guns

Configuration: 60.6 in. x 30 in. x 29 in.

Features: DX-90 Monster Mech over-center cam technology; 90 minutes fire protection; 95,000 BTU fire rating; Palusol Heat Activated door seal; U.L. Residential Security Container burglary classification; 1.24 in. bolts with anti-pry tabs; up to 16 locking bolts; S & G group II lock; Clearview Interior Lighting; premium door panel; dehumidifier; available in 25, 35, and 50 size models; multiple finishes

From: $2369

LIBERTY SAFES HOME SAFES LH12 NATIONAL SECURITY MAGNUM 50

Gun Capacity & Configuration: 39 Long Guns

Configuration: 72.5 in. x 42 in. x 32 in.

Features: GX-480 gear drive mechanism; U.L. Residential Security Container burglary classification; 131,000 BTU and 2.5 hour fire rating; Palusol heat Activated door; interlocking dead lock system; triple relockers; 26 active locking bolts; gear-drive off-set handle; premium accessory door panel; dehumidifier; 4-in-1 Flex velour interior; Clearview Wand Lighting system; available in 25, 40, 50, and 56 size models

From: $6209

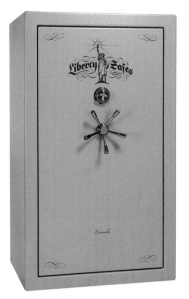

LIBERTY SAFES HOME SAFES LH12 LINCOLN 25

LIBERTY SAFES HOME SAFES LH12 VOYAGER 23

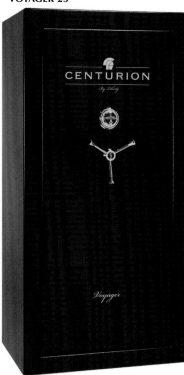

LIBERTY SAFES HOME SAFES LH12 NATIONAL SECURITY MAGNUM 50

LIBERTY SAFES HOME SAFES LH12 REVERE 20

LIBERTY SAFES HOME SAFES LH12 REVERE 20

Gun Capacity & Configuration: 22 Long Guns

Configuration: 60.5 in. x 28 in. x 23 in.

Features: Palusol heat-expanding seal; 62,000 BTU fire protection; U.L. Residential Security Container burglary classification; triple case hardened steel plates; S & G Group II mechanical lock; seven-eight locking bolts; two-piece roll-form body; added steel gussett; 3-in-1 Flex fabric interior; made in the U.S.; available in RV20, RV23, and RV30 models

From: $999

LIBERTY SAFES HOME SAFES LH12 VOYAGER 23

Gun Capacity & Configuration: 25 Long Guns

Configuration: 59.25 in. x 30 in. x 25 in.

Features: Palusol heat-expanding seal; 45 minute fire protection; 12-gauge three-piece body; one-inch composite fire and security door with up to eight locking bolts; tripple hardplates to protect lock; slip clutch handle mechanism; 3-in-1 Multi-Flex interior fabric

From: $1159

SENTRY SAFES G0135 GUN SAFE

Gun Capacity & Configuration: 5 Long Guns
Configuration: 55 in. x 12 in. x 11.5 in.
Features: Eight lever security key with double bit key; solid steel door with concealed hinges; two live-locking bolts; carpeted interior; meets California DOJ standards
Available upon request

SENTRY SAFES G1459DC GUN SAFE

Gun Capacity & Configuration: 14 total
Configuration: 59 in. x 21 in. x 17.8 in.
Features: Combination lock and key; meets California DOJ standards; dual lock system; solid steel pry-resistant door; five live-locking and three dead bolts; bolt-down hardware; adjustable shelves; carpeted interior
Available upon request

SENTRY SAFES G1464E GUN SAFE

Gun Capacity & Configuration: N/A
Configuration: 64 in. x 21 in. x 17.8 in.
Features: Electronic lock, also available in combination lock; meets California DOJ standards; pry-resistant door; three live-locking and three dead bolts; two adjustable shelves; hardened steel plate; carpeted interior; chrome hardware
Available upon request

SENTRY SAFES GM2459E FIRE-SAFE

Gun Capacity & Configuration: 24 total
Configuration: 59 in. x 28.3 in. x 24.2 in.
Features: Electronic lock, also available in combination lock; Etl verified 30 minute fire protection; pry-resistant door with external hinges; three live-locking and three dead bolts; four way adjustable configuration; bolt-down hardware; carpeted interior
Available upon request

SENTRY SAFES G0135 GUN SAFE

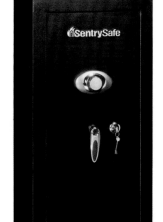

SENTRY SAFES G1459DC GUN SAFE

SENTRY SAFES G1464E GUN SAFE

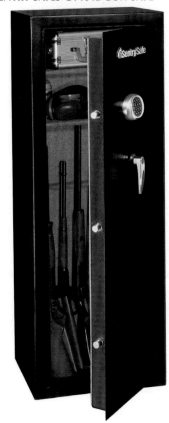

SENTRY SAFES GM2459E FIRE-SAFE

Gun Safes

SENTRY SAFES GM3659C FIRE-SAFE

Gun Capacity & Configuration: 36 total

Configuration: 59 in. x 38 in. x 26.7 in.

Features: Combination lock, also available in electronic lock; ETL verified 30 minute fire protection; pry-resistant door; five live-locking and three dead bolts; hardened steel plate; four way adjustable configuration; carpeted interior

Available upon request

SENTRY SAFES GS1459C FIRE-SAFE

Gun Capacity & Configuration: 14 total

Ext. Dimensions: 59 in. x 22.8 in. x 23.6 in.

Features: Combination lock, also available in electronic lock; ETL verified 30 minute fire protection; lever handle and external hinges; three live-locking and three dead bolts; hardened steel plate; bolt-down; four way adjustable configuration; carpeted interior; high gloss finish

Available upon request

**SENTRY SAFES
GM3659C FIRE-SAFE**

**SENTRY SAFES
GS1459C FIRE-SAFE**

SENTRY SAFES GS3659C FIRE-SAFE 36 GUN

Gun Capacity & Configuration: 36 total

Ext. Dimensions: 59 in. x 38 in. x 26.7 in.

Features: Combination lock, also available in electronic lock; ETL verified 30 minute fire protection; five live-locking bolts and three dead bolts; hardened steel plate; bolt-down hardware; four way adjustable configuration; pry-resistant door; meets California DOJ standards; carpeted interior

Available upon request

SENTRY SAFES HDC11E HOME DEFENSE CENTER

Gun Capacity & Configuration: N/A

Ext. Dimensions: 54.4 in. x 11.1 in. x 12 in.

Features: Included bolt-down kit; quick-entry electronic lock, no audible feedback; pistol stand; barrel containment system; one-inch corner bolts; hidden floor compartment; adjustable shelving; integrated personal defense tray

Available upon request

**SENTRY SAFES
GS3659C FIRE-SAFE 36 GUN**

**SENTRY SAFES HDC11E
HOME DEFENSE CENTER**

CENTRAL SPY SHOP HOUSTON CAR REAR MIRROR SELF-POWERED SPY CAMERA

Features: One piece fully functional car rear view mirror; one piece camera and DVR unit with Sony color CCD; one set high power rechargeable battery; one piece battery charger; one piece 2GB SD card; human body thermal detector (PIR)
MSRP $499

CENTRAL SPY SHOP HOUSTON CAR REAR MIRROR SELF-POWERED SPY CAMERA

CENTRAL SPY SHOP HOUSTON COVERT SMOKE DETECTOR

CENTRAL SPY SHOP HOUSTON COVERT SMOKE DETECTOR

Features: Covert color camera in the form of a smoke detector; side view camera provides greater distance than regular birdseye view; 480 TVL, 1/3 in. super HAD CCII; DC 12v500mA battery
MSRP $109.99

CENTRAL SPY SHOP HOUSTON DIGITAL WIRELESS DVR SECURITY SYSTEM

CENTRAL SPY SHOP HOUSTON DIGITAL WIRELESS DVR SECURITY SYSTEM

Features: Digital wireless DVR security system with seven-inch LCD monitor; SD card recording; two-way intercom; long range night vision; 24/7 lifetime live customer support
MSRP $279.99

CENTRAL SPY SHOP HOUSTON MAIL BOX MESSENGER SPY CAMERA

CENTRAL SPY SHOP HOUSTON MAIL BOX MESSENGER SPY CAMERA

Features: Camera hangs on a wall, posing as a normal mail box; requires AT&T or T-Mobile prepaid SIM card; sends MMS images to your phone whenever someone walks in to the house; MMS sends pictures automatically in 60 second increments as long as activity in area continues; AES GSM Remote Camera supports motion detection and PIR body detector
MSRP $699

DIY Systems

CENTRAL SPY SHOP HOUSTON SVAT 4CH SMART SECURITY DVR

CENTRAL SPY SHOP HOUSTON SVAT 4CH SMART SECURITY DVR

Features: This system is a 4 Channel Smart Security DVR with four outdoor 75 ft. nightvision cameras and a 500gb HDD with smartphone compatibility; 4 x 480TVL security cameras; 4 x 65 ft. security extension cable; two BNC to RCA connectors; 10 ft. RJ-45 ethernet cable; 6 ft. power adapter; 6 ft. RCA video cable; USB mouse; IR remote controller with batteries; window warning stickers; instruction manualand softwre CD
MSRP **$449.99**

CENTRAL SPY SHOP HOUSTON
ULTRA MINIATURE COLOR CAMERA

CENTRAL SPY SHOP HOUSTON ULTRA MINIATURE COLOR CAMERA

Features: Small "Sony Chip" black miniature camera; 380TVL resolution; automatic white balance/gain control; usable illumination 4 LUX/F1.2; backlight compensation; .25 in. color CCD sensor; pinhole lens camera; 10 foot RCA cable - retail box; 92 degree lens and RCA jack
MSRP **$129.99**

CENTRAL SPY SHOP HOUSTON
XTREME LIFE LANDSCAPE STONE

CENTRAL SPY SHOP HOUSTON XTREME LIFE LANDSCAPE STONE

Features: SleuthGear Xtreme Life product; hidden camera; up to one year of operation in standby mode on a battery charge; wireless operation; motion activated; water resistant;designed for outdoor, long term use;capable of recording up to 20 hours of continuous video action; frame counter stamped; 480 TV Lines resolution
MSRP **$649**

CENTRAL SPY SHOP HOUSTON
ZONE SHIELD NIGHT VISION
IPOD DOCK QUAD LCD

CENTRAL SPY SHOP HOUSTON ZONE SHIELD NIGHT VISION IPOD DOCK QUAD LCD

Features: Zone Shield Night Vision hidden cameras; Complete Covert USB Receivers; 20-30 foot camera range in complete darkness; SD recording capability; USB and RCA output; connects with 1-4 cameras to one receiver and any SleuthGear hidden cameras
MSRP **$549**

SECURITY DEPOT 4 CAMERA SURVEILLANCE SYSTEMS

Features: Stand-alone four channel H.264 DVR with 500GB HDD; cameras accessible via the internet on your PC, tablet, and smartphone; 12v AC/DC power supply; two-piece 50 ft. Plug-n-Play cable; two-piece 100 ft. Plug-n-Play cable; CD manual; remote control; mouse; available four-piece camera options: Weatherproof IR Night Vision CMOS 600TVL cameras with 24 LEDS, Weatherproof IR Night Vision Sony 700TVL cameras with 24 LEDs or 42 LEDs & 2.8-12mm zoom, Weatherproof IR Night Vision Sony 500TVL cameras with 42 LEDs & 2.8-12mm zoom, VandalProof IR Night Vision CMOS 600TVL cameras with 24 LEDs, VandalProof IR Night Vision Sony 420/480TVL cameras with 24 LEDs, VandalProof IR Night Vision Sony 700TVL cameras with 36 LEDs & 2.8-12mm zoom, and VandalProof Low-Light Sony Effio-P 700TVL WDR cameras with 2.8-12mm zoom

From: **$599**

SECURITY DEPOT 8 CAMERA SURVEILLANCE SYSTEMS

Features: Stand-alone eight channel H.264 DVR with 500GB HDD; cameras accessible via the internet on your PC, tablet, and smartphone; DIY Plug-n-Play Kit or Installer's Choice Kit; available eight-piece camera options: Weatherproof IR Night Vision CMOS 600TVL cameras with 24 LEDS, Weatherproof IR Night Vision Sony 700TVL cameras with 24 LEDs or 42 LEDs & 2.8-12mm zoom, Weatherproof IR Night Vision Sony 500TVL cameras with 42 LEDs & 2.8-12mm zoom, VandalProof IR Night Vision CMOS 600TVL cameras with 24 LEDs, VandalProof IR Night Vision Sony 420/480TVL cameras with 24 LEDs, VandalProof IR Night Vision Sony 700TVL cameras with 36 LEDs & 2.8-12mm zoom, and VandalProof Low-Light Sony Effio-P 700TVL WDR cameras with 2.8-12mm zoom

From: **$1149**

SECURITY DEPOT 16 CAMERA SURVEILLANCE SYSTEMS

Features: Stand-alone sixteen channel H.264 DVR with 500GB HDD; cameras accessible via the internet on your PC, tablet, and smartphone; DIY Plug-n-Play Kit or Installer's Choice Kit; available sixteen-piece camera options: Weatherproof IR Night Vision CMOS 600TVL cameras with 24 LEDS, Weatherproof IR Night Vision Sony 700TVL cameras with 24 LEDs or 42 LEDs & 2.8-12mm zoom, Weatherproof IR Night Vision Sony 500TVL cameras with 42 LEDs & 2.8-12mm zoom, VandalProof IR Night Vision CMOS 600TVL cameras with 24 LEDs, VandalProof IR Night Vision Sony 420/480TVL cameras with 24 LEDs, VandalProof IR Night Vision Sony 700TVL cameras with 36 LEDs & 2.8-12mm zoom, and VandalProof Low-Light Sony Effio-P 700TVL WDR cameras with 2.8-12mm zoom

From: **$1599**

SECURITY DEPOT CMOS 600TVL IR NIGHT VISION WEATHERPROOF CAMERA

Features: DC Auto Iris Drive; 600TVL resolution; 0 Lux infrared sensitivity; 24 high powered LED illuminators; Automatic Gain Control (AGC); automatic white balance; tamper proof feed-through mounting bracket; IP66 weatherproof rating; other available Bullets Cameras: Sony Effio 700TVL IR Night Vision Weatherproof Camera, Sony 420/480TVL IR Night Vision 2.8-12mm Weatherproof Camera, Sony Effio 700TVL IR Night Vision 2.8-12mm Weatherproof Camera, and Sony S-HAD 500TVL IR Night Vision 2.8-12mm Weatherproof Camera

From: **$79**

SECURITY DEPOTPROFESSIONAL SONY PTZ 432X SPEED DOME

Features: Digital color pan, tilt, zoom camera; Sony CCD Wide-D Technology Zoom module; 36x optical zoom; 540 Max TV Lines resolution; high spped pan/tilt operation; high speed digital signal processing; progressive scan; Digital Slow Shutter (DSS); Wide Dynamic Range (WDR); electronic image stabilizer; .01 Lux Rating; IR cut filter; 128 user-defined presets; six auto cruise modes; advanced on-screen display; IP66 Weatherproof rating; corrosion-free housing
MSRP **$1499**

SECURITY DEPOT PROFESSIONAL SONY PTZ 432X SPEED DOME

SECURITY DEPOT SONY 420/480TVL IR NIGHT VISION VANDALPROOF DOME CAMERA

Features: Digital signal processing; 420 Max TV Lines resolution; IP66 Weatherproof rating; 65 ft. Zero Lux illumination; UL Listed Vandal-proof; compact housing; other available Dome Cameras: CMOS 600TVL IR Night Vision VandalProof Dome Camera, Sony Effio 700TVL IR Night Vision 2.8-12mm VandalProof Dome Camera, and Sony Effio-P 700TVL WDR 2.8-12mm VandalProof Dome Camera
From: **$65**

SECURITY DEPOT SONY 420/480TVL IR NIGHT VISION VANDALPROOF DOME CAMERA

SECURITY DEPOT SONY EFFIO 700TVL PIR COVERT CAMERA

Features: Hi-res color CCD camera designed to look like a PIR Motion Detector Alarm Module (non-functional PIR); .001 Lux rating; 12v DC power; Sony Exview CCD-II Effio-E sensor; 3.7mm pinhole lens; BNC video output
MSRP **$129**

SECURITY DEPOT SONY EFFIO 700TVL PIR COVERT CAMERA

SECURITY DEPOT SONY EFFIO 700TVL WDR PROFESSIONAL BOX CAMERA

SECURITY DEPOT SONY EFFIO 700TVL WDR PROFESSIONAL BOX CAMERA

Features: Low-light wide dynamic range camera; hi-res Sony Effio 700TVL; Sony Exview Super HAD CCD-II; DC VD Lens Drive with OSD button; 2D/3D-NR; BLC/MD/Demist/SLR; automatic white balance
MSRP **$179**

ADT PULSE CHOICE

Included items: one monitored security system, two door/window sensors, and one motion detector; 24/7 Monitoring from ADT Fast Responders; cellular connection service; fire and smoke monitoring; remote web and mobile access; email and text alerts/ notifications; lighting and thermostat control; QSP warranty; six month money back guarantee; optional carbon monoxide monitoring, water detection and temperature monitoring, and remote lock/unlock door control

Installation: $349;
Service: $49.99/mo

ADT PULSE PREMIER

Included items: one monitored security system, two door/window sensors, one motion detector, one small appliance module, two indoor video cameras, one home control touchscreen, one thermostat, and one light control module; 24/7 Monitoring from ADT Fast Responders; cellular connnection service; fire and smoke monitoring; remote web and mobile access; email and text alerts/ notifications; lighting and thermostat control; remote secure video; QSP warranty; six month money back guarantee; optional carbon monoxide monitoring, water detection and temperature monitoring, and remote lock/unlock door control

Installation: $999;
Service: $57.99/mo

ADT QUICKCONNECT PLUS

Included items: one monitored security system, two door/window sensors, one motion detector, one key chain remote, and one sounder; 24/7 Monitoring from ADT Fast Responders;

ADT PULSE CHOICE

fire and smoke monitoring; QSP Warranty; six month money back guarantee; optional cellular connection service, carbon monoxide monitoring, and water detection and temperature monitoring

Installation: $299;
Service: $42.99/mo

ADT QUICKCONNECT PLUS

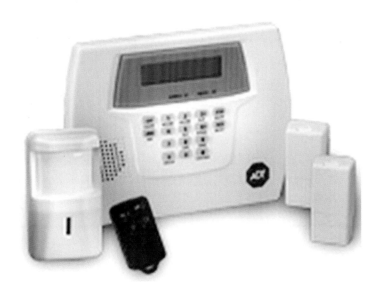

Cameras and Monitoring

FRONT POINT SECURITY GLASS BREAK SENSOR

Features: Sensor detects unique sound frequency of breaking glass; wireless signal transmission; 360 degree coverage; detection range of 20 ft. with a clear line-of-sight; "peel-and-place" adhesive for areas near windows; battery life up to five years; tamper-resistant GE components
From: **$74.99**

FRONT POINT SECURITY INTERACTIVE MONITORING

Features: Crash-and-Smash protection for control panel tampering; instant security alerts via phone, email, or text; Geo Services for mobile tracking and reminder options; automated light control system; remote access and control; monitoring center is 100 percent cellular based; burglar intrusion system; fire protection and monitoring; environmental protection including carbon monoxide poisoning and flooding; medical emergency monitoring; 24/7 professional monitoring
Service: **$42.99/mo**

FRONT POINT SECURITY OUTDOOR WIRELESS CAMERA

Features: Streams live video to you online; runs on home internet connection and wireless router in conjunction with security system; weatherproof; visibility in the dark up to 40 ft.; motion triggered video recording; resolution options from 176x144-1280x800; high, medium, and low compression; wireless encryption; 12v DC, 6.6 W; up to ten simultaneous viewers
From: **$399.99**

FRONT POINT SECURITY PROTECTION MONITORING

Features: Monitoring center is 100 percent cellular based; burglar intrusion system; fire protection and monitoring; environmental protection including carbon monoxide poisoning and flooding; medical emergency monitoring; 24/7 professional monitoring
Service: **$34.99/mo**

FRONT POINT SECURITY ULTIMATE MONITORING

Features: Wireless video surveillance; home automation for door locks, light control, or thermostat settings; monitoring center is 100 percent cellular based; burglar intrusion system; fire protection and monitoring; environmental protection including carbon monoxide poisoning and flooding; medical emergency monitoring; 24/7 professional monitoring; Crash-and-Smash protection for control panel

FRONT POINT SECURITY GLASS BREAK SENSOR

FRONT POINT SECURITY OUTDOOR WIRELESS CAMERA

tampering; instant security alerts via phone, email, or text; Geo Services for mobile tracking and reminder options; remote access and control
Service: **$49.99/mo**

FRONT POINT PAN TILT

FRONT POINT TALKING REMOTE TOUCHPAD

GUARDIAN PROTECTION SERVICES BASIC

Features: GE Simon XT Home Control Unit/Keypad; built-in siren; micro door/window sensors; motion sensor; 24-hour monitoring; Theft Protection Guarantee deductible; Quality Installation Guarantee; Relocation Guarantee; fire and medical emergency monitoring; yard signs and window stickers; personalized Customer Care Dashboard for online interfaces; official Certificate of Installation for insurance purposes
Service from: $29.95/mo

GUARDIAN PROTECTION SERVICES ESSENTIAL

Features: Remote management ability; Extended Service Plan warranty; Digital Cellular Communication; weather updates; smartphone and computer notifications; Smash-and-Crash panel tampering protection; Geo-Service tracking; optional pan-and-tilt, standard, or infrared wireless camera surveillance; optional motion sensing still shot security cameras; GE Simon XT Home Control Unit/Keypad; built-in siren; micro door/window sensors; motion sensor; 24-hour monitoring; Theft Protection Guarantee deductible; Quality Installation Guarantee; Relocation Guarantee; fire and medical emergency monitoring; yard signs and window stickers; personalized Customer Care Dashboard for online interfaces; official Certificate of Installation for insurance purposes
Service from: .$29.95/mo-$55.95/mo

GUARDIAN PROTECTION SERVICES PLUS

Features: Guardian VoiceLink connectivity; severe weather alert;

remote management ability; Extended Service Plan warranty; Digital Cellular Communication; smartphone and computer notifications; Smash-and-Crash panel tampering protection; Geo-Service tracking; optional pan-and-tilt, standard, or infrared wireless camera surveillance; optional motion sensing still shot security cameras; GE Simon XT Home Control Unit/Keypad; built-in siren; micro door/window sensors; motion sensor; 24-hour monitoring; Theft Protection Guarantee deductible; Quality Installation Guarantee; Relocation Guarantee; fire and medical emergency monitoring; yard signs and window stickers; personalized Customer Care Dashboard for online interfaces; official Certificate of Installation for insurance purposes
Service from: .$29.95/mo-$55.95/mo

GUARDIAN PROTECTION SERVICES PREMIUM

Features: Always on Guard Tacking for when your system is unarmed; Guardian VoiceLink connectivity; severe weather alert; remote management ability; Extended Service Plan warranty; Digital Cellular Communication; smartphone and computer notifications; Smash-and-Crash panel tampering protection; Geo-Service tracking; optional pan-and-tilt, standard, or infrared wireless camera surveillance; optional motion sensing still shot security cameras; GE Simon XT Home Control Unit/Keypad; built-in siren; micro door/window sensors; motion sensor; 24-hour monitoring;

Theft Protection Guarantee deductible; Quality Installation Guarantee; Relocation Guarantee; fire and medical emergency monitoring; yard signs and window stickers; personalized Customer Care Dashboard for online interfaces; official Certificate of Installation for insurance purposes
Service from: $55.95/mo

GUARDIAN PROTECTION SERVICES EMPOWER

Features: Remote management of emPower Locks, Lights, and Thermostats; Always on Guard Tacking for when your system is unarmed; Guardian VoiceLink connectivity; severe weather alert; remote management ability; Extended Service Plan warranty; Digital Cellular Communication; smartphone and computer notifications; Smash-and-Crash panel tampering protection; Geo-Service tracking; optional pan-and-tilt, standard, or infrared wireless camera surveillance; optional motion sensing still shot security cameras; GE Simon XT Home Control Unit/Keypad; built-in siren; micro door/window sensors; motion sensor; 24-hour monitoring; Theft Protection Guarantee deductible; Quality Installation Guarantee; Relocation Guarantee; fire and medical emergency monitoring; yard signs and window stickers; personalized Customer Care Dashboard for online interfaces; official Certificate of Installation for insurance purposes
Service from: $55.95/mo

Cameras and Monitoring

LOREX LH340-8CH-TOUCH-SERIES

Features: Complete security camera system Edge3 DVR 8 channel series; Triple Touch Technology monitor; pentaplex operation; Mirror Hard Drive Recording; PTZ cameras supported; Instant Mobile Viewing; Easy Connect Internet Set-up Wizard; email alerts; VESA mount; 21.5 in. LED touch monitor; eight cameras with Super+ resolution sensing, BrightNight, and all-purpose build for indoor and outdoor use

Available upon request

LOREX LNB2151

Features: HD IP camera for netHD security NVR; full HD 1080p resolution; Power over Ethernet providing video and power; night vision up to 100 ft. in total darkness; weatherproof IP66 rated; wide-angle lens; compatible with Lorex Network Video Recorder

MSRP **$329.99**

LOREX LW338LED-4PK

Features: Wireless security surveillance system with four outdoor wireless cameras and monitor; real time video with MPEG-4 compression; adaptive FHSS digital wireless technology; built-in auto-mechanical infrared camera; Triple Touch Technology monitor; pentaplex operation; Swipe-to-Switch viewing; PTZ cameras supported; Instant Mobile viewing; Easy Connect Internet Set-up Wizard; email alerts; Scroll-to-Search function; 13.3 in. color LED monitor; eight channel DVR with 1TB hard drive

MSRP **$1499.99**

LOREX LW2230 SERIES

Features: Wireless security surveillance camera; VGA resolution; 90 ft. night vision; listen-in audio; indoor and outdoor use; SignalGuard Technology; real-time video with MPEG-4 compression; Frequency Hopping Spread Spectrum to reduce

interference; auto-mechanical infrared camera

Available upon request

LOREX SD9+ SERIES

Features: Wireless video monitoring system; all-in-one monitor and recorder; view remotely via Skype; dual motion detection technology; digital zoom; secure wireless signal; Two-way audio intercom; four channels; 9 in. LCD monitor; SD recording; two indoor/outdoor cameras

Available upon request

LOREX DIGITAL WIRELESS SYSTEM

LOREX INDOOR-OUTDOOR NIGHT VISION

LOREX BABY MONITOR

PINNACLE SECURITY ENHANCED PERIMETER PROTECTOR

Features: Simon XT panel; cell unit if required; six standard door/window sensors; motion sensor; yard sign and window stickers; 24/7 monitoring for police, fire, and medical; lifetime warranty; customer relocation program; two-way voice system; mobile control

Installation: **$299**

PINNACLE SECURITY ESSENTIAL PACKAGE

Features: Simon XT panel; cell unit if required; two standard door/window sensors; motion sensor; yard sign and window stickers; 24/7 monitoring for police, fire, and medical; lifetime warranty; customer relocation program; two-way voice system; mobile control

Installation: **$199**

PINNACLE SECURITY FREQUENT TRAVELER PACKAGE

Features: Simon XT panel; cell unit; two standard door/window sensors; motion sensor; yard sign and window stickers; touchscreen keypad; pan/tilt camera; 24/7 monitoring for police, fire, and medical; lifetime warranty; customer relocation program; two-way voice system; mobile control; camera service

Installation: **$599**

PINNACLE SECURITY SECURITY GURU PACKAGE

Features: Simon XT panel; cell unit; motion sensor; yard sign and window stickers; touchscreen keypad; two recessed door sensors; smoke detector; glass break detector; image sensor; 24/7 monitoring for police, fire, and medical; lifetime warranty; customer

relocation program; two-way voice system; mobile control; image sensor service

Installation: **$399**

PINNACLE SECURITY STAY AT HOME PACKAGE

Features: Simon XT panel; cell unit if required; two standard door/window sensors; key remote; yard sign and window stickers; touchscreen keypad; Glass Break Detector; wall fob; 24/7 monitoring for police, fire, and medical; lifetime warranty; customer relocation program; two-way voice system; mobile control

Installation: **$299**

Cameras and Monitoring

PROTECT AMERICA BRONZE SECURITY

Features: GE Simon XT Control Panel; seven door/window sensors; one motion detector; three security stickers; one security yard sign; owner's manual; landline, broadband, or cellular monitoring options; customizable

Service from: **$35.99/mo**

PROTECT AMERICA GOLD SECURITY

Features: GE Simon XT Control Panel; twelve door/window sensors; one motion detector; three security stickers; one security yard sign; owner's manual; landline, broadband, or cellular monitoring options; customizable

Service from: **$39.99/mo**

PROTECT AMERICA COPPER SECURITY

Features: GE Simon XT Control Panel; three door/window sensors; one motion detector; three security stickers; one security yard sign; owner's manual; landline, broadband, or cellular monitoring options; customizable

Service from: **$19.99/mo**

PROTECT AMERICA PLATINUM SECURITY

Features: GE Simon XT Control Panel; fifteen door/window sensors; one motion detector; three security stickers; one security yard sign; owner's manual; landline, broadband, or cellular monitoring options; customizable

Service from: **$42.99/mo**

PROTECT AMERICA SILVER SECURITY

Features: GE Simon XT Control Panel; ten door/window sensors; one motion detector; three security stickers; one security yard sign; owner's manual; landline, broadband, or cellular monitoring options; customizable

Service from: **$37.99/mo**

PROTECTION 1 BASIC HOME SECURITY

Features: Two-way Voice system; color touchscreen keypad; all digital, all wireless system of three intrusion sensors, one motion detector, and keychain remote; professional installation; 24/7 Professional UL Listed Monitoring

Free installation, contact for quote

PROTECTION 1 DIGITAL HOME SECURITY

Features: Web alarm and event history; text and email notifications; 24/7 Professional UL Listed Monitoring; Professional installation; all digital, all wireless system of three intrusion sensors, one motion detector, and keychain remote; color touchscreen keypad; two-way voice system; Extended Service Plan with Tech Tracker; Advanced Protection Logic; WiFi compatible; eSecure web and mobile control; five-day weather forecast

Free installation, contact for quote

PROTECTION 1 DIGITAL & ENERGY

Features: Energy and automation Z-Wave Touchscreen Thermostat; Web alarm and event history; text and email notifications; 24/7 Professional UL Listed Monitoring; Professional installation; all digital, all wireless system of three intrusion sensors, one motion detector, and keychain remote; color touchscreen keypad; two-way voice system; Extended Service Plan with Tech Tracker; Advanced Protection Logic; WiFi compatible; eSecure web and mobile control; five-day weather forecast

Free installation, contact for quote

PROTECTION 1 DIGITAL & VIDEO

Features: Indoor video camera with wireless access points; Web alarm and event history; text and email notifications; 24/7 Professional UL Listed Monitoring; Professional installation; all digital, all wireless system of three intrusion sensors, one

motion detector, and keychain remote; color touchscreen keypad; two-way voice system; Extended Service Plan with Tech Tracker; Advanced Protection Logic; WiFi compatible; eSecure web and mobile control; five-day weather forecast

Free installation, contact for quote

PROTECTION 1 DIGITAL & ENERGY & VIDEO

Features: Indoor video camera with wireless access points; energy and automation Z-Wave Touchscreen Thermostat; Web alarm and event history; text and email notifications; 24/7 Professional UL Listed Monitoring; Professional installation; all digital, all wireless system of three intrusion sensors, one motion detector, and keychain remote; color touchscreen keypad; two-way voice system; Extended Service Plan with Tech Tracker; Advanced Protection Logic; WiFi compatible; eSecure web and mobile control; five-day weather forecast

Free installation, contact for quote

Cameras and Monitoring

SAFEMART ADEMCO VISTA-20P INSTALLER PACK

Features: Ademco Vista 20P Alarm Panel; Ademco 6150 Fixed Display Touchpad; Ademco Wave2 Interior Siren; 12v 4AH 12-Hour backup battery; transformer; RJ31X jack; installation, programming, and end user manuals; 2K Eol resistors
From: $149.95

SAFEMART GE SECURITY CONCORD 4 CUSTOM STARTER KIT

Features: Concord 4 Panel; Interactive Cellular Communicator; 1st month of LiveWatch Interactive Monitoring Service; programmable Alpha Display Keypad; power supply with 6 ft. cord; RJ31X jack and cord; installation and user manuals; 96 zones maximum, either hardwired, wireless, or combination; two onboard programmable outputs; compatible with GE Security crystal and SAW Learn Mode sensors; SIA CP-01 False Alarm Reduction Standard compliant; 2- and 4-wire smoke detector compatible; built-in 12 watt siren driver
MSRP **$499**

SAFEMART GE SECURITY NEXT GENERATION SIMON XTI WIRELESS HOME SECURITY SYSTEM

Features: Supports 40 wireless zones; built-in touchscreen; supports phone line, cellular, and IP communication; alarm system control from Internet enabled smart devices; chime features for monitoring door, window, and motion activity; Two-way Voice capable; compatible with wireless video cameras; supports home automation and control features
MSRP **$299**

SAFEMART HONEYWELL SECURITY LYNX TOUCH L5000 WIRELESS ALARM SYSTEM

Features: Full color touchscreen; supports 64 wireless zones; phone line, cellular, and IP communication supported; control alarm system from iPhone, Android, or computer with Total Connect; chime feature for door, window, or motion sensors; Two-way Voice capable; compatible with Honeywell wireless video cameras; supports home automation with Total Connect
MSRP **$499**

SECURITY LABS
SLC-154C BULLET CAMERA
Features: Weatherproof; high resolution color; 1/3 in. Micro Pitch CCD imager; 540 Line resolution; (24) IR LEDs with Halo Diffuser; automatic white balance and gain control; swivel mount; 12v DC
Available upon request

SECURITY LABS SLC-176 PTZ DOME CAMERA
Features: Pan/Tilt/Zoom camera; 27x optical zoom; upper casing constructed of high-intensity flame retardant ABS; acrylic optical dome housing; automatic fan and heater; 24v AC; ¼ in. Super HAD CCD camera; color to b/w with day-night feature for low light; auto electronic shutter and white balance
Available upon request

SECURITY LABS SLM433
Features: SLD264 - 4 CH Internet DVR with 500 GB HD; pentaplex operation; dual stream H.264; HDMI and VGA output; 16MB of pre-alarm storage per event; still image snapshot and portable video converter with time stamp; two USB ports; email notification and event trigger for motion detection, alarm, and video loss; MyDVRView connection through the Internet; optical mouse; IR remote; LAN and BNC video cable; four SLC-3130 weatherproof IR CCD bullet cameras, cables, and mounting
Available upon request

SECURITY LABS SLC-154C BULLET CAMERA

SECURITY LABS SLC-176 PTZ DOME CAMERA

SECURITY LABS SLM433

Cameras and Monitoring

SECURITY LABS SLM451

Features: SLD265 - 8 CH Internet DVR with 2TB GB HD; pentaplex operation; dual stream H.264; HDMI and VGA output; 16MB of pre-alarm storage per event; still image snapshot and portable video converter with time stamp; two USB ports; email notification and event trigger for motion detection, alarm, and video loss; MyDVRView connection through the Internet; optical mouse; IR remote; LAN and BNC video cable; two SLC-1055 weatherproof Sony Ex-View II with Effio DSP IR dome cameras; four SLC-159 weatherproof Sony Super HAD IR bullet cameras
Available upon request

SECURITY LABS SLM461

Features: SLD266 - 16 CH Internet DVR with 2TB HD; dual stream H.264; port for additional eSATA external hard drive; pentaplex operation; HDMI and VGA output; 16MB of pre-alarm storage per event; picture-in-picture; snapshot and portable video converter with time stamp; email notification and event trigger for motion detection, alarm, and video loss; MyDVRView from internet enabled device; optical mouse; IR remote; LAN and BNC cable; five SLC-1055 weatherproof IR dome cameras; four SLC-159 weatherproof IR bullet cameras; all

cameras contain Sony Ex-View II with Effio DSP; 22 in. Class LED monitor with VGA video input, cable, and power supply
Available upon request

SECURITY LABS TEMPAL PRO

Features: Add temperature and humidity display to any video source; module incorporated into video connection without loss of signal; reading overlaid on top of video; alarm and notification function for minimum and maximum levels;
Available upon request

SECURITY LABS TEMPAL PRO

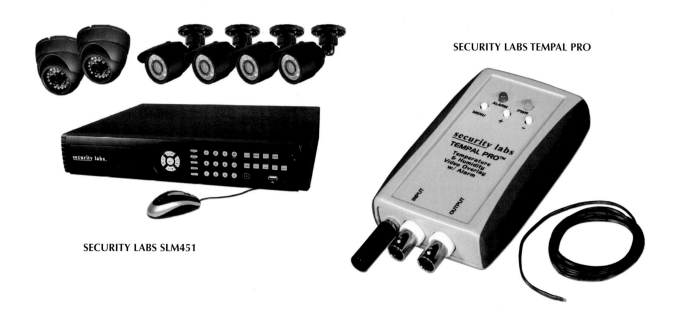

SECURITY LABS SLM451

SECURITY LABS SLM461

SVAT
MODEL 11005

Features: Ultra resolution 100 ft. night vision security camera; weather-resistant housing; anti-vandal mount; easily connects to DVR; power adapter; 65 ft. extension cable; mounting hardware; window warning stickers

Available upon request

SVAT CV503-8CH19M-002

Features: All-in-one security system; 19 in. LCD monitor; four hi-res indoor/outdoor surveillance cameras; view footage online and with smart devices; 500GB hard drive; supports up to eight cameras; 24/7 lifetime live support; USB mouse; remote control; power adapter for DVR and cameras; BNC to RCA connectors; keys for removable HDD; RJ-45 ethernet cable; four window warning stickers; software CD

Available upon request

SVAT GX301-011

Features: Two wireless, long range night vision cameras; 7 in. LCD monitor with SD Card recording; 8 ft. power adapter for camera; 6 ft. power adapter for monitor; camera mounting brackets; AV to RCA wire; remote control; four window warning stickers; instruction manual; 24/7 lifetime live customer support; two-way intercom; motion detection settings

Available upon request

SVAT PI1000

Features: All-in-one security recording system; records only when movement is detected; MPEG-4 Compression; 1GB SD recording card; SD DVR; power adapter; RCA wire; mounting bracket and hardware; manual; built-in color pinhole surveillance camera hidden in a motion sensor

Available upon request

Cameras and Monitoring

VIVINT HOME AUTOMATION PACKAGE

Features: Touchscreen panel; video surveillance; electronic door lock; smart thermostat; remote Internet and smartphone access; window sensors; door sensors; key fob; Glass Break Detector; motion detector; smoke alarm; carbon monoxide alarm; energy-efficient bulbs; lighting controls; small appliance controls; non-emergency alerts; optional medical pendant
Activation: **$199;**
Service: **$68.99/mo**

VIVINT HOME SECURITY PACKAGE

Features: Touchscreen panel; three door/window sensors; motion detector; key fob; remote Internet and smartphone access; Glass Break Detector; smoke alarm; carbon monoxide alarm; optional non-emergency alerts and medical pendant
Activation: **$99;**
Service: **$49.99/mo**

BULLET GUARD BULLET RESISTANT DOOR

Options: solid core doors in plastic laminate and paint or stain grade veneer with optional view windows; all clear door made from UL-752 Acrylic or Polycarbonate in level 1-3; full lite aluminum stile and rail protection levels 1-8; ½ lite aluminum stile & rail doors protection levels 1-8; door frame available in aluminum, slip in steel, and steel wrap around, packed with ballistic fiberglass
Available upon request

BULLET GUARD HOLLOW METAL DOOR

Features: Bullet resistant hollow metal doors and frames; manufactured to UL-752 standards, levels 1-8; capable of withstanding medium powered small arms up to high-powered rifles with 7.62 mm ammunition; frames available in aluminum, slip in steel, and steel wrap around, packed with ballistic fiberglass; available in standard hollow metal doors, doors with view window, narrow-lite doors, half-lite doors, and double door configurations
Available upon request

BULLET GUARD TRANSACTION WINDOWS

Features: Bullet resistant transaction windows; two standard sizes - 24 in. x 36 in. and 30 in. x 36 in.; sliding windows available in UL levels 1-3 materials; voice port options: horizontal, rectangular, circular, vertical offset, arched, voice surround, and sliding window; aluminum frame
Available upon request

LARSON DOORS SECURITY STORM DOORS

Availble in the following models and styles: Secure Elegance, Standard, Garden View, Courtyard, Presidential, River Oak, Canterbury, Mississippi Oak, Corner Oak, and Butterfly; aluminum frame or 16-gauge steel depending on the model
Available upon request

BULLET GUARD HOLLOW METAL DOOR

BULLET GUARD BULLET RESISTANT DOOR

BULLET GUARD TRANSACTION WINDOWS

LARSON DOORS SECURITY STORM DOORS

Doors and Windows

NORTH AMERICAN BULLET PROOF BALLISTIC ALUMINUM DOORS (ADR)

Features: Built in bullet resistant U.L. Levels 1-8; narrow and wide stile doors; mill finish, clear, dark bronze anodized, Kynar, or powder coated finishes
Available upon request

NORTH AMERICAN BULLET PROOF BALLISTIC HOLLOW METAL DOORS (HMDR)

Features: Lightweight; available in handgun performance levels with a U.L. Label; standard flush and common viewlite options; standard and custom sizes
Available upon request

NORTH AMERICAN BULLET PROOF BALLISTIC SLIDING TRANSACTION WINDOW (SLTW)

Features: Available in aluminum, prime finish steel, or stainless steel frames; usually built with plastic laminate, stainless steel, or solid surface shelves; available in U.L. Levels 1-3; customization available
Available upon request

NORTH AMERICAN BULLET PROOF BALLISTIC STEEL DOORS (SDR)

Features: Available in U.L. Levels 1-8; custom configurations and performance levels up to and including .50 calibers and 30.06

armor piercing; minimum 12-guage steel framework; secure forced entry characteristics
Available upon request

NORTH AMERICAN BULLET PROOF BALLISTIC WOOD DOORS (WDR)

Features: Capable of visually matching ballistic doors with existing non-ballistic doors; standard slab, rail and stile, or panel doors available; U.L Levels 1-8; view lite frames available; standard or custom sizes, single or paired doors
Available upon request

SWISS SHADE SECURITY SECURITY DOOR

Features: In-swing only; key-only operated from outside; also available in sliding and French style doors; steel reinforced aluminum frame for bullet resistant security levels

Available upon request

SWISS SHADE SECURITY SECURITY WINDOW

Features: Multi-chamber frame with steel inlays and A three burglar proof security glass; minimum seven internal security locks; lockable handle; drill protection; installed with hardened steel bolts; completely foamed in with high grade Polyurethane Foam; Level A, Level B, and Level C Bullet Proof security glass available; optional grilles, transoms, screens, blinds, and tempered interior glass

From: **$882**

SWISS SHADE SECURITY SECURITY DOOR

SWISS SHADE SECURITY SECURITY WINDOW

Doors and Windows

U.S. BULLET PROOFING USAD 1000
Features: Forced entry, bullet, and blast resistant aluminum door; narrow or monumental stiles; single or double door, swinging or sliding configuration; available sidelights and transoms; full vision, half, double, and opaque options; ballistics U.L. Levels 1-8; blast protection exceeds GSA DOD
Available upon request

U.S. BULLET PROOFING USAW 100
Features: Aluminum frame, sliding blast and ballistic window; U.L. Levels 1-8; GSA C & D blast levels; retrofit or new construction; clear and dark bronze anodized finish, custom colors, Kynar paint, brass, and stainless steel cladding available
Available upon request

U.S. BULLET PROOFING USSD 4000
Features: Forced entry, bullet, and blast resistant steel door; single or double door, swinging or sliding configuration; available sidelights and transoms; half vision, view, narrow, and opaque options; ballistics U.L. Levels 1-8; blast protection exceeds GSA DOD; meets ASTM forced entry rating; full flush unit
Available upon request

U.S. BULLET PROOFING USAW 500
Features: Thermally broken, operable, aluminum framed blast and ballistic window; in- or out-swing; ballistics U.L. Levels 1-3; exceeds GSA DOD blast requirements; clear or bronze anodized finish, custom options available
Available upon request

U.S. BULLET PROOFING USAW 800
Features: Forced entry, bullet, and blast resistant fixed steel frame window; DOS 15 minute forced entry rating; U.L. Levels 1-8; available as a single-lite, multi-lite, and transaction window; blast protection exceeds GSA DOD DOS
Available upon request

U.S. BULLET PROOFING USWD 2000
Features: Bullet resistant wood door; single or double door, swinging or sliding configuration; available sidelights and transoms; half vision, view, narrow, and opaque options; good for interior applications where aesthetics and protection are both important; ballistics U.L. Levels 1-8; laminated construction of fiberglass or steel armor
Available upon request

U.S. BULLET PROOFING USSD 3000
Features: Forced entry, bullet, and blast resistant steel door; single or double door, swinging or sliding configuration; available sidelights and transoms; half vision, view, narrow, and opaque options; ballistics U.L. Levels 1-8; blast protection exceeds GSA DOD; 60 minute forced entry rating; glazing is totally restrained within armor sheeting; full flush unit
Available upon request

AFTERWORD

The goal of the *Shooter's Bible Guide to Home Defense* was to provide contemporary information about how to address one of the most basic and universal needs faced by mankind. Please note that the word "contemporary" should not be skipped over or taken lightly. The specifics in this book have much to do not only with our right to defend ourselves but also the freedom to choose any weapons we deem necessary to do so. That seems natural enough to me. Yet these rights continue to be challenged by those who would profit from having us think we are better off outsourcing our personal security. Call us arrogant, but as Americans the birth of our nation was based on being independent and knowing how to take care of ourselves.

When we think of heroes, leaders or just the toughest guy on the block, it's natural to wonder how they got that way. Were they always the toughest, the biggest, or the strongest? No, not necessarily. Ask a cop or a firefighter or a professional fighter and you'll hear stories like, "I moved into a new neighborhood and I used to get beat up a lot." Or, "I got a bloody nose once and I decided it wasn't going to happen again."

Perhaps from the beginning the world was meant to be a giant stage upon which the conflict of good versus evil would be played out. Will good triumph over evil? Will evil rule the world? Perhaps the only conclusion is that we must continue to defend, for that struggle alone is what sustains existence. Does this mean actual hand-to-hand fists, knives, and bullets? Sometimes it does. In the meantime there is much to be done to fortify the home and discourage trespass and much to be diagnosed in the daily routine that may unwittingly make us more vulnerable. There is much to be understood about conditioning our reactions to stay calm in the face of danger and decisive in the throes of chaos. There is much to be done about making friends with the weapons that deserve both our fear and our respect. But always remember that predators fear those weapons, too.

In the preceding pages I have tried to put forth information in a different way than has been done before. I hope it has offered inspiration, as well as facts. If the contents of this book cannot teach you everything you need to know about defending your home (and no book really can), I hope that it might serve as an inoculation against self-doubt and assist in preserving the will to fight the one enemy that threatens our safety above all others: the urge to give up.

REFERENCE

Preface

p. vii "A Racer's Life: Richard Petty." First broadcast February 18, 2013 by Speed TV.

p. vii Eckstine, Roger. "Going 1911: How a PD Changed and How They Trained." *American Cop.* January/February 2008.

p. vii Cirillo, Jim. *Guns, Bullets, and Gunfights: Lessons and Tales from a Modern-Day Gunfighter.* Boulder, CO: Paladin Press, 1996.

Introduction

p. xi *Escape From New York*. Directed by John Carpenter. Goldcrest Films, 1981.

p. xi Giuliani, Rudolph J. *Leadership*. New York: Hyperion, 2002.

p. 3 Webb, Walter Prescott. *The Texas Rangers: A Century of Frontier Defense.* 1935. Facsimile of the first edition, with a foreword by Lyndon B. Johnson. Austin, TX: Univ. of Texas Press, 1996.

p. 35 https://www.osha.gov/doc/outreachtraining/htmlfiles/extmark.html

p. 41 http://www.nononsenseselfdefense.com

p. 42 Halforty, Damian. *Carjacking Countermeasures.* Grand Junction, CO: Executive Security International, 2002. CD-ROM.

p. 43 *Guns in South Africa: Facts, Figures and Firearm Law*. Alpers, Philip and Marcus Wilson. Sydney School of Public Health, The University of Sydney 2013.

p. 53 "Edith's 50th Birthday: Part 1." *All in the Family.* Episode no. 162, first broadcast October 16, 1977 by CBS. Directed by Paul Bogart.

p. 53 "Shaolin Monk vs. Maori." *Deadliest Warrior.* Episode no. 7, first broadcast May 19, 2009 by Spike. Directed by F. Paul Benz.

p. 60 Image courtesy of Patrick Edwin Moran. Accessed June 27, 2013, http://en.wikipedia.org/wiki/File:OODA.Boyd.svg

p. 61
http://abcnews.go.com/US/georgia-mom-hiding-kids-shoots-intruder/story?id=18164812

http://www.wsbtv.com/news/news/local/woman-hiding-kids-shoots-intruder/nTm7s

http://www.waltontribune.com/news/article_eac-0b0ec-745e-11e2-a312-001a4bcf887a.html

p. 124 Jordan, William H. *No Second Place Winner.* 1965. Concord, NH: Police Bookshelf, 2000.

p. 128 Watson, James and Kevin Dockery. *Point Man*. 1993. New York: Avon, 1995.